Prologues and Epilogues of Restoration Theater

Prologues and Epilogues of Restoration Theater

Gender and Comedy, Performance and Print

Diana Solomon

UNIVERSITY OF DELAWARE PRESS

Newark

Published by University of Delaware Press
Co-published with The Rowman & Littlefield Publishing Group, Inc.
4501 Forbes Boulevard, Suite 200, Lanham, Maryland 20706
www.rowman.com

10 Thornbury Road, Plymouth PL6 7PP, United Kingdom

British Library Cataloguing in Publication Information Available

Library of Congress Cataloging-in-Publication Data
Solomon, Diana, 1970–
  Prologues and epilogues of Restoration theater : gender and comedy, performance and
print / Diana Solomon.
    pages cm
  Includes bibliographical references and index.
  ISBN 978-1-61149-422-8 (cloth : alk. paper) — ISBN 978-1-61149-423-5 (electronic)
  1. English drama—Restoration, 1660–1700—History and criticism. 2. Prologues and
epilogues—History and criticism. 3. Theater—England—History—17th century. I.
Title.
  PR698.P68S65 2013
  822'.052—dc23   2012047557

Printed in the United States of America

Contents

~

Acknowledgments

This project first benefited from the superb stewardship of my advisor at the University of California Santa Barbara, Elizabeth Heckendorn Cook, and my committee members, Robert A. Erickson, William Warner, and Kay Young. Many scholars in the UCSB community also helped my work develop, including Rob Adlington, Carolyn Butcher, Marc Coronado, Jody Enders, Robert Hamm, Sheila Hwang, David Schuster, and Melissa Stevenson. I also thank Craig Howes and professors at the University of Hawaii for preparing me to write it. And my postdoc colleagues at Duke: Ben Albers, Alex Block, Betsy Verhoeven, and Rebecca Walsh helped me refine the manuscript.

Fellowships from the American Society of Eighteenth-Century Studies, the Clark, Folger, Huntington, and Noel libraries, and the Duke University Writing Program's Mellon fund have made the archival research for this book possible. Many librarians including Sara Seten Berghausen, Sue Hodson, Scott Jacobs, Bob Leitz, Mona Shulman, Suzanne Tatian, and Georgianna Ziegler provided great assistance. At Simon Fraser, the President's Research Startup Grant, the small Social Science and Humanities Research Council grant, and the Department of English's FIC fund have provided generous support. The oversight of Beverly Neufield helped me obtain these grants. Cameron Duder and Dania Sheldon helped prepare the final manuscript, and the editors at the University of Delaware Press and Rowman & Littlefield Publishers have provided capable guidance.

At last I get to boast about my Simon Fraser University colleagues in print. The members of the "pre-1800" reading group: Ronda Arab, David Coley,

Matt Hussey, and Tiffany Werth, plus Scott Mackenzie and Tiffany Potter from UBC, have offered invaluable feedback on the manuscript, as have Peter Cramer and Peter Dickinson. For rich discussions that have helped shape my work, I wish to thank Lara Campbell, Colette Colligan, Leith Davis, Michael J. Everton, Carole Gerson, Carolyn Lesjak, Michelle Levy, Betty Schellenberg, and Jon Smith, and for their insights on women and comedy I thank Peter Dickinson, Anne Higgins, Paul St. Pierre, and Sean Zwagerman. For support and collegiality I thank the entire department, including Maureen Curtin, Elaine Tkaczuk and the rest of our terrific staff. Rebecca Dowson and the interlibrary loan librarians have been a great help, while Sarah Creel, Heather Ritzer, and Amy Russell-Coutts have performed admirably as research assistants. And it has been a great benefit to me to work with Sarah Creel, Erin Keating, and David Weston on the development of their own dissertations.

In the scholarly community I have benefited from the help and encouragement of Roberto Alvarez, Misty Anderson, Paula Backscheider, Regina Barreca, Debra Bronstein, Michael Burden, Kevin Cope, Bärbel Czennia, Rob Hume, George Justice, Elisabeth Le Guin, Devoney Looser, Elizabeth Morgan, Felicity Nussbaum, Leslie Ritchie, Albert Sheen, Elaine Showalter, Judith Bailey Slagle, and Laura Stevens. Writing exchanges and conference collaborations with Fiona Ritchie have greatly enriched my work. And this project would have been vastly more difficult without Pierre Danchin's immensely helpful prologue and epilogue collections.

Portions of chapter four were previously published in *1650–1850: Ideas, Aesthetics, and Inquiries in the Early Modern Era*. Portions of chapter five were published in *Prologues, Epilogues, Curtain-Raisers and Afterpieces: The Rest of Eighteenth-Century English Theatre*, ed. Daniel Ennis and Judith Slagle. I thank the AMS and University of Delaware Presses for permission to reprint this material.

My parents, Aileen and Henry Solomon, my brother and sister in-law, Matthew Solomon and Kathrina Peterson, my niece Callie and nephew Gavin, my aunt Hedda Marcus, and my extended family have provided wonderful sustenance. And my friends have given me good cheer throughout the process: Cherie Abrahams, Carl Ackerman, Candace Beale, Christine Beaule, Jane D. Bonifazzi, Laura Caldwell-Aden, Kathy Cassity, Jim Clarke, Christine David, David Liney, Krista C. Fleming, Karen Ferguson, Brandy Gibb, Anne-Marie Gillon, Padma Jairam, Kristina Kim, Shelley and Mel Klatt, Helen Leung, Julie Goldsmith Reiser, Elizabeth Rivlin, Susan Schultz, Michael Silverman, Erika Smith, Gail K. Smith, Mika and Eric Smith, Abby and Buster Solomon, Michele Strano, Eric Wredenhagen, and especially Elizabeth, Ben, Denise, and John Benskin, who long ago sparked my love of comedy at their dinner table.

~

Introduction

London, late June, 1669. An audience that includes King Charles II sits in the Drury Lane theater, watching the first performance of John Dryden's latest tragedy, *Tyrannick Love*. Some audience members are buying oranges, selling or purchasing postperformance sex, or commenting on their neighbors' attire. Those watching the play see a dictator storming the stage. The emperor Maximin has returned home from war to find others ruling Rome in his stead. Angry, he wants to kill his wife and marry the woman he loves: St. Catherine. But when she rejects him, he murders her and three others before receiving a fatal blow. Maximin has also offered to marry his daughter Valeria to his stellar captain, but while this outcome would please Valeria, the captain covets her mother instead. At the end, Valeria (played by Nell Gwyn) stabs herself from unrequited love and joins a litter of bodies strewn across the stage. The stage quiets; the only movement comes from a pair of pallbearers loading Valeria's corpse onto a stretcher. Just as they start to carry her off, however, she suddenly sits up and says:

> *To the Bearer.* Hold, are you mad? you damn'd confounded Dog,
> I am to rise, and speak the Epilogue.
> *To the Audience.* I come, kind Gentlemen, strange news to tell ye,
> I am the Ghost of poor departed *Nelly.*[1]

In delivering these lines, Nell Gwyn caused a metatheatrical sensation that resonates to this day. Her words trumpet the slippage between character and actress that became a mainstay of Restoration and eighteenth-century actresses' prologues and epilogues. Here the character and situation of the dead Valeria combine with the bawdy public persona of Gwyn, resulting in comic incongruity and foregrounding hitherto-ghosted layers of audience–performer identification. Gwyn's apparent usurping of Dryden's authority in this epilogue supposedly sparked the love of King Charles II, a myth that many contemporary critics perpetuate despite evidence that the two had become lovers over a year before this performance.[2] While *Tyrannick Love* was revived several times in the seventeenth and eighteenth centuries, today it is rarely performed or studied. The epilogue, however, is referenced in numerous studies of Restoration theater and in texts further afield. It is a scholarly favorite.

Although a theatrical touchstone, the epilogue remains underanalyzed. Earlier critics quoted blocks of couplets and left them untouched.[3] Today, some critics cite the epilogue as an example of typecasting, while others use it to reflect biographically on Gwyn or the king; all avoid examining the epilogue's style or content.[4] A few Restoration scholars even take for granted that readers recognize this epilogue sans context; discussing the fitness of Mrs. Knep for the role of Lady Fidget in *The Country Wife*, for example, Anthony Kaufman comments that her suitability is "[t]ypecasting you might say; just the opposite of Nell Gwyn as 'a Princess, acting in S. Cathar'n'."[5] While critics have long assumed the importance of this epilogue to an understanding of Dryden's play, and of Restoration theater more generally, they have yet to explain what that importance is, and more largely how the circulation and reception of this and other Restoration prologues and epilogues might render more complex our scholarly accounts of author–performer–audience relations during the period. Critics, in short, have treated the epilogue like a favorite passage that they wish to savor, rather than a text ripe for interpretation.

To find such a rich text lacking sustained analysis is unusual in literary criticism; such is the case, however, with nearly *every* Restoration prologue and epilogue. And there are many. Dramatic prologues and epilogues—poetic bids for the audience's favor—first appeared in ancient Greek and Roman theater, and developed through the medieval and early modern English stage until reaching their apotheosis in the Restoration. There are 1,570 extant prologues and epilogues written between the years under discussion here, 1660 to the death of Anne on 1 August 1714. Overall numbers are much lower for Renaissance plays, with fewer than half containing a prologue or epilogue, yet scholars routinely consider Shakespeare's two inductions, five prologues, and seven epilogues alongside his plays, and have also treated prologues *qua* prologues. Dryden wrote over eight times as many prologues and epilogues as Shakespeare (fifty-nine prologues and forty-four epilogues), yet even within Dryden scholarship these rarely receive more than a mention.[6] When cited, prologues and epilogues are usually treated as factual references—used, for example, to document a royal's presence at the theater that night—but they remain largely bereft of critical analysis. While their utility as documentation is valuable, their political and social commentary, elucidation of theater practices and conditions, and customization for celebrated players are just three reasons that prologues and epilogues are vital to understanding Restoration theater and culture.

But before shedding critical light on the significance of prologues and epilogues, we must deal with the methodological confusion they raise. Specifically, are they or are they not parts of the plays they flank? When analyzing plays, should we attend to them or not? Restoration audiences, both theatrical and literary, provide the answer: yes. Spectators often took elaborate measures to attend performances of prologues and epilogues, either along with or at the expense of their plays. Yet to preserve the illusion of the play, particularly a tragedy, other audience members made a point of leaving before the epilogue—a practice later debated in *The Spectator*.[7] Their departures reflect the significance of the epilogue as mediating audience impressions of the play. And on this point I wish to be clear: Restoration audiences viewed prologues and epilogues as consequential aspects of the theatrical performance, and therefore so should we. In print, prologues and epilogues circulated as broadsides to advertise performances, and normally accompanied their playtexts in published quartos. Play revivals occasioned new prologues and epilogues, yet Restoration publishers almost invariably printed the originals in subsequent play editions. The vogue for prologues and epilogues endured throughout the eighteenth century, as favored examples turned up in miscellanies and comprised whole anthologies.[8] It is thus time for prologues and epilogues to be treated systematically, analytically, culturally, and theoretically as documents that shaped the viewing and reading of plays for audiences. That is the goal of this book.

What Can Prologues and Epilogues Tell Us about Restoration Theater?

When Gwyn says "Hold!" does our suspension of disbelief end? The conventions of prologues and epilogues force this question: When does the make-believe world of performance start and finish? In conventional auditoriums today, the most evident signal is the curtain. We are accustomed to instances of preperformance address taking place in front of the curtain, and such was also the case in the Restoration, when the two curtain-tunes and then the prologue were performed while the curtain was still down. But once the curtain was up, it stayed up for the duration of the performance. The epilogue is, accordingly, not separated from the end of act 5, and even the prologue can create interpretive complications because its performer usually plays a role in the mainpiece.[9] Clearly, then, Restoration prologues and epilogues should be examined alongside the plays to which they were most commonly attached.

Given the limited archives of Restoration theater, it may be tempting to read prologues and epilogues New Historically, as records of theater conditions and conventions. This approach, however, sidesteps the fact that most prologues and epilogues not only were designed for specific actors but also were promotional and thus profit-driven. Before seeking factual information from them, we must ask: is a prologue likely to contain an accurate record of historical events if it is designed specifically for, say, Nell Gwyn? Harold Love speaks to this question when he warns that prologues and epilogues are "so often mistaken for photographs from the stage," when their primary motive is "to secure a favourable hearing for the play in order to secure profit for the house and the dramatist."[10] These two purposes are not antithetical but, due to their profit motive, prologues and epilogues cannot be uncritically taken as documentary evidence. This is not to say that we cannot derive rich information from them; the frequency with which prologues and epilogues refer to the Popish Plot during the years 1679–1682, for example, speaks to the cultural preoccupation with this issue. Extraction of such information, however, requires a new critical methodology more attuned to prologues' and epilogues' textual content *and* the formal conventions of their performance, to the authors who wrote them *and* the actors who spoke them—not to mention the audiences who received them.

The lack of such a methodology is evident in present-day publication of the plays. While Restoration editions consistently published prologues and epilogues, the same cannot be said for some contemporary editions that either lop them off altogether or, disorientingly, publish some and not others within the same text. The latter practice occurs in the much-used *Broadview Anthology of Restoration and Eighteenth-Century Drama*, which includes only ten prologues, two introductions, and three epilogues alongside its forty-three plays. The editor justifies the decision as follows: "More reluctantly, we have, in the main, omitted prologues and epilogues, since, witty and entertaining as they are, they rarely contribute to the thematics of the plays to which they are attached but rather most often carry on a banter with the audience over the state of the theater, the plight of the actors, and so forth."[11] Putting aside for a moment the comment about thematics, why would we want to avoid teaching our students about the state of the theater and the plight of the actors? But my main concern here is the randomness of editorial practice. Did the *Broadview* editors select the thirteen prologues and epilogues because they were deemed consistent with their plays' thematics? Were they considered the most "witty and entertaining"? To take one example from the anthology, what purpose does it serve to explore the wit of Horner in the main play of Wycherley's *The Country Wife* yet exclude the ingenuity of Lady Fidget/actress Mrs. Knep's retort in the epilogue?

While taking their data at face value is dangerous, sticking to a purely historical consideration can also prevent prologues and epilogues from providing any meaning at all. Too often critics have eschewed a thematic analysis of the prologues and epilogues in relation to their plays, in favor of a narrow discussion of them as simply a convention of the Restoration stage. Even sophisticated critics have opted for such traditional approaches. In "Playwrights, Prologues, and First Performances in the Early Modern Theatre," for example, Tiffany Stern asks how we should interpret prologues and epilogues: "So how should the presence or absence of prologues and epilogues affect our reading of printed plays? Unfortunately, as stage-orations can have a different heritage from the play they are attached to, they cannot be used to make statements about the underlying nature of the text they adjoin."[12]

This approach unnecessarily separates prologues and epilogues from their texts. In performance, prologues are commonly spoken by actors wearing costumes designed for the characters they will soon incarnate in the main stage play, while epilogues frequently feature actors still wearing their costumes and speaking as their character, or their public persona, or both at once. In such prologues and especially epilogues, we encounter characters who offer additional perspectives on the mainpiece. Quarto publications of Restoration plays most often reprinted the prologues and epilogues delivered at the play premiere, thus giving readers the option to interpret the play alongside them as initial theater audiences might have done. So dividing prologues and epilogues from their plays prevents us from considering how their performance and publication may have shaped audiences' and readers' experiences of the plays. To separate the *Tyrannick Love* epilogue from its play would cost the opportunity to understand the line "I am the Ghost of poor departed Nelly" in context. That line breathes new life into Valeria and begins the course of Valeria/Gwyn supposedly laughing at Dryden for casting her in a tragedy. As such, it provides a critical perspective on the play's genre, a comic remaking of the concluding bloodbath, an insight into relations between player and playwright, and a depiction, underexplored in critical analyses, of Restoration theater as a collaborative endeavor.

Such elements demonstrate why a new methodology for treating prologues and epilogues is essential. The approach I propose is influenced by performance and print culture theories, feminist and gender studies (especially as they have intersected with, and helped revise, theater history and reception), and theories of comedy. I argue that we should treat prologues and epilogues as performances that shaped the audience's reception of the play, and as material artifacts published in a variety of formats before and after the play's premiere. Both methods find direction from Gerard Genette's theory of the paratext: a part of the text that can exist independently of its main text yet stands to influence the reception of that text. We also need to consider prologues and epilogues as differentiated by their speaker's gender. This watershed moment in English theater history, when women finally performed on the public stage, coincided with the high point of dramatic prologues and epilogues, and both actress and genre developed in tandem through specific modes of comic address. By considering them in performance and print, and alongside their performers and authors, we can understand how prologues and epilogues offer insightful interpretations about the plays they adjoin and the audiences they address.

Prologues and Epilogues as Paratexts

Genette's theory of the paratext as an intermediary between text and reader helps us understand how prologues and epilogues negotiate similar spaces within both play performances and publications. In *Paratexts: Thresholds of Interpretation*, Genette defines the paratext as "what enables a text to become a book and to be offered as such to its readers and, more generally, to the public."[13] As he explains:

> More than a boundary or a sealed border, the paratext is, rather, a *threshold*, or . . . a "vestibule" that offers the world at large the possibility of either stepping inside or turning back. . . . [T]his fringe, always the conveyor of a commentary that is authorial or more or less legitimated by the author, constitutes a zone between text and off-text, a zone not only of transition but also of *transaction*: a privileged place of a pragmatics and a strategy, of an influence on the public, an influence that—whether well or poorly understood and achieved—is at the service of a better reception for the text and a more pertinent reading of it (more pertinent, of course, in the eyes of the author and his allies).[14]

Designating as paratexts such disparate items as book titles, epigraphs, and transcripts of authorial interviews, Genette claims that the paratext offers readers methods of controlling their reading experience. Readers may proceed either informed by or willfully ignorant of the paratext and its supposed authorial endorsement. To readers, one attraction of the paratext is precisely this illusion of authorial intention. Whether or not the author wrote it, the reader often senses that the paratext offers clues to interpretation. Paratexts authored by others nevertheless create interpretive proximity.

Genette designates his theory for a specific generic framework—narratology—at the expense of another, theater studies. But theater, too, contains paratexts. Like the preface and afterword of a book, the Restoration prologue and epilogue help the text make a play of itself. This becomes clearer if we consider two subcategories of paratexts that Genette identifies: *peritexts*, indicating paratexts that physically accompany their texts, such as prefaces, dedications, and subtitles; and *epitexts*, which exist outside of the book, such as statements from the author or publisher, rough drafts, and correspondence. Within such a schema, prologues and epilogues reveal their versatility; they function as both peritexts, performed and published alongside their plays, and epitexts, printed separately as broadsides that circulated to advertise the performance and collectively in eighteenth-century anthologies. Theatrical paratexts also offer up elusive, though no less mediated, glimpses of the author. Their language can be seen to channel an author's point of view, whether monologically, with the author's voice apparently speaking through the actor's body, or dialogically, with the actor, speaking in his or her own voice, either promoting or protesting the author. Restoration prologues and epilogues also condition the audience's response to the play. When printed with plays, they are easily read or skipped. Less apparently, in performance they permitted similar options, as audiences had a high degree of choice over what parts of a theatrical evening they attended. When applied to theater, Genette's theory of the paratext as threshold emphasizes the agency Restoration audiences possessed over their playgoing. Those audience members enjoyed the same choices as readers over when, where, and how to consume texts and paratexts.

A quality of narrative that Genette identifies prior to his work on the paratext signals the deconstruction a prologue or epilogue can reap on a play. In *Narrative Discourse: An Essay in Method*, Genette discusses how a novel's narrator can create a metanarrative that interrupts the flow of the narrative, thereby introducing "a comical or fantastic" effect; the narrator in Sterne's *Tristram Shandy* is one such example.[15] This "metalepsis" befits the destabilization caused by a prologue that diverts the audience from the subject of the play, or an epilogue where a character reflects back on the play's events. Thus, Charlotte Butler, who played the titular role in Aphra Behn's *The City-Heiress*, reflects back on her character sarcastically in the epilogue: "My Part, I fear, will take with but a few, / A Rich young Heiress to her first Love true!"[16] In the opening couplet of her epilogue, Butler's incredulity about a character the audience may have sympathized with during the past three hours implicitly questions how they could have done so. This and many other epilogues—predominantly performed by women—create what I call a "retroactive metalepsis," a directing of the audience to reflect on (or in Butler's case, to laugh off) characterizations and other elements of the play. As the Gwyn and Butler examples demonstrate, performed epilogues can unsettle characterizations. When occurring after tragedies, this retroactive metalepsis also interrupts genre, as demonstrated by the comic epilogue to *Tyrannick Love*.

Printed prologues and epilogues similarly disrupted the reading experience. Their publication as both peritexts and epitexts occasioned various paths of readerly consumption, which in turn toyed with character and genre. Readers of the precirculated broadside may have then anticipated a comic role from Butler, thereby influencing their reception of the performance. With postperformance play publications, the number and placement of paratexts meant that readers experienced plays differently according to the edition they read. Prologues in play quartos appeared before the play, mirroring the location they held onstage, but the quartos often included additional prologues, as well as dedications, encomiums to the author, and other peritexts. Epilogues often followed act 5, matching the performance order, but at other times, especially in the late Restoration and increasingly throughout the eighteenth century, they appeared right after the prologue, before the dramatis personae and the playtext. So if readers read the publication through from first leaf to last, they stood to have different conceptions of character and genre, based on the number and ordering of peritexts. Readers of the 1702 edition of *Tyrannick Love*, for example, encountered the epilogue right after the prologue, thus experiencing Valeria's revival before she actually died.[17]

These apparent disruptions do, however, suit Genette's sense of paratexts as providing a "better" interpretation of the main text.[18] But we must reorient the notions of "better" and "more pertinent" for the particular milieu of the Restoration period. Better, for Restoration theater, must first and foremost indicate commercial success. Before all other objectives, the prologue and epilogue flatter, cajole, insult, and take any number of approaches to draw their audiences back to the theater for successive performances.[19] And because of their metaleptical relationship to the play, "more pertinent" includes interfering with the play's characters, genre, and affect. These paratexts accordingly supply entertainment in the form of often-disruptive commentary that may or may not concern the play at all. There are no ghosts, devils, or sprites in *Tyrannick Love*, for example, yet Gwyn references them all in the epilogue.

Although Genette defines the paratext in ways useful for conceptualizing dramatic prologues and epilogues, some theater scholars have favored alternate approaches. The authors of *Prologues to Shakespeare's Theatre*, Douglas Bruster and Robert Weimann, for example, cite three reasons for rejecting Genette: he only considers a text circulating within a literate world; he acknowledges but does not explore paratexts produced by others besides the author; and he focuses on the novel.[20] While these are legitimate criticisms, I wish to argue that there is enough flexibility and applicability in Genette's theory to address the important issues that Bruster and Weimann identify. I seek to do so by considering, first and foremost, the genders of Restoration performers, and the ways in which the relationship between gender and genre necessitates, in the theatrical and print cultural contexts of the Restoration, a revision of what Genette identifies above as "the author and his allies." In the paratextual world of Restoration theater, the play's author should not be singled out as the primary agent; the prologue and epilogue may have come from another writer, circulated before the first performance and without the author's name on it, been grafted to the performance without the author's consent, and benefited the company as a whole. And as Restoration playwrights could not yet profit from the public sale of their works by printers and booksellers (who might better substitute here for "author" in Genette's conceptualization of that term), arguably their greatest allies were the actors and actresses who spoke their prologues and epilogues, inducing audiences not just to stay but also to return again and again to watch the performance of their work. In this respect, I further contend that the Restoration actress was the author's best friend of all.

Gender as a Defining Element

Could a male actor have delivered Gwyn's epilogue? Comparatively, the male paratextual orator had a more limited range of stances: he could discuss or satirize the same subjects of cultural and theatrical politics; he could innocuously, or wryly, welcome audiences; or he could adopt clownish poses such as riding an ass onstage (as did Joseph Haines; see chapter 1). But Gwyn also scoffs at her character and the play, and jokes with sexual irreverence: two actions beyond the scope of male paratexts. Her epilogue is gender-representative in this respect; the disruptions prologues and epilogues perform on character, plot, and genre almost always emanate from female examples.

In her groundbreaking essay "Decomposing History (Why Are There So Few Women in Theatre History?)," Susan Bennett calls for a new strategy for studying women's historical contributions to theater.[21] Bennett argues that revisionism, as a feminist strategy, adds female playwrights to a conventional narrative of theater history but fails to challenge that narrative. Elsewhere, she identifies "the search for truth," typically a male model, as omitting theater's "narratives, theories, and imagination."[22] Now, argues Bennett, we need to "decompose" that conventional model itself to rewrite the history of women's participation in theater.

An irony of Restoration prologues and epilogues is that since, as a sub-genre, they have garnered little thorough treatment, analyses of them have not actively contributed to the demotion of women's theatrical history. In fact, the title of Autrey Nell Wiley's pioneering article, "Female Prologues and Epilogues in English Plays" (1933), points to the significance of gender for Restoration paratexts. In addition to tracing their origins, topics, style of delivery, and publishing history in her important follow-up, *Rare Prologues and Epilogues, 1642–1700* (1940), Wiley singles out female paratexts for consideration and identifies the 1670s and 1690s as decades particularly hospitable to their performances. The insightful and example-replete book by Mary Knapp, *Prologues and Epilogues of the Eighteenth Century* (1961), discusses paratexts written for both female and male performers and identifies the "indecent" aspect of some female epilogues, an important observation that in this study I rename "bawdy" and treat at length in chapters 2 and 5.[23] But while several other articles have offered insights about prologues and epilogues, their limited scopes de-emphasize or misconstrue gender.[24] In "Rhetorical Patterns in Restoration Prologues and Epilogues," for example, Emmett Avery selects nearly all of his examples from the first half of the Restoration, before the heydays of the greatest Restoration actresses and performers of paratexts: Elizabeth Barry, Anne Bracegirdle, and Anne Oldfield.[25] And while David Roberts discusses prologues and epilogues in his important book on Restoration female playgoers, his inattention to their speakers provokes misinterpretations of their content.[26] Articles and books that do not make prologues and epilogues their main subject, moreover, cannot do justice to the great number of prologues and epilogues written during this time, given that 1,570 examples survive from between 1660 and 1714. Meanwhile, the compilations by Pierre Danchin—*The Prologues and Epilogues of the Restoration* (1981–1988) and

The Prologues and Epilogues of the Eighteenth Century (1990–1994)—beautifully lay out the field for all future analyses of these paratexts, with helpful glosses that grow more extensive in each successive volume and minimal editorializing.[27] In short, the majority of my critical forebears' work has let the paratexts be, without creating a tradition that excludes women but also—to refer back to Bennett—without attempting to theorize about or imagine the role women may have played, through this form, in shaping the narrative of the Restoration stage.

My own theory in this book is that although there are more male than female prologues and epilogues (just as there were many more male than female writers and actors), a comprehensive discussion of Restoration theatrical paratexts must emphasize the female variety as the more versatile form and must note the groundbreaking opportunity they afforded women to speak out in public. By and large, it is the female examples that create new kinds of relationships with the audience. The content of these first actresses' paratexts ranges more widely than that of their male counterparts, and they demonstrate huge leaps in female public participation. Prologues and epilogues often contained political and cultural commentary. This meant that actresses critiqued politics, generic conventions, and cultural attitudes toward women and received approbation, as testified by the proliferation of such paratexts. Whether the prologues and epilogues were *in propria persona* is largely irrelevant. The manner of downstage direct address might lead the audience to interpret the ideas as belonging to the actress, not the playwright. But the more significant point is that the woman is given a voice.

We also need to stop and recognize this cultural moment: Restoration prologues and epilogues presented the first sanctioned spaces for nonmonarchical British women to voice ideas, theirs and others', in public. The eighth of December 1660 was a landmark day in British theater history, when the first professional actress stepped onto the public stage to play Desdemona. But to this we should add the date of the first female speaker of a paratext in a public theater—if only we knew it. What we do know is that the latest possible date is 23 February 1663, at Lincoln's Inn Fields theater, when Mrs. Gibbs spoke the epilogue to a production of Sir Robert Stapylton's *The Slighted Maid* wearing breeches and making a pun on "clap." From then on, prologues and epilogues offered opportunities for women to create comedy, comment on politics and culture, address both male and female audiences, and receive applause for their outspokenness. While the content of female prologues and epilogues varies from protofeminist to misogynist, they nevertheless represent the first licensed opportunity for British women to participate in the public sphere.

And the extensive print dissemination of prologues and epilogues, with their speakers' names attached, means performances were circulated and preserved.

Can we say that their paratexts represented actresses' points of view? Some critics have argued that an actor is merely the empty vessel that the (usually male) playwright filled with words. But besides the common retort that such an approach overlooks the actor as creating a role, this claim contradicts the critical commonplace that the Restoration theater was an "actors' theater," where playwrights wrote parts for specific actors to perform throughout their careers, and that it gave birth to celebrity culture, whetting appetites for details of actors' personal lives. These aspects hold especially true for performances of prologues and epilogues. Roles such as Horner in *The Country Wife* and Millamant in *The Way of the World* have survived the actors for whom they were originally created. But in performance, prologues and epilogues lived and died with the performer; my research has turned up only twelve Restoration prologues and epilogues that were passed down to other performers.[28] Finally, during the Restoration a paratext occasionally provoked arrest; for example, Aphra Behn and actress Mary Lee, Lady Slingsby, were apprehended for the epilogue to *Romulus and Hersilia, or, the Sabine War* (1682), which made fun of the Duke of Monmouth during the Exclusion Crisis.[29] We do not know whether this epilogue reflected Lee's politics, but we should consider her to have been much more than an empty vessel—as did the people who authorized her arrest.

Of particular interest are the connections that prologues and epilogues enabled actresses to make with female audiences. Between 1660 and 1714, a minimum of 115 prologues and epilogues feature actresses either directly addressing female spectators or more generally implying community with them.[30] In twelve of what I call "solidarity" paratexts, actresses ask women for support because male spectators "dare not disapprove when you applaud."[31] While paratexts base female authority on the notion that upper-class women have a more developed sense of virtue—a belief stronger at the end of the Restoration than at the beginning—many instead appeal to women's wit or charm, or simply assume that women can influence men. Forty-one paratexts feature the actress representing her gender collectively, one being the prologue by Dryden to Lee's *The Princess of Cleve* (1682) where the actress complains, "There's Treason in the Play against our Sex."[32] Many solicit female favor by laughing at men, such as the second prologue to Vanbrugh's *The Relapse* (1696), in which Susannah Mountfort Verbruggen says that female spectators can anticipate the play's many pleasures, including the silly beaux who will entertain them between the acts.[33] Seven court women by appealing to their sexuality, such as Anne Bracegirdle's epilogue to *The Maid's Last Prayer* (1693), which urges women not to stay virginal for too long.[34] Through such prologues and epilogues, actresses cultivated an active and varied body of female spectators, offering these viewers many more ways of experiencing theater than has previously been thought.

Not surprisingly, female prologues and epilogues were frequently exploitative and sometimes misogynistic. And yet this can be seen as a further confirmation of the expressly gendered aspect of prologues and epilogues, not least in their frequent focus on the female body. We have, for example, the "breeches" paratext, where the actress, clothed in that masculine vestment, delivered supposedly self-referential double entendres. Such paratexts may have lured the audience into feeling what Joseph Roach calls "public intimacy," here indicating an illusory sexualized bond with the performer.[35] Revealing the actress's calves and ankles, and separating the legs, the titillating breeches costume was at least artistically merited in plays, when female characters cross-dressed to advance their own interests. But no such motivations existed in paratexts. Female bodily exploitation is especially apparent when one considers that at least six plays featured a breeches prologue or epilogue when no character cross-dressed in the play.[36] And yet, as the next section elucidates, I argue that women performing comedy onstage was itself a protofeminist act.

Comic Performance

The first word of Gwyn's epilogue, "Hold," must have sent a shock through the Restoration audience, for it violates numerous rules of genre and gender. It interrupts the somber death scene and the potential for audience catharsis; it disorients the audience; it reanimates a character; and, perhaps most shockingly, it represents a woman reprimanding a man (albeit a presumed servant). The emphatic directive reverses gender privilege; a woman arrests a man's range of motion. The subsequent incredulous "are you mad?" augments her power at his expense, while "you damn'd confounded dog" confirms him as the butt of a joke.

After the opening couplet, Gwyn addresses the audience full-frontally and downstage, typical blocking for Restoration prologues and epilogues and akin to that of modern-day standup comedy. Allowing for significant cultural differences in the joke fodder and the audience makeup, it is useful to compare prologues and epilogues to standup's performance-oriented, typically single-clown style of comedy. A comedian's routine consists of mini-narratives, each of which can in different performances be emphasized or minimized according to the audience's reception and with no necessary connection to each other save that they develop and trade on the comedian's persona. Successful standup comedians create personae that the audience should be able to imagine in a variety of situations. While usually the province of a solo comedian, standup, like theatrical paratexts, is sometimes performed in pairs or groups. The audience either knows beforehand or else quickly learns the comedian's persona or "shtick." The comedian can target a mixture of present individuals or groups, or absent third parties. Audience members may feel excitement and trepidation if they sense that they may become involved in the act. Either the comedian generates material, or another writes it and tailors it to that performer. Shows vary nightly; performance theorists remind us of the lack of fixedness between any text and performance, but the degree of vacillation in standup is especially wide due to the emphasis on eliciting audience response.[37] Philip Auslander implies this when he describes standup as "a fundamentally old-fashioned, labor-intensive, low-tech performance mode" that depends upon the "human presence" of performers and audience.[38] Regarding the connection between comedian and audience, established in part because of the customary direct address to the audience, Lawrence E. Mintz says it is founded on paradox: pathos generates the audience's pity and superior laughter, but also their investment and promotion, so that the comedian becomes their spokesperson.[39]

Restoration and early eighteenth-century prologues and epilogues share many features with standup. First and foremost, persona dominates. The comic content and the delivery style must appear either consistent or blatantly inconsistent with the persona. The number of performers is also regular; usually delivered solo, prologues and epilogues were sometimes performed in duos, and occasionally in other groupings, especially during their evolution in the mid-1660s through the 1670s.[40] Targets were similarly topical. The *eiron* predominates; there is no triumphant "green world" of the kind that Northrop Frye imagines.[41] The performer's physical relationship to space also remains consistent; especially for prologue speakers, who performed in front of the curtain, there was little need for a complex background scene. There is similarly little need for depth; to have the best chance of connecting with the audience, performers would mostly have used the forestage (illustrations of prologue and epilogue performers confirm this convention). Finally, as Auslander points out for standup, prologues and epilogues used little, if any, of the Restoration theater technology, such as flying machines and moveable scenery, depending instead on the persona and the word.

Historical circumstances gave Restoration actresses access to such come-dic personae and words. The marginalization of Puritanism, the reopening of the theaters, and the king's patronage helped make possible the advent of the actress, and her position was popularized and sustained, as Katherine Eisa-mann Maus says, because of prurient interest in her sex life, most frequently alluded to in prologues and epilogues.[42] This made room for the actress to represent the exception to steady prohibition of female public involvement. Through such motions as wearing breeches or putting fingers on her forehead to indicate the cuckold's horns, the actress is sexualized. The conditions that supported the rise of the actress reflect a new receptiveness toward women as comic practitioners.

Yet to have an audience laughing at a joke, whether the target is another or oneself, is to control many people at once; for women, this position remains difficult to obtain. Standup comedy poses particular challenges and stigmas for female performers. In his study of humor, anthropologist Mahadev Apte ob-serves cross-cultural limitations on women as comic practitioners. Apte finds that especially in situations where men are present, women avoid aggressive jokes such as witty attacks, insults, and pranks.[43] Because the words "aggres-sive" and "dominant" carry negative connotations when assigned to women, it is not surprising that women often avoid behavior that might fall under these labels. In *Jokes and Their Relations to the Unconscious*, Freud theorizes a joke triangle consisting of joker, target, and audience—a configuration that can help determine agency in paratextual relationships between actor, author, and audience—but he envisions women inhabiting only the role of target.[44] Studies confirm that historical and cross-cultural social conditions limit the opportuni-ties and range of female jokers.[45] To succeed, Restoration actresses needed to develop such "male" behaviors associated with delivering comedy, becoming comfortable using their bodies as joke fodder and running the risk of giving of-fense that might provoke retaliation (or arrest). Especially in light of such en-during and cross-cultural obstructions, as scholar and former standup comedian Joanne Gilbert claims, the mere presence of women "standing onstage and speaking can be construed as 'feminist.' A woman onstage taking up time and space and getting paid is rhetorically and economically empowered."[46]And in performing comedy, women, as Regina Barreca says, "are exploring their own powers; they are refusing to accept social and cultural boundaries that mark the need or desire for closure as a 'universal.'"[47] Given such issues, for a woman to stand onstage in Restoration England and perform comedy, no matter the content, was a remarkable achievement, and it also indicated an audience will-ing to recognize the female performer as comedian.

Audience Taste and Influence

Tyrannick Love was a smash hit in 1669, running for fourteen straight days.[48] And while we don't know whether Gwyn performed the epilogue every night—scholars still differ over whether prologues and epilogues usually were performed on a play's first night, first three nights, or entire first run—several subsequent materials confirm the epilogue's endurance in the Restoration.[49] One measure of its popularity was an allusion six years later in the epilogue to the tragedy *Piso's Conspiracy*:

> It is a Trick of late grown much in Vogue,
> When all are Kill'd, to raise an *Epilogue*.
> This, some Pert Rymer wittily contriv'd
> For a Surprize, whil'st the Arch Wag believ'd;
> 'Twould please You to see Pretty *Miss* reviv'd.[50]

Alluding directly to Dryden and Gwyn and to the one intermediary example, *Herod and Mariamne* (1673), these lines help establish the endurance of the revived epilogue. In a pamphlet exchange in 1673, the author of the misleadingly named *The Friendly Vindication of Mr. Dryden* complains about the ghosts in *Tyrannick Love* singing and dancing and having shrill voices. A response, *Mr Dreyden Vindicated*, defends these cabaret ghosts by citing two lines from Gwyn's epilogue.[51] And, as the appendix to this study shows, there were seventeen subsequent revived epilogues.

How did audiences feel about prologues and epilogues more generally, and how influential were their opinions? In the sections of *Paratexts* devoted to the preface (a term he extends beyond the prefix "pre-" to apply to texts "consisting of a discourse produced on the subject of the text that follows or precedes it"), Genette stresses that, unlike other paratexts such as the title, prefatory paratexts are not essential.[52] Yet to Restoration audiences, such paratexts became mandatory. Following their predecessors Thomas Dekker and Thomas Middleton, Dryden and Colley Cibber sold prologues and epilogues to other, less experienced playwrights, demonstrating demand.[53] We have several instances of authors complaining about the need to write prologues and epilogues, and the difficulty in creating original documents due to the huge body of forerunners. The prologue to Alexander Greene's *The Polititian Cheated* (1663) includes the lines:

> Poets have harder dealings amongst men
> In these our days than ever; for they'll have
> Forsooth of late that which they never gave,

> Prologues before, and Epilogues succeeding
> And they not like'd, unless they be exceeding
> Rarely compos'd.[54]

Such demands affirm the great influence audiences wielded, an agency augmented by theatrical structures and conventions. Audiences in general, and Restoration audiences in particular, influence the direction and success of a performance. Vsevolod Meyerhold promotes the idea of audiences as "co-creators" of plays, a concept Susan Bennett develops at length in her important book, *Theatre Audiences*.[55] While conventions of naturalistic theater such as the darkened auditorium and the maintenance of the fourth wall promote audience passivity, many contemporary practices, such as call-and-response theater, nevertheless activate the audience into the role of cocreator. The chance noises and related occurrences within any performance, moreover, are just as likely to be "contributed" by audience members. But in Restoration theater, Meyerhold's concept is even more integral. As the opening lines of Gwyn's epilogue exemplify, the prologue and epilogue speakers break and remake the fourth wall with each different line of dialogue, sustaining an intimacy with the audience members and building on their fascination with the actor-stars' personae and private lives.

Restoration and eighteenth-century theatergoing practices demonstrate the priority audiences put on seeing, or avoiding, prologues and epilogues.[56] Performance theorists such as Richard Schechner argue that how audiences travel to and from the theater, where they sit, how early they arrive and how late they stay, and how much they pay for admission shapes their experience of the play and is therefore key to understanding the performance.[57] Restoration and eighteenth-century audiences saw themselves and each other as part of the entertainment, a practice enabled in part by theater design, from theaters such as the original Drury Lane through its many reincarnations. A few aspects of such stagecraft were that the lighting was equally distributed throughout the theater, audience members sat onstage until 1762 (meaning other audience members looked at them alongside the players), and box seats were geared more toward displaying their occupants than providing the best views of the stage. Also, the audience's comings and goings necessarily led to varied interpretations of the play and its prologue and epilogue. Restoration theater audiences could visit the theater for the two curtain-tunes and the prologue, then depart with a full refund; many patrons considered these three short performances worth the effort. Audiences similarly could pay "after-money" (normally one-half the price of a full ticket) to attend acts 4 and 5, the epilogue, and any subsequent performances such as afterpieces.[58]

And scholarship has expanded Restoration audiences well beyond the upper classes; Judith Milhous, for example, has pointed out that Christopher Rich admitted servants of upper-class attendees to the upper gallery for free.[59] In short, various audiences attended the theater in various ways, some of which did not prioritize watching an intact narrative. In considering Restoration theater in performance, it therefore may be appropriate to think of the theatrical evening as featuring not only narratives but also a series of momentary performances. Such an approach prioritizes the prologue or epilogue.

Erving Goffman's description of the curtain call further complicates the role of prologue and epilogue: "At curtain calls actors routinely maintain the costume they wore when the curtain came down, but now the costumes are worn by individuals who do not fill them characterologically but slackly serve as mere hangers, a hat off or a scarf missing, as though to make a point that nothing real is to be attributed to the guise."[60] An extension of Goffman's point is that the imperfect costuming of the curtain call may make the audience feel that they are closing in on the supposedly "real" person underneath. Restoration theater predates the curtain call but, to use Goffman's terms, the epilogue represents a new personage who fills the clothes half characterologically and half slackly. In epilogues featuring "betweenness," the player complicates character by combining with it a second performance of a certain kind of slackness, a guise of reality. The character is still partially present, but the actress also performs a persona who may be hyperaware of her odd attire (such as when wearing breeches) or sexually self-advertising through—or in spite of—the costume.

Betweenness, the Actress, and the Epilogue

The slippage of character and persona described above formed a third figure that inhabited what I call a state of "betweenness": a moment of staged liminality. In this role, perspective changed without warning, so the meaning of the self-reference, the "I," continuously fluctuated. The fourth line of Gwyn's epilogue exemplifies this state: "I am the Ghost of poor departed *Nelly*." The word "Ghost" alludes to both the dead Valeria and the fact that someone onstage, dressed as her, is suddenly animate. And "Nelly" refamiliarizes the audience with this entity, evoking the character's demise while reminding them of their affection for the actress.[61] She simultaneously performs her character, who has just died in the play, and her persona as a wit unsuited to solemn roles. Betweenness, a deliberate hybridization of her onstage role and offstage public persona, is thus a primary source of the epilogue's comedy.[62]

As a concept, betweenness is not gendered. Whenever a player delivers a line referring to both character and persona, a comic betweenness occurs.

A case of male betweenness occurs, for example, in the epilogue of Thomas D'Urfey's *The Virtuous Wife* (performed 1679; published 1680). The 1680 quarto says the epilogue was spoken "By Mr *Nokes*, Representing my Lady *BEARDLY*," and toward the end this entity says, "I'le change my *Sex*, and then/Cast my *Snakes-Skin*, and thus turn *Nokes* agen."[63] The speaker's self-reference thus encapsulates the character of Lady Beardly and the persona of Nokes, reinforced by the subsequent stage direction: *"Pulls off all his Head-cloaths."*

Betweenness, however, chiefly occurs in female epilogues. In prologues the incidence is lower, in part because they occur before the play, and so only if the audience had previously attended or read the play would they be acquainted with the player's character. Epilogues, though, were both rife with betweenness and more frequently delivered by actresses. The epilogue as framing device meant that the speaker could simultaneously perform and reflect on her character, in what Felicity Nussbaum has called a "double consciousness."[64] In uniting the actress's persona and character, betweenness created a rich, innuendo-laden language wherein every word and gesture invited the audience to decipher, moment by moment, which entity it reflected.

Because these female epilogues populated tragedies, they in turn challenged generic integrity. *Tyrannick Love* and many other tragedies frequently took a prominent, suffering female character and reconceived her as a comedian within their epilogues. Still wearing her act 5 costume, the actress combined two entities: her tragic role in the play and her sexualized public persona. In reinterpreting the play's tragic content as comic, the epilogue blends incongruity and innuendo, with the result degrading the original character. It likewise revises the play's subject matter, lessening the villain's magnitude, the hero's fall, and the lover's sorrow. Thus in *Tyrannick Love*, by abandoning filial loyalty to save her lover but then ridiculing in the epilogue the dramatic construct that occasioned her death, Valeria/Gwyn breaks the rules of generic rule-breaking.

This type of ending indicates that many authors and theater managers sacrificed principles of neoclassicism to audience demand. Although the performance structure of prologue-play-epilogue might seem a neoclassical symmetry, the epilogue's skewing of character creates an incongruity. The epilogue also abbreviates the play's tragic catharsis. The primary characters' grief and death, the audience's purgation of its flaws, and the restoration of an ordered society all precede the epilogue, whose speaker reintroduces disorder by interrupting the audience's prior conception of the heroine. The epilogue greets the heightened emotionalism of catharsis with flippant comedy born of betweenness. And out of this betweenness emerges a distinctive brand of theatrical agency that in some senses is unique to the Restoration stage.

Agency: Actor, Author, Audience

Prologues and epilogues illustrate a key element of Restoration theater: its collaborative nature and shared agency between actor, author, and spectator. First there is the matter of their composition. While it has been argued that late seventeenth-century playwrights rarely wrote collaboratively, prologues and epilogues demonstrate otherwise. In *Authorship and Appropriation: Writing for the Stage in England, 1660–1700*, Paulina Kewes states that of the four hundred plays written during the Restoration, only two were composed through a professional partnership (Dryden and Lee) and that the scarcity represents a growing valuation of the solitary writer.[65] This is, however, the narrowest definition of collaboration and one that makes less sense when considering writing for performance. Plenty of writers contributed prologues and epilogues to other writers' plays; many did this out of friendship, while others sold prologues for two to three guineas apiece.[66] Numerous other prologues and epilogues are designated as "written by a person of quality" or, especially in the 1690s, "sent from an unknown hand." Regarding the extant paratexts between 1660 and August 1714, outsiders supplied prologues and epilogues 229 times. Some of these documents read as if their contributors knew next to nothing about the play to which they were contributing their paratexts; others integrate an element of the play, such as a specific character or theme; and still others read as if written by the playwright.[67] In a similar scenario, prologues and epilogues were sometimes delivered by actors who did not otherwise act in the play.

Then there is the matter of their performance, a flexible and always-shifting site in which author, actor, and audience together make meaning. The author of the prologue and epilogue has in many cases customized it for a particular actor, so while the author is responsible for the words on a page, the actor is also a cocreator. In many cases, the performer also adopts a persona—such as Gwyn, the bawdy flirt who laughs at Dryden for miscasting her in a tragedy. In these cases—occurring especially for women and more frequently in epilogues—the persona matters as much as the performer herself. The public's perception of the persona takes on life almost as a fourth entity, in this case the betweenness of Valeria and the persona of Gwyn. What the author writes clearly matters here, but it relies on the actress's role and independent persona. Compelled by her celebrity and by audience demand, the author thus disappears into the actress, investing her with an unusual amount of agency.

Just as prologues and epilogues have different performance and publication histories, and interact both with and independently of their plays, so too do they give different levels of agency to their authors, speakers, and

audiences. Within the collaborative meaning-making circuit of author, actor, and audience, in individual prologues and epilogues two of these entities frequently possess agency at the expense of the third. The actor's stage
persona and the audience's expectations often exert a collective agency that,
in and through performance, trumps the writer's textual authority. Agency
combines in different ways according to the type of paratext, the gender of
the actor and audience member, and the author's identity.

Certainly in several Restoration paratexts, more agency accrues to the
author than to the actor. In such cases the actor serves as a cipher, representing or defending the author's ideas without giving them personal in-
flection. The prologue to George Farquhar's *The Recruiting Officer* (1706),
for example, features no acknowledgment of the speaker and concentrates
on a sly reinterpretation of *The Odyssey*, where British playwrights outwrite
blind Homer because "so many Hellens" in the audience inspire them.[68]
In many paratexts spoken by women, however, strong actresses embody
and exploit the tension and dynamic interplay between their gendered
presence onstage and the male playwright's ghosted hand; the epilogue to
Tyrannick Love features the lines "O Poet, damn'd dull Poet, who could
prove/So sensless! to make *Nelly* dye for Love," where Dryden and Gwyn
create a joke at Dryden's expense.[69] Betweenness also enlarges the actor's
agency, since there are now two combined entities to consider. "I am the
Ghost of poor departed *Nelly*" crowds the author out of shaping this figure.
And paratexts where the actor addresses parts of the audiences (such as an
actress addressing women) even emphasize female agency at the expense
of the male audience. Thus, when the female speaker of the prologue to
Lee's *The Princess of Cleve* tells women, "There's treason in the play against
our sex," she builds a comic and agential solidarity with them at the expense—although probably also the amusement—of the male audience.
And then there is the question of outside contributors of prologues and
epilogues, who can further advance a play's theme or write for a specific
actor, thus weighting agency toward the former or the latter, most often the
latter in the case of female performers. Add to this the audience members,
who possess the ultimate agency. They may call for encores, commanding
Anne Oldfield, for example, to repeat her epilogue to Ambrose Philips's
The Distrest Mother (1712). Or their boos may chase an actor off the stage.
Later in the book I offer a taxonomy of paratexts, but here I want to clarify
that even more than the authority of the plays themselves, the authority
of any given paratext emerges from a collaborative nexus developed among
author, audience, and actor. The shifts and slippages within that nexus
inevitably complicate but also partially define the overarching project of

this study—especially with respect to questions of gender identification on the stage and issues of genre interpretation on the page.

In Print: Broadsides, Quartos, Compilations, and Pictures

Despite their divergent publication formats, and contrary to Stern's claim that prologues and epilogues in the early modern theater cannot affect play interpretations, I argue that Restoration and eighteenth-century play publication facilitated reading and thus potentially interpreting the original prologue and epilogue alongside its play. In most cases throughout the Restoration, new editions of plays retained the original prologue and epilogue. These editions thus conveyed theater history lessons, especially since they also usually contained the original dramatis personae. This publishing practice prevailed even though play reprinting coincided with performance revivals and their accompanying new casts. *Tyrannick Love* exemplifies the connection maintained between a play, its paratext, and the original speaker; the epilogue appears in all nine quarto editions between 1717 and 1735, and in several (but not all) of the eighteenth-century Dryden anthologies, with "Mrs *Ellen*" (Gwyn) listed as speaker.[70]

But there are other factors to consider when reading these plays. In addition to some printers' heterotaxic approach, relocating epilogues to the front matter, certain plays also featured more than one prologue or epilogue, contributed by another playwright or "person of quality." The publication history of Congreve's *Love for Love* demonstrates the mutability of reading experiences that can arise from the number and location of paratexts. I have inspected forty-eight play publications (all but two of which are distinct editions) of Congreve's *Love for Love*, from its first publication in 1695 to its most recent, in 2011. The early editions include two prologues: one "Sent from an unknown hand" for Bracegirdle, and another written by Congreve for actor Thomas Betterton, usually published in that order. Among these editions, fifteen print both prologues, twenty-nine (beginning in 1710, when Congreve famously collaborated with printer Jacob Tonson) print only the Betterton prologue, and four omit both paratexts. Fifteen also place the epilogue up front, following the prologue(s). D. F. McKenzie has argued that in the 1710 edition, Congreve and Tonson used printing elements such as "decorative head-pieces and tail-pieces, ornamental drop initials for each act, and type ornaments to separate the scenes," to capture more of the performance within the text.[71] All of this emphasizes the great disparity in how playtexts were presented to readers, and demonstrates that prologues and epilogues often, but not always, play important roles in textual presentation and thus readers' meaning-making processes.

Prologues and epilogues also possessed the potential to sway the play's reception when they circulated as broadside advertisements. Bennett discusses how, today, people who have reserved tickets can prepare for the performance by perusing its marketing, reading the playtext, and soliciting the opinions of friends and reviewers.[72] In the Restoration, one method of preparation consisted of reading broadside publications of prologues and epilogues. Autrey Nell Wiley has compiled a helpful list of the sixty prologues and forty-five epilogues still extant that were published individually between 1642 and 1872, showing the frequency and endurance of this practice.[73]

Some broadsides, however, provide strange counterexamples. One might expect that a precirculated prologue and epilogue would condition viewers for the genre of the forthcoming play: either comedy or tragedy. But several broadsides of comic prologues and epilogues advertised tragedies. Amassing during the Exclusion Crisis, these include the prologues and epilogues to *Mithridates, King of Pontus* (1681), Settle's *The Heir of Morocco* (1682), Southerne's *The Loyal Brother* (1682), Dryden's *The Duke of Guise* (1683; two epilogues), and Lee's *Constantine the Great* (1683), all of which featured female speakers. Another is the aforementioned epilogue to Behn's tragedy, *Romulus and Hersilia* (1682), which resulted in the arrests of author and speaker. This last example is a "revived" epilogue, like Gwyn's where the dead character comes back to life, so those who read the epilogue in advance of the performance would already have the ending "spoiled," as they would know that her character was going to die. But circulated during the thick of the Exclusion Crisis, the political epilogue might have also tipped off opponents ahead of time to have the actress arrested after she finally spoke the epilogue. Prologue and epilogue broadsides influenced public reception, sometimes in unexpected ways.

Both their inclusion within miscellanies and the existence of collections of prologues and epilogues throughout the Restoration and eighteenth century also demonstrate that the paratexts could thrive independently. Between 1660 and 1714 were printed forty-seven miscellanies containing prologues and epilogues, and the practice continued throughout the eighteenth century. Beginning with Thomas Jordan's *A Rosary of Rarities Planted in a Garden of Poetry* (1663), some poetry collections featured prologues and epilogues, as did drolleries such as the *Covent Garden Drollery* (1672). Newspapers and magazines also published prologues and epilogues. The eighteenth century, moreover, saw several anthologies consisting entirely of prologues and epilogues, the most significant of which is the four-volume *Collection and Selection of English Prologues and Epilogues, Commencing with Shakespeare and*

Concluding with Garrick (1779), which includes the epilogue to *Tyrannick Love* and many others by Dryden.

Additional evidence of their endurance comes from pictures of prologue and epilogue speakers. The *Tyrannick Love* epilogue appears in pictorial form (see figure 1.1). Buckingham's *Works* (1715) includes a picture, titled "The Key to the Rehearsal," of Gwyn rising from the dead.[74] Surrounded by three people, two of whom support her body, Gwyn appears front and center on a gurney. The picture represents the moment when Gwyn reawakens: her arms stretch out like wings and her left hand shoves away the head of one of the pallbearers, who grimaces from the contact. On the extreme right a shadowy figure watches her with his one visible arm extended, mirroring hers. He casts a shadow toward her, but her radiant body diverts the darkness underneath the gurney. Light shines through the Bridges Street Theatre windows from what looks to be scenic stage left, and two aristocratic men casually lean on the columns, taking her reanimation in stride. Gwyn is draped like a Botticelli heroine, with cloth falling between her legs and revealing her navel. The artist has comically aligned her pelvis with a spouting fountain. The moment being represented is evident; one can almost hear Gwyn say, "Hold!"

The Restoration featured three types of theatrical illustrations: portraits of individual actors in elegant clothing, with no obvious connection to the theater; pictures of actors playing roles, without their lines included; and players delivering prologues and epilogues, which often include between one and four of their lines. Additional Restoration-era pictures of actors and actresses delivering prologues and epilogues include Anne Marshall Quin delivering the epilogue to Behn's *Sir Patient Fancy*, accompanied by two lines; and two pictures of Joseph Haines delivering his "ass epilogue" to Thomas Scott's *The Unhappy Kindness* (1696)[75] (see figure 1.2). While the sample size is too small to support universal claims, it should be noted that these pictures not only highlight the fact that popular actors were chosen to deliver prologues and epilogues but also solidify the connection between specific actors and customized paratexts.[76]

Engaging issues of gender, genre, and audience reception in performance and print, the study of female prologues and epilogues fundamentally changes our understanding of Restoration theater. Through betweenness and its frequently resultant retroactive metalepsis, which reformulated the plot and the audience's theater experience, female prologues and especially epilogues alter our understanding of genre. As chapter 5 shows, attempts by eighteenth-century critics such as Joseph Addison and Jeremy Collier to define paratexts' inconsistent and murky relationship to the play indicate

"The Key to the Rehearsal." The Works of His Grace, George Villiers, Late Duke of Buckingham, vol. 2 (London: Sam Briscoe, 1715), frontispiece.
By permission of the Folger Shakespeare Library.

Jo Haines delivering an "ass epilogue." From Thomas Brown, The Fifth Volume of the Works of Thomas Brown (London, 1721), opposite page 233.
By permission of the Huntington Library, San Marino, California.

that they could transmit as either pleasure or threat. That prologues and epilogues employ comedy to promote the play and that actresses delivered so many of them indicate that they provided for women rare settings of a vast comic agency. But comedy requires an audience; that women were able to perform comedy and gain applause and celebrity status indicates that prologues and epilogues represented an unprecedented space in British cultural history for female public expression. Studying actresses' paratexts also changes our perception of female spectatorship. Whereas many critics have elided differences in female audience receptivity by assuming that women spectators' purpose was to certify the virtue in plays, when we study actresses' communication with those spectators via prologues and epilogues we find a wider range of options. The study of costume, theater architecture, and audience demographics helps us understand the transmission and popularity of female prologues and epilogues, and the application of performance and spectatorship theories allows us to see that the precirculation of prologues and epilogues may have conditioned audiences to anticipate the comic even when attending tragedies. So when title pages proclaim their plays tragedies, prologues and epilogues demonstrate that we cannot take them at their word.

Chapter Overview

The following chapters begin the process of rewriting Restoration theater history in light of actresses' prologues and epilogues. The book is divided into two parts. Part I explores the range of Restoration prologues and epilogues, examining a variety of speakers and styles. To trace the styles and themes of the 1,570 extant prologues and epilogues written between 1660 and 1714, chapter 1 proposes a taxonomy with two overall categories of prologues and epilogues, which I call the "cloaked" and the "exposed." Named after the costume typically worn by pre- and early Restoration prologue speakers, the "cloaked" type metaphorically conceals the speaker's identity, thus positioning the speaker as neutral, authoritative, and disembodied. It is a paratext where the audience cannot easily identify markers of the speaker's politics, religion, or appearance. The "exposed" paratext, by contrast, features gendered, bodily centered, and often personalized comedy that capitalizes on the speaker's public persona. This chapter features readings of select male and female cloaked paratexts to plays, including Behn's *The City-Heiress* and *The Young King*, Congreve's *The Way of the World*, Dryden's *The Conquest of Granada, Part I*, Pix's *The Different Widows*, and Rochester's *Valentinian*, and closes by examining two male exposed examples: Dryden's "drunken" prologue, written for Joseph Harris's *The Mistakes*, and the series of "ass epilogues" inaugurated by actor-playwright Jo Haines.

Because I define six subcategories within female exposed paratexts, chapters 2 and 3 divide and discuss these types. Focusing on comic bodily manipulation, chapter 2 examines the "breeches," "revived," and "virgin" types, and explores how their comedy derives from scrutinizing the female body. All three types rely on physical comedy, with the breeches and virgin synecdochically objectifying the body. Chapter 2 concludes by examining a more generic category of "tendentious" paratexts, which features female objectification in a less regionalized way. Here I am referencing Freud's useful term from *Jokes and Their Relations to the Unconscious*, where he claims that the effectiveness of a joke is related to the size of the taboo it breaks.[77] Jokes in this category range in their tendentiousness, from simplistic puns like the association of "die" with orgasm, to extreme moments where figures of betweenness complain that they missed out on getting raped in the play. Close readings of Dryden's *Tyrannick Love*, Otway's *Alcibiades*, D'Urfey's *Don Quixote Part II*, Cibber's *Love's Last Shift*, Vanbrugh's *The Relapse*, Pix's *Ibrahim*, and Hopkins's *Boadicea* demonstrate how these types of prologues and epilogues provide new interpretations of their plays.

Whereas chapter 2 focuses on paratexts that tend to generate comedy by exploiting the bodies of their female speakers, chapter 3 then examines how female-delivered paratexts promote connections between actresses and female audiences, especially through a critique of social issues such as marriage and male sexuality. Readings of Rochester's *Valentinian* and Lee's *The Princess of Cleve* interpret these particularly vicious plays alongside the prologues that court female audiences. And considerations of the epilogues to Behn's *The City-Heiress*, Wycherley's *The Country Wife*, and the anonymous *The Constant Nymph* demonstrate how their speakers intervened with issues from the plays and recast them from female points of view. My appendix supplements chapters 1, 2, and 3 by categorizing every extant female prologue and epilogue between 1600 and 1714.

Part II contains two case studies: one exploring how the delivery of prologues and epilogues shaped one actress's career, and the second tracing the impact that a particular epilogue had on the eighteenth-century theater world. The study of Anne Bracegirdle in chapter 4 shows how one performer's sexually customized prologues and epilogues advanced her career and, ironically, her reputation for virginity. As the foremost actress of "she-tragedies"—plays that centered on female sexual violation—Bracegirdle showed more skin than any other Restoration actress. She also delivered the highest number of female prologues and epilogues, nearly all of which were of the bawdy, "exposed" variety. How did Bracegirdle create and sustain her reputation as the "Virgin Actress" when her performances suggested the opposite? Prologues and epilogues, I argue, contributed to Bracegirdle's fame and proved the sustainability of her reputation. Her roles—particularly when she played a raped heroine—so affirmed her virginal reputation that her bawdy prologues and epilogues derived much of their comedy from the widespread belief in her virtue. A discussion of her roles in she-tragedies by Dryden, Mountfort, and others, and a reading of her prologue to Congreve's *Love for Love*, demonstrate how this combination of roles paradoxically reinforced Bracegirdle's virgin persona.

Chapter 5 traces a bawdy epilogue Joseph Addison wrote for Anne Oldfield to perform in Ambrose Philips's tragedy, *The Distrest Mother*. This lewd paratext, which celebrates female masturbation, prompted a debate in *The Spectator* about epilogues' relationships to plays. Later on, Samuel Richardson has Pamela attend a performance of the play and single out the epilogue for condemnation; by contrast, Samuel Johnson calls it the greatest epilogue ever written. It became a set piece for actresses throughout the century, delivered even by such famously chaste actresses as Sarah Siddons. The epilogue therefore necessitates a revision of eighteenth-century theater censorship as being, at times, surprisingly permissive. Prologues and epilogues were not subject to the same level of censorship as playtexts, and thus, in addition to suggesting new readings of the plays they flank, they challenge current critical arguments about eighteenth-century efforts to censor the stage. The book concludes with an appendix that categorizes actresses' prologues and epilogues according to the taxonomy.

Notes

1. Pierre Danchin, *The Prologues and Epilogues of the Restoration 1660–1700* (Nancy: Presses Universitaires de Nancy, 1981–1988), 1:321. All subsequent quotations of prologues and epilogues come from Danchin's editions, except where noted.

2. Although Samuel Pepys writes that their affair began over a year earlier, this story is recounted as fact by Peter Cunningham and Henry B. Wheatley, Edmund Curll, and Percy Fitzgerald, and in the twentieth century, by Arthur Dasent, Pierre Danchin, Lewis Melville and Kitty Shannon, and John Harold Wilson. (Derek Parker, Gwyn's recent biographer, disputes it.) If the play had in fact sparked their affair, the irony is, as Max Novak observes, that despite its dedication to James, Duke of Monmouth, Dryden had written the play for the queen. See Maximillian E. Novak and George R. Guffey, *The Works of John Dryden*, vol. 10 (Berkeley: University of California Press, 1970), 382.

3. A typical example of the use critics make of this epilogue comes from Autrey Nell Wiley, "Female Prologues and Epilogues in English Plays," *Publications of the Modern Language Association (PMLA)* 48 (1933): 1077–78. Wiley quotes twenty-four

lines and then quickly comments that such rebirths became frequent in epilogues. For additional examples of critics who quote but do not discuss the epilogue, see Katharine Eisaman Maus, "'Playhouse Flesh and Blood': Sexual Ideology and the Restoration Actress," *English Literary History* 46 (1979): 599–600; John Harold Wilson, *All the King's Ladies; Actresses of the Restoration* (Chicago: University of Chicago Press, 1958), 89. The exception is David Vieth, who within his insightful essay "The Art of the Prologue and Epilogue," spends a paragraph describing the clash of character, Gwyn's public image, and her "real" self. See David M. Vieth, "The Art of the Prologue and Epilogue: A New Approach Based on Dryden's Practice," *Genre* 5, no. 3 (1972): 281.

4. See, for example, Joseph R. Roach, "The Performance," in *The Cambridge Companion to English Restoration Theatre*, ed. Deborah Payne Fisk (Cambridge: Cambridge University Press, 2000), 31; Katherine M. Quinsey, "Introduction," in *Broken Boundaries: Women and Feminism in Restoration Drama*, ed. Katherine M. Quinsey (Lexington: University Press of Kentucky, 1996), 7–8; Elizabeth Howe, *The First English Actresses: Women and Drama, 1660–1700* (Cambridge: Cambridge University Press, 1992), 98.

5. Anthony Kaufman, "The Smiler with the Knife: Covert Aggression in Some Restoration Epilogues," *Studies in the Literary Imagination* 17, no. 1 (1984): 68.

6. Autrey Nell Wiley claims that 48 percent of plays between 1558 and 1642 feature a prologue or epilogue. See Autrey Nell Wiley, *Rare Prologues and Epilogues 1642–1700* (London: George Allen and Unwin, 1940; reprint, Port Washington, NY: Kennikat, 1970), xxvii. Pierre Danchin agrees with Wiley's percentage; see Danchin, *Restoration*, 1:xxiv–xxv. Douglas Bruster and Robert Weimann cite this figure in their recent book. See Douglas Bruster and Robert Weimann, *Prologues to Shakespeare's Theatre: Performance and Liminality in Early Modern Drama* (London: Routledge, 2004), 4; In calculating these numbers I have followed *The Works of John Dryden*, which includes the prologue to *Julius Caesar* but excludes the epilogue to *Calisto* and the prologue and epilogue to *The Mistaken Husband*. I am also counting *Secret-Love* (1667) as having one two-part prologue rather than two separate prologues.

7. For my discussion of this subject and *Spectator* papers 338 and 341, see chapter 5.

8. During the 1660s, the total number of prologues and epilogues per year never went into double digits. That changed after Gwyn's epilogue; there were a total of three prologues and epilogues in 1669, but the number in 1670 had more than quintupled, and in 1696 reached forty-six.

9. An example of the latter occurs when actress Mary Lee (later Lady Slingsby), performing in *The Constant Nymph* (1677), uses the prologue to introduce her part in the play, a cross-dressed role, and then delivers some of her lines in a female and others in a male voice. For further discussion of this prologue, see chapter 3.

10. Harold Love, "Who Were the Restoration Audience?," *Yearbook of English Studies* 10 (1980): 24, 23.

11. J. Douglas Canfield, ed., *The Broadview Anthology of Restoration and Eighteenth-Century Drama, Concise Edition* (Peterborough: Broadview, 2001; reprint, 2004), xx. In fact, Broadview president Don LePan says that he has received many complaints about this editorial methodology. Conversation with LePan, 3 June 2008.

12. Tiffany Stern, "'A Small-Beer Health to His Second Day': Playwrights, Prologues, and First Performances in the Early Modern Theater," *Studies in Philology* 101, no. 2 (2004): 197. See also her *Documents of Performance in Early Modern England* (Cambridge: Cambridge University Press, 2009), chapter 4; Shirley Strum Kenny, "The Playhouse and the Printing Shop: Editing Restoration and Eighteenth-Century Plays," *Modern Philology* 85, no. 4 (1988): 412. Kenny claims that in the eighteenth century, prologues and epilogues were published with plays, "although they . . . ordinarily have nothing to do with the contents of the play."

13. Gerard Genette, *Paratexts: Thresholds of Interpretation*, trans. Jane E. Lewin (Cambridge: Cambridge University Press, 1997), 1–2.

14. Genette, *Paratexts*, 1–2.

15. Gerard Genette, *Narrative Discourse: An Essay in Method*, trans. Jane E. Lewin (Ithaca, NY: Cornell University Press, 1980), 234.

16. Danchin, *Restoration*, 2:403.

17. John Dryden, *Tyrannick Love* (London: T. W. for Jacob Tonson and Thomas Bennet, 1702), 5.

18. Genette, *Paratexts*, 2.

19. Previous critics of prologues and epilogues have categorized them by tone; thus, we have huffing, begging, defiant, and other types. This approach can be helpful, particularly when assessing the relationship between a paratext's author and speaker, but only represents one aspect of each paratext. In addition, tones within paratexts often fluctuate. See Wiley, *Rare Prologues*, xxxvii.

20. Bruster and Weimann, *Prologues*, 38.

21. Susan Bennett, "Decomposing History (Why Are There So Few Women in Theater History?)," in *Theorizing Practice: Redefining Theatre History*, ed. W. B. Worthen and Peter Holland (Hampshire: Palgrave Macmillan, 2003), 73.

22. Susan Bennett, "Theatre History, Historiography and Women's Dramatic Writing," in *Women, Theatre and Performance*, ed. Maggie B. Gale and Viv Gardner (Manchester: Manchester University Press, 2000), 51.

23. Mary Etta Knapp, *Prologues and Epilogues of the Eighteenth Century* (New Haven, CT: Yale University Press, 1961), 103.

24. See Emmett Avery, "Rhetorical Patterns in Restoration Prologues and Epilogues," in *Essays in American and English Literature Presented to Bruce Robert McElderry, Jr.*, ed. Max Schulz, with William D. Templeman and Charles R. Metzger (Athens: Ohio University Press, 1967); James Sutherland, "Prologues, Epilogues, and Audience in the Restoration Theatre," in *Of Books and Humankind: Essays and Poems Presented to Bonamy Dobree*, ed. John Butt, J. M. Cameron, D. W. Jefferson, and Robin Skelton (London: Routledge and Kegan Paul, 1964); Vieth, "Art of the Prologue and Epilogue."

25. Avery, "Rhetorical Patterns."

26. For further discussion of Roberts's treatment of prologues and epilogues, see chapter 3. Fiona Ritchie points out, for example, that Roberts cites five lines from John Crowne's epilogue to *Juliana, or, The Princess of Poland* (1671), implying that playwrights court male at the expense of female spectators, but neglects to mention that the female speaker then reverses this hierarchy. See David Roberts, *The Ladies: Female Patronage of Restoration Drama, 1660–1700* (Oxford: Clarendon, 1989); Fiona Ritchie,

"'Jilting Jades'? Perceptions of Female Playgoers in the Restoration, 1660–1700," in *Theatre and Culture in Early Modern England, 1650–1737: From Leviathan to Licensing Act*, ed. Catie Gill (Surry, UK: Ashgate, 2010), 131–32.

27. Occasionally Danchin incorrectly reads a paratext as impugning an actress's reputation. Of Thomas Duffett's prologue to *The Mock Tempest* (1674), for example, spoken by Jo Haines and Betty Mackarel, he writes: "The sexual innuendoes in [the prologue] seem to imply that Mrs. Mackerel's reputation was not for virtue." Danchin, *Restoration*, 1:600.

28. These are: the prologues to *The Faithful Shepherd* (1663) and *Mr Anthony* (1669), both paratexts to *The Double Marriage* (1671 or 1672), a "prologue to a reviv'd play" (1671 or 1672), the epilogues to *Pastor Fido* (1676) and *A True Widow* (1678), the prologues to *Sophonisba* (1680-1), *The Injur'd Princess* (1682), and *Titus Andronicus* (1685), Joseph Haines's "ass epilogue" to Thomas Scott's *The Unhappy Kindness* (1696; see chapter 1), the epilogues to *Ignoramus* (1704) and *The Fatal Marriage* (1710), and Anne Oldfield's epilogue to Ambrose Philips's *The Distrest Mother* (1712; see chapter 5). Other prologues and epilogues were occasionally printed with more than one play, but there is no evidence that they were performed by different actors.

29. For more on this epilogue, see chapter 1.

30. This subject is discussed further in chapter 3. For a list of confirmed examples, see the appendix. Of course, since in numerous cases the speaker's gender is unknown, this number is potentially much larger.

31. Pierre Danchin, *The Prologues and Epilogues of the Eighteenth Century*, 8 vols. (Nancy: Presses Universitaires de Nancy, 1990), 1:167.

32. Danchin, *Restoration*, 2:442.

33. Danchin, *Restoration*, 3:346–47.

34. This is ironic in Bracegirdle's case; for more on Bracegirdle's virgin persona, see chapter 4. Also see Sarah Cooke's prologue to Rochester's *Valentinian*, which stresses the author's sex appeal (discussed in chapter 3).

35. Joseph R. Roach, *It* (Ann Arbor: University of Michigan Press, 2007), 3.

36. These include: Elkanah Settle, *The Heir of Morocco, with the Death of Gayland* (1682); William Congreve, *Love for Love: A Comedy*, (1695); Catharine Trotter, *Agnes de Castro* (performed 1695; published 1696); Thomas Dilke, *The Lover's Luck* (1696); Elkanah Settle, *The World in the Moon* (1697); Robert Owen, *Hypermnestra*, (1703; reprint, 1722).

37. Andrew Parker and Eve Kosofsky Sedgwick remind us that the connection between text and performance can never be seen as fixed. See Andrew Parker and Eve Kosofsky Sedgwick, *Performativity and Performance*, Essays from the English Institute (New York: Routledge, 1995), 13.

38. Philip Auslander, "Comedy about the Failure of Comedy: Stand-Up Comedy and Postmodernism," in *Critical Theory and Performance*, ed. Janelle G. Reinelt and Joseph R. Roach (Ann Arbor: University of Michigan Press, 1992), 199–200.

39. Lawrence E. Mintz, "Standup Comedy as Social and Cultural Mediation," in *American Humor*, ed. Arthur P. Dudden (New York: Oxford University Press, 1987), 89.

40. A pair delivered the prologue to Behn's 1670 play, *The Forc'd Marriage; or, The Jealous Bridegroom*: a man complained about women until line 41, when a woman wittily responded. Catherine Gallagher reads this prologue as a "woman's version of sexual conquest"; see Catherine Gallagher, *Nobody's Story: The Vanishing Acts of Women Writers in the Marketplace, 1670–1820* (Berkeley: University of California Press, 1994), 20. The prologue to 1664's *The Ungrateful Favourite* featured a large cast: it began with a dance by "a Drunkard, a Morice-dancer, a Buffoon, a Bawd, a Whore, and a She-Gypsie." The author of the latter may be Thomas Southland. See Danchin, *Restoration*, 1:169.

41. Northrop Frye, *Anatomy of Criticism; Four Essays* (New York: Atheneum, 1966), 182.

42. Maus, "Playhouse," 599.

43. Mahadev Apte, *Humor and Laughter: An Anthropological Approach* (Ithaca, NY: Cornell University Press, 1985), 69.

44. Sigmund Freud, *Jokes and Their Relation to the Unconscious* (New York: Norton, 1960), 118. I discuss Freud's triangle in more detail in chapter 2's "tendentious" categorization of prologues and epilogues.

45. For an excellent overview of the subject, see Helga Kotthoff, "Gender and Humor: The State of the Art," *Journal of Pragmatics* 38 (2006): 4–25.

46. Joanne Gilbert, *Performing Marginality: Humor, Gender, and Cultural Critique* (Detroit: Wayne State University Press, 2004), 171.

47. Regina Barreca, *Last Laughs: Perspectives on Women and Comedy* (New York: Gordon and Breach, 1988), 14.

48. This information comes from a lawsuit against the play's scene painter, Isaac Fuller. Managers of the Kings Company—Thomas Killigrew, Charles Hart, and Michael Mohun—accused Fuller of delivering the scene late and poorly; they claimed that this cost them the king's patronage, which would have worked out to 500 pounds. In response, Fuller claims that the play was a great success because it performed "about 14 days together." For further discussion of this issue, see Novak and Guffey, *The Works of John Dryden*, 10:380 and appendix.

49. In their introduction to *The London Stage*, Emmett Avery and Arthur Scouten note the lack of proof that all play performances featured prologues and epilogues, but give evidence from Samuel Pepys and John Downes that this seems to have been common practice. Danchin cites *Spectator* no. 341, which singles out the epilogue to Ambrose Philips's 1712 tragedy, *The Distrest Mother*, by saying "Contrary to all other Epilogues, which are dropt after the third Representation of the Play, this has already been repeated nine times." For further discussion of responses to this particular epilogue, see chapter 5. Tiffany Stern concurs that Restoration prologues and epilogues expired after three days, an extension from 1630s and 1640s plays where, she claims, they were only staged at play premieres. Harold Love argues, in contrast, that "[t]he audience addressed and described is that of the first day only." See Emmett L. Avery and Arthur H. Scouten, "Introduction," in *The London Stage*, ed. William Van Lennep (Carbondale: Southern Illinois University Press, 1965),

cxxxii; Danchin, *Eighteenth*, 1:xxviii; Love, "Who Were the Restoration Audience?" 24; Tiffany Stern, *Rehearsal from Shakespeare to Sheridan* (Oxford: Clarendon, 2000), 190–91; 116.

50. Danchin, *Restoration*, 1:680.

51. Anon., "The Friendly vindication of Mr Dryden from the censure of the Rota," (Cambridge, 1673), 4; Charles Blount, "Mr Dreyden vindicated in a reply to The friendly vindication of Mr Dreyden: with reflections on the Rota" (London: T. D., 1673), 6.

52. Genette, *Paratexts*, 161, 163.

53. Wiley, *Rare Prologues*, 67–69.

54. Danchin, *Restoration*, 1:131. Danchin discusses the pressure on poets to be original in 1:xxxvi–xxxviii.

55. Vsevolod Emilevich Meyerhold, *Meyerhold on Theatre*, trans. Edward Braun (New York: Hill and Wang, 1969), 256; Susan Bennett, *Theatre Audiences: A Theory of Production and Reception*, 2nd ed. (London: Routledge, 2001). In the new preface, Bennett introduces the idea that "[i]t is at the nexus of production and reception that the spectator exists," a concept that runs throughout her book (vii).

56. Nos. 338 and 341 of the *Spectator* debate whether audiences should leave before seeing epilogues to tragedies.

57. Richard Schechner, *Essays on Performance Theory, 1970–1976* (New York: Drama Book Specialists, 1977), 122.

58. Avery and Scouten, "Introduction," liii.

59. Judith Milhous, *Thomas Betterton and the Management of Lincoln's Inn Fields, 1695–1708* (Carbondale: Southern Illinois University Press, 1979), 149.

60. Erving Goffman, *Frame Analysis: An Essay on the Organization of Experience* (Cambridge, MA: Harvard University Press, 1974), 132.

61. In his all-too-brief discussion of epilogues, Manfred Pfister refers to them as creating an "additional fictional role." See Manfred Pfister, *The Theory and Analysis of Drama* (Cambridge: Cambridge University Press, 1994), 78.

62. It should be noted that Bruster and Weimann casually use the word "betweenness" twice as a synonym for "liminality," but they do not define or call attention to the word. See Bruster and Weimann, *Prologues*, 26, 33.

63. Danchin, *Restoration*, 2:202.

64. Felicity Nussbaum, *Rival Queens: Actresses, Performance, and the Eighteenth-Century British Theater* (Philadelphia: University of Pennsylvania Press, 2010), 22.

65. See Paulina Kewes, *Authorship and Appropriation: Writing for the Stage in England, 1660–1710*, Oxford English Monographs (Oxford: Clarendon Press, 1998), 154–55.

66. Avery and Scouten, "Introduction," cxxxvi.

67. For an example of a completely detached epilogue, see Jo Haines's "ass epilogue" to Thomas Scott's *The Unhappy Kindness*, discussed in chapter 1. For an example of a prologue written by an outsider that somewhat involves a play element, see Dryden's prologue to Lee's *The Princess of Cleve*, discussed in chapter 3. For an

epilogue that sounds as if the author wrote it, see my discussion of Aphra Behn's *The City-Heiress* in chapter 3.

68. Danchin, *Eighteenth*, 1:321.

69. Danchin, *Restoration*, 1:321.

70. The epilogue appears in the 1717, 1717–1718, 1725, 1735, and the 1735–1763 editions, but not Tonson 1701 or Brown 1701.

71. D. F. McKenzie, *The London Book Trade in the Later Seventeenth Century*, Sandars Lectures (Cambridge: Typescript, British Library, 1976), 30.

72. Bennett, *Theatre Audiences*, 142. Lars Fodstad has extended this point to include theater programs, which in introducing the plot and explaining the director's staging choices also influence the spectator's reception. See Lars August Fodstad, "Refurbishing the Doll's House?," *Ibsen Studies* 6.2 (2006): 159.

73. Wiley, *Rare Prologues*, 313–21.

74. George Villiers and Duke of Buckingham, *The Works of His Grace, George Villiers, Late Duke of Buckingham*, vol. 2 (London: Sam Briscoe, 1715), frontispiece.

75. There are also pictures of two prologue performances with unidentified performers, which help affirm the popularity of prologues if not the connection between paratexts and specific actors. Accompanying the 1674 opera *Ariane, ou Le Mariage de Bacchus* by Pierre Paulin, the first picture depicts one nymph beckoning to two others across the forestage; the sung prologue describes this action. The other picture, from 1707, is titled "Prologue to the Dogs" and shows seven dogs in costume and dancing on their hind legs. See Wiley, *Rare Prologues*, 313–21.

76. Danchin, *Restoration*, 1:opp. 584; Danchin, *Eighteenth*, 1:381.

77. Freud, *Jokes and Their Relation to the Unconscious*, 167.

PART I

PROLOGUES AND EPILOGUES: A GENDERED TAXONOMY

CHAPTER ONE

~

Male and Female Cloaked, and Male Exposed, Paratexts

On 10 August 1682, the Duke's Company premiered the anonymous play *Romulus and Hersilia*. The play reimagines the aftermath of the rape of the Sabines as a loose allegory of the Exclusion Crisis; at this date, the question of whether King Charles II's Catholic brother would be excluded from inheriting the throne had yet to be determined. Although the play's references to it are oblique, the prologue and epilogue directly engaged this political imbroglio. Written by Aphra Behn and spoken by Mary Lee, Lady Slingsby, the epilogue transmits differently according to its medium. In performance, and in its subsequent publication in the play quarto, the epilogue seems a benign reflection on the play; a "revived" epilogue, the speaker evaluates her military role and ridicules the way that her character's morality precluded sexuality. But in its advance circulation in broadside form during the height of the Exclusion Crisis, two couplets read as slurs against the Duke of Monmouth. What happened next attests to prologues' and epilogues' potential to inflame: both author and actress were arrested.[1]

While the above is an extreme example, it attests to this point: both within and beyond the theater, prologues and epilogues had consequences. The epilogue that accompanied *Romulus and Hersilia* represented inflammatory political discussions that implicated both author and player. Nor is it the only example of a performed prologue or epilogue provoking arrest; on 18 June 1677, Joseph Haines was arrested for delivering "a scurrilous & obscene Epilogue."[2] These examples should dispel once and for all the argument of the player as empty vessel for the playwright's words, a concept that has been applied disproportionately to the male playwright–female player combination. Even though she did not write them, Lady Slingsby was held legally responsible for the words she uttered onstage, as could be any performers of paratexts. Such incidents also challenge the codicil offered by J. L. Austin in his theory of speech acts, that lines from plays offer only a "hollow" citationality—that performative statements uttered onstage remain circumscribed within the theater and lack consequence in any other context.[3] In their spoken and written forms, prologues and epilogues circulated within and without the theater and, as this example indicates, possessed the power to impact many worlds.

In this and the following two chapters, I offer a comprehensive taxonomy of prologues and epilogues. To understand the great range and impact of prologues and epilogues, we must necessarily survey the entire body of examples. By compiling two comprehensive collections of prologues and epilogues, Pierre Danchin has done a laudable service for scholars of Restoration and eighteenth-century British theater, and he has also suggested several categories of prologues and epilogues.[4] Yet until now, nobody has surveyed his collections and provided an overarching structure for their contents. Such a structure is what my next three chapters provide. My taxonomy categorizes the themes and styles of prologues and epilogues. It demonstrates, most importantly, that prologues and epilogues enabled actresses and actors to deliver a remarkable range of performances, whether abetting or resisting objectification, pandering to or attacking the audience, or advancing their stardom within the theatrical public sphere.

One of the two most fundamental categorizations within my schema is the division of prologues and epilogues by their speakers' gender. Coincident with the rise of the actress, the percentage of plays containing prologues and epilogues ballooned from roughly 40–48 percent in the late Renaissance to 90 percent during the Restoration, and the years 1660 through to the death of Anne on 1 August 1714 generated 1,570 extant prologues and epilogues, 372 of which feature confirmed female speakers.[5] In context, this number is more significant, as there are 691 paratexts for which we do not know the identity, and thus the sex, of the speaker. Capitalizing on the female body and voice in ways impossible for male examples to do, these 372 paratexts in turn supply the greatest variety of tone and content.

Given that there are many prologues and epilogues for which the speaker is unknown, how viable is a taxonomy based upon the speaker's gender? In fact, this dilemma is coincident with the growth of information about Restoration theater, and therefore is far from being unique to prologues and epilogues. Within this time period, we generally know the least about 1660s performances and the most about those of early eighteenth-century plays. As such, we cannot allow incomplete records to determine this pivotal aspect of prologues and epilogues. As the form develops throughout the Restoration, moreover, published paratexts more frequently include speakers' names. Whereas for paratexts from the 1660s we do not know the gender of the speaker 69 percent of the time, that figure grows progressively smaller, dropping to 13 percent between 1710 and 1 August 1714.[6] Those percentages, moreover, coincide with the rising frequency of women delivering paratexts. There is a direct relationship between the number of paratexts women perform and the percentage of paratexts with known speakers. The heyday of women's performances was in the 1690s, when women performed 123 prologues and epilogues, or 29 percent of the total; accordingly, during this decade (i.e., 1690–1699), the seventy-nine paratexts with unknown speakers accounted for only 19 percent.[7] While the gaps in our knowledge of prologue and epilogue speakers are significant, they can be accommodated, and thus should not preclude a gender-based taxonomy.

A word on methodology. In selecting examples from the taxonomic categories, I have prioritized the prologues and epilogues that accompanied the play's first run. These paratexts faced the do-or-die burden of selling the play, pleasing the audience, and enabling subsequent performances. After the play performed for three nights (or, in later years, six nights), the pressure was off; plays with longer initial runs might occasion prologues or epilogues suited to subsequent special occasions such as a royal's attendance that evening, but they no longer faced the acute marketing need. Because only successful plays occasioned revivals, new paratexts written for revived plays faced no such burden but might instead explain some facet of the revival, an example being the epilogue to the 1672 restaging of Dryden's *Secret-Love*, which promoted the all-female cast. Beginning in the late Restoration, audiences themselves requested that certain plays be revived and thus granted them a measure of financial success. New editions and reissues of plays, moreover, customarily republished the original prologue, epilogue, and the dramatis personae (which frequently provided the actors' names), fostering reading experiences that mirrored premier performances. These initial prologues and epilogues are likeliest to qualify as what Gerard Genette has called "peritexts" because they normally accompany most (if not all) editions of the play.[8] My occasional deviations from this policy focus on paratexts that shaped the careers of their performers; all others emphasize the initial performance and propose new readings of the plays they accompany.

Cloaked and Exposed Paratexts: Some Definitions

Most prologues in medieval and Renaissance English plays featured a standardized form: the solitary actor wearing a long black cloak.[9] The cloak gave the speaker a shapeless, sober appearance and an authority to make credible declamations, and both text and performer were known as "the prologue." In the character of a messenger, for example, the prologue to *Everyman* promises that audiences, if they pay attention to the play, will receive moral edification. During the Renaissance, while the cloaked figure remained prevalent in prologues, several writers grew more exploratory with both prologues and epilogues. Shakespeare's most famous example, the epilogue to *As You Like It*, features the character Rosalind offering to trade the male audience's approval of the play for kisses—if only "she" was a woman. Antecedents to the extraordinary creativity of the Restoration, the prologue to *Everyman* and the epilogue to *As You Like It* exemplify the two categories I propose for Restoration prologues and epilogues: the "cloaked" and the "exposed."

The cloaked category is named for this sober and impersonal vestment. Worn onstage, the cloak connotes authority. James Gousseff describes the Renaissance prologue so attired:

> He was dressed in black from head to foot. His suit was of fashionable cut. It was surmounted by a long, black, velvet cloak. His hat was swept from his head in a gesture of respect. Around his brow was a wreath of bay leaves in token of his task as representative of the play's poet. In contrast to the custom of the gentlemen of the period, he wore no sword . . . [and] no makeup. In one of his hands it is quite likely that he carried a book, a scroll, or one or more sheets of paper. In other cases he apparently carried a staff, a banner with the name of the play inscribed upon it, or a placard of some sort giving the same piece of information.[10]

Douglas Bruster and Robert Weimann argue for the standardization of these details in the Renaissance by pointing out that when prologues deviate, they call attention to their own exceptional status.[11] This can be seen through a Renaissance-era prologue by a female character. It seems that in the Renaissance, female characters who delivered prologues and epilogues did not wear cloaks; in addition to Shakespeare's Rosalind in *As You Like It*, the female prologue to Shirley's *The Coronation* (1635, published 1640) confirms both the expectation of the prologue speaker wearing a cloak and the costume's gender affiliations:

> Since tis become the Title of our Play,
> A woman once in a Coronation may

> With pardon, speake the *Prologue*, give as free
> A welcome to the Theater, as he
> That with a little beard, a long blacke cloke,
> With a starch'd face, and supple legge hath spoke
> Before the Playes the twelvemonth, let me then,
> Present a welcome to these Gentlemen,
> If you be kind, and noble, you will not
> Thinke the worse of me for my petticote.[12]

Although there are no pictures of cloaked Restoration actors delivering prologues, and although the rise of the actress suggests a movement away from cloaked paratexts, textual references confirm that, at least sporadically, actors continued to wear cloaks. The first Restoration playwright/managers toyed with the convention: In Sir William Davenant's *Love and Honour* (published 1649; performed 1661), the male prologue complains of having to wear "this grave long old Cloak"; and the epilogue to Sir Thomas Killigrew's *Pandora* (1662 or 1663) mentions that if the audience pans the play, the author "In's Cloak, thus muffl'd . . . will sneak away."[13] *The Rehearsal* mentions a prologue wearing "a long black Veil," but he does so to approach the gallows and offer his head should the audience not like the play.[14] By the early eighteenth century, the cloak costume was not in regular use, as the opening lines to the prologue of Anthony Aston's *The Coy Shepherdess* (1709) demonstrate: "Perhaps few here, Remember, in a *Cloke*, / They ever heard there was a Prologue Spoke."[15] Aston's prologue implies that, while prologue speakers no longer habitually wore cloaks, that costume had enough resonance that some audience members would remember the association. There are, moreover, several subsequent prologues that provide evidence that the costume, or at least its memory, endured. In 1756 Garrick wrote a prologue for Mr. Murphy to speak "dressed in black," and the prologue to Arthur Murphy's *The Citizen* (1793), spoken by Mr. O'Brien, declares, "You see I come in black—the usual form!"[16] One example specifies that its performer wears "a Black Coat closely buttoned" and says:

> Behold me in the usual prologue dress,
> Though why it should be black, I cannot guess;
> Custom the law of fools—improvement's foe,
> Has long establish'd that it shall be so;
> But say, is slavish custom to controul,
> The active vigor of my free-born soul;
> I'll break the statutes—and her laws deface,
> [Unbuttoning his coat and displaying a gold laced waistcoat.]
> Behold the glare of deviating lace.[17]

Yet his cloak is the deviation among eighteenth-century prologues, not the norm. The references to the black cloak are sparse, and the pictures of eighteenth-century performers of prologues and epilogues do not depict the costume; nevertheless, the idea and the occasional presence of the cloaked prologue speaker endured throughout the century.

Despite the cloak's fading use in the Restoration, its declarative credibility flourished in what I term the "cloaked" style of paratext. As a costume, its color, material, and effacement of the speaker's identity made the cloak symbolize sobriety, authority, and neutrality.[18] It represents communication untainted by the speaker's personality. The metaphorical cloak enabled both actors and actresses to appear trustworthy, through the customary absence of self-reference. Because it usually avoided discussing specific details of the play directly, such as character or setting, the cloaked style lent itself especially well to prologues, where due to their performance order the affiliation between prologue and play had not yet solidified. Staged epilogues, in contrast, maintained a closer relationship to the play, due to both their chronological sequence and their greater likelihood of being delivered by a cast member. Since audience members frequently attended plays more than once, they may have already associated the prologue with that play. The time lag between performances, however, and the fact that the prologue was expressly written to initiate a new play and beg for subsequent performances, demonstrate that the prologue was less immediately connected to the play than the epilogue.

Cloaked paratexts' impersonal, often ceremonial style suits their subject matter. Topics include political pronouncement, celebration of the royals' health and the openings of new theaters, disparagement of theatrical trends such as animal acts and Italian opera, and more. Many of them deliver important details and perspectives on current events, such as the Anglo–Dutch Wars and the Exclusion Crisis. A few reflect interestingly on prologues and epilogues themselves: their popularity with audiences and the difficulty of writing original ones. The epilogue to a c.1670–1671 revival of Samuel Tuke's *The Adventures of Five Hours*, for example, indicates that audiences at that moment seemed to favor them over prologues: Speaker William Smith says, "But since that *Epilogues* are so much in vogue, / Take this as *Prologue* to the *Epilogue*."[19] When in Buckingham's *The Rehearsal* the character Bayes considers whether to use a paratext as either prologue or epilogue, he evokes such discussions in cloaked prologues and epilogues themselves.[20]

While male examples were vaster in number, sometimes actresses adopted the metaphorical (if not the physical) cloak and addressed political and related issues from such a theoretically disembodied stance. The minimum of fifty occasions where women performed cloaked paratexts indicates their authoritative speech. When actresses had opportunities to speak about political matters, they staked out a remarkable new and culturally sanctioned place for women's participation in the public sphere.[21] Later in this chapter, "The Female Cloaked Style" focuses on the paratextual interventions of actresses on two of the most significant political events of the Restoration: Elizabeth Barry on the Exclusion Crisis, and Mary Porter on Jeremy Collier's antitheatrical attack.

As the cloak costume fell out of fashion, another vestment, breeches, gained popularity. In the Restoration, the so-called breeches part fitted this staple of the male wardrobe to the female body, and thus reimagined the plot device of a woman masquerading as a boy. When playing cross-dressed roles, actresses wore breeches that emphasized the feminine body, especially that Restoration-era erogenous zone between the knee and ankle. Approximately one-quarter of Restoration plays and at least forty prologues and epilogues feature a cross-dressed woman.[22] Several paratexts even employ the breeches costume gratuitously, where an actress wears it to deliver the prologue or epilogue but her character does not do so in the play.[23] Because of the proscenium stage, not to mention the practice of seating select audience members onstage, breeches prologues and epilogues meant that not only was an actress revealing more of her body than usual, but she was also doing so at close range.

The breeches part is one example of the second category of prologues and epilogues, which I call the "exposed" style. In this type, the speaker creates comedy based on a specific concept or characterization. In the epilogue to Catharine Trotter's initially anonymous tragedy, *Agnes de Castro* (performed 1695; published 1696), for example, breeches-clad actress Susannah Verbruggen flaunts the prospect of her nudity and compares revealing the play's authorship to removing the author's clothes.[24] Because of their more immediate connection to the play, epilogues were much more likely to be exposed than prologues, and while actresses sometimes cross-dressed only for the epilogue, male and female speakers frequently remained in the costume of the part they had just played and provided metacommentary—what in the introduction I call "retroactive metalepsis"—about the play. Thus we have epilogues delivered by characters such as "Ignoramus the lawyer," "Lysandra, in the Habit of a Nun," and "Frisco, Just Return'd from Whipping."[25] Occasionally, nonhuman characters deliver exposed paratexts, the strangest of which comes in *Il Pastor*

Fido (1647), where the prologue speaker is "Alfeo, a River of Arcadia." From time to time, spirits appear, most commonly the ghosts of Shakespeare and Jonson. As the Restoration progresses, the percentage of exposed paratexts rises; accordingly, we more frequently know the identity of their speakers. As opposed to their cloaked counterparts, exposed paratexts divide more neatly by gender. Some of the most outrageous male exposed paratexts involve a prop, such as the run of epilogues beginning in 1694 that featured actors riding asses, and occasionally other animals, onstage. Female exposed prologues and epilogues, by contrast, most often feature the actress investigating her body as simultaneously object and agent. Her body turned the actress into both a sexual spectacle and a critic of the ideology that made her so. Ruptures of the gender dichotomy expanded performance possibilities for women. A gendered taxonomy attends to this critically overlooked space whereby actresses negotiated object-hood and opportunity, sexual exploitation and celebration, conformity and critique. Although not all prologues and epilogues fit neatly into one of these categories, between 1660 and 1714, the majority are readily categorized. While prologues and epilogues followed trends chronologically, and varied in style and substance from the beginning to the end of the Restoration, the cloaked and exposed categories nevertheless encompass the entire archive. In the rest of this chapter I examine male and female cloaked, and then male exposed, prologues and epilogues. Chapters 2 and 3 then examine the six varieties of female exposed paratexts.

The Male Cloaked Paratext

When prologues and epilogues are categorized into cloaked and exposed, gender functions differently. Male and female exposed examples differ quite clearly by subject matter and style, as the final part of this chapter and the entirety of chapters 2 and 3 show. Cloaked paratexts, by contrast, differ less by subject matter and style and more by proximity. That is, the male examples vastly outnumber the female, thereby suggesting that actresses had less access to the authoritative stance this type required. It was in playwrights' interest to have charismatic men speak their words authoritatively. This section of the chapter accordingly states the stylistic aspects present in cloaked paratexts of both genders, while the following section traces several of the rarer female examples.

Male cloaked examples are the paratexts most likely to give authors more agency than actors. One way this happens is through pronouns. The biggest grammatical difference between the cloaked and exposed paratexts concerns the former's use of the first person plural versus the latter's first person singular.[26] Befitting a theoretically objective authority, the cloaked speaker's routine use of the first person plural implies representation of the author, the other actors, and/or the entire theater company. The following couplet from Dryden's epilogue to John Banks's *The Unhappy Favourite* (1682) is typical: "We Act by Fits and Starts, like drowning Men, / But just peep up, and then drop down again."[27] Yet even at times when the male speaker uses the first person singular, he is not calling attention to his subjectivity. Most often, he does so for emphasis; exclamations such as "I gad," "I dare say," and the like were tossed-off expressions rather than personalized phrases. Many examples begin with a token "I" and then barely, if ever, return to the stance. Another technique that emphasizes the author's agency is cloaked paratexts' frequent employment of epic similes to defend the playwright, such as treating a playwright's inaugural dramatic effort as a first-born child and requesting mercy toward the babe. In "Rhetorical Patterns in Restoration Prologues and Epilogues," Emmett Avery identifies several common moves.[28] One frequent conceit compares the playwright to a powerful figure, such as a king, captain, pilot, merchant, or military officer. Another represents the inverse: a subservient pose, where the playwright or speaker is like a prisoner or a religious sinner before the audience/jury, a cook or host offering the audience a feast, or a man wooing a woman. Avery also mentions the poet being compared to a virgin, mistress, or mother, usually stances of subjugation. Avery's study, however, is unrepresentative of Restoration prologues and epilogues, because almost all of his examples feature such similes that make the author a larger presence than the actor. As indicated by their different grammars, such a condition does not represent exposed paratexts.

Male cloaked paratexts represent the least difference of perspective between author and actor. Often the actor defends the author either directly or "ventriloquized," where the author speaks through the actor.[29] In the first epilogue to Otway's *Venice Preserv'd* (1682), for example, the speaker invokes a war metaphor to rally audience members around the author, while in Etherege's *The Comical Revenge, or, Love in a Tub* (1664) the speaker channels the author, who says he wants to distract the audience since there is little wit in the play. Another approach established by cloaked paratexts is that of the speaker abandoning the author. In the prologue to Congreve's *The Mourning Bride* (1697), Betterton complains that actors pay the price for authors' lack of wit—"Our Authors Sin, but we alone repent"—while in Shadwell's *The Virtuoso* (1676), the epilogue speaker abandons the playwright to his own fate.[30] A final common tactic involves the speaker bypassing the author to insult sections of the audience. In the prologue to Southerne's *The Wives Excuse* (1691), for example, Betterton accuses men in the pit of paying more attention to "Vizard Masks" than the play, while the speaker of the epilogue to Lee's *The Rival Queens* (1677) complains that the theater company keeps losing actresses as "prey" to male audience members. Considering their relatively confined range of material, male cloaked paratexts nevertheless adopt varied strategies that play with power dynamics within the author–actor–audience triangle. Authors of male cloaked paratexts are much more likely to retain agency in a cloaked than an exposed paratext.

Female playwrights had a particular reason to write male cloaked paratexts: so that there was a "neutral" (uninflected) male body backing their work. Behn most often used male cloaked or female exposed paratexts to defend her plays. Her prologue and epilogue to *Sir Patient Fancy* (1678) are instructive: the prologue features Thomas Betterton lightly mocking the playwright as someone who "Knows better how to juggle then to write," while in the epilogue Anne Quin complains about patrons who damn the play because of the author's gender: "Ah, Rott it—'tis a Woman's Comedy."[31] The male cloaked paratext can help anonymous authors; returning to playwrighting anonymously in 1706 after a ten-year hiatus, Delarivier Manley writes male cloaked paratexts for her play *Almyna, or, The Arabian*—the prologue for Cibber and the epilogue for Betterton—which refer to the author as male.[32] And having just recently started publishing her plays under her own name, Susanna Centlivre features a male cloaked prologue written "by a Gentleman" to open her play *The Man's Bewitched* (1709), where Robert Wilks defends Centlivre as a credit to her sex, as opposed to a recent female satirist (Delarivier Manley) who "so abus'd the Town."[33] Male cloaked paratexts provided female playwrights with various self-protective strategies, even if one of the strategies was to criticize other women.

The player who delivered the greatest number of known prologues and epilogues until Garrick, Colley Cibber, lauds Thomas Betterton's skill at delivering what I consider cloaked prologues:

> To speak a good Prologue well, is, in my Opinion, one of the hardest Parts, and strongest Proofs of sound Elocution; of which, I confess, I never thought, that any of the several who attempted it, shew'd themselves, by far, equal Masters to *Betterton*. *Betterton*, in the Delivery of a good Prologue, had a natural Gravity, that gave Strength to good Sense; a temper'd Spirit, that gave Life to Wit; and a dry Reserve, in his Smile, that threw Ridicule into its brightest Colours.[34]

Gravity and a tempered spirit suggest the rhetorical move of avoiding self-reference. The "dry reserve" implies the pose of the satirist, who in presenting unstable targets keeps the audience alert and ready to appreciate ridicule at another's expense. Accordingly, the roll call of male cloaked speakers includes some of the period's actors: Barton Booth, Charles Hart, William Mountfort, William Smith, and John Wilks.

In addition to demonstrating his gravity and dry reserve, Betterton's prologue to Congreve's *The Way of the World* (1700) exemplifies the cloaked paratext's primary maneuver: the passing off of opinion as truth. The piece first meditates on the difficulty for distinguished playwrights to maintain their reputation; its theme is that fortune is fleeting. These lines affect to wax philosophical while they set up a sympathetic reception for Congreve. Poets are doubly damned: by nature, who aligns them with cuckolds, and by the town, whose respect they risk losing by continuing to write after their earlier successes. The next stanza features an apparent lack of defensiveness by Congreve. The couplet "This Author, heretofore, has found your Favour, / But pleads no Merit from his past Behaviour" presents an appealing lack of presumption while more subtley reminding the audience of their favorable past treatment. Congreve must "in *Parnassus . . .* lose his seat" if he fails to recapture the audience's favor. The first two stanzas thus refer only generally to the writer's plight, and both the lack of pronouns and the use of the famous Betterton established the transparent and impartial tone.

It is in the extended third stanza that Betterton and Congreve strategically separate. Avoiding any reference to himself, Betterton nevertheless grows dictatorial in an audience-pleasing stance:

> He owns, with Toil, he wrought the following Scenes,
> But if they're naught ne're spare him for his Pains:
> Damn him the more; have no Commiseration
> For Dulness on mature Deliberation.[35]

Betterton's apparent impartiality is typical of the cloaked style, and timely. Two years earlier, in *A Short View of the Immorality, and Profaneness of the English Stage* and subsequent pamphlets, Jeremy Collier had inveighed against smut in the theater and had taken umbrage at Congreve's plays. At the time, Congreve had responded with *Amendments of Mr. Collier's False and Imperfect Citations*, and his prologue to *The Way of the World* cleverly continues that earlier response. In *Amendments*, Congreve advanced the "qui s'excuse s'accuse" argument; in the prologue, he continues this logical progression by presenting the play as potentially inducing boredom, not profanity, and Betterton as its impartial and indifferent host. Since Betterton also stars in the play, the prologue infers, the play too must be innocuous.

Betterton's deferential tone thus offers the power of discrimination to the audience, yet conditions them to find nothing immoral in the forthcoming play. The last five couplets demonstrate this coexistence:

> Satire, he thinks, you ought not to expect,
> For so Reform'd a Town, who dares Correct?
> To please, this time, has been his sole Pretence,
> He'll not instruct lest it should give Offence.
> Should he by chance a Knave or Fool expose,
> That hurts none here, sure here are none of those.
> In short, our Play, shall (with your leave to shew it)
> Give you one Instance of a Passive Poet.
> Who to your Judgments yields all Resignation;
> So Save or Damn, after your own Discretion.[36]

Phrases like the opening couplet and "sure here are none of those" depict relief and sarcasm at once—the audience is reassured for the moment that the satire treats a different target, yet careful listeners can deduce the sarcasm and anticipate additional targets. The subsequent closing couplets comprise the strategy: The player tells the audience members that they have free will to judge because the author is malleable and not prone to grudges. The author's supposed relinquishing of agency and the player's licensing of audience castigation belies the prologue's cocreatorship by Congreve and Betterton. Their apparent disunion ironically limits the range of audience members' response and reminds the audience of their indebtedness to both. And the use of generalities, the supposedly impartial method of pleading the poet's case, and the polite yet cunning treatment of the audience are hallmarks of the male cloaked prologue and epilogue.[37] While a promising rhetorical strategy, the apophasis in the third couplet above could not ensure against failure, with one critic (who attended at least three of its performances) noting that the play, "being too Keen a Satyr, had not the Success the Company Expected."[38]

A similar strategy appears in the epilogue to Dryden's The Conquest of Granada, Part 1 (1670). Despite its beautiful final couplet, this epilogue has received less critical attention than other paratexts in the play. Trading on her celebrity, the prologue to Part 1 featured Nell Gwyn wearing an oversize hat and belt as a response to comedian James Nokes of the Duke's Company, who had worn such a costume to mock French fashion.[39] And accompanying the epilogue to Granada, Part 2 is Dryden's "Defence of the Epilogue, or, An Essay on the Dramatique Poetry of the last Age," where the author expounds on his claim in the epilogue that the Restoration age is more refined than that of Ben Jonson. But Buckingham's *Rehearsal*, which parodies many aspects of *Granada 1* and *2*, mocks Dryden's supposed insensitivity to the qualities of *all* prologues and epilogues by having his representative, the character Bayes, say: "I have made a Prologue and an Epilogue, which may both serve for either: (do you mark?) nay, they may both serve too, I gad, for any other Play as well as this."[40] *The Rehearsal's* subject matter and timeliness (late 1671) indicates the importance of prologues and epilogues in general.

The epilogue was most likely spoken by Charles Hart, who played Almanzor, the play's most controversial character.[41] In his essay prefacing Part 1, "Of Heroique Plays," Dryden defends heroic plays in general and Almanzor in particular, the latter for switching sides during the war.[42] As befits a cloaked epilogue, there is no apparent carryover of Hart's character into the epilogue; Almanzor, the beheader of bulls, is nowhere in sight. Instead, the epilogue allies Hart with Dryden, who makes comic excuses for his play. The union of Dryden and the ambassador Hart makes the epilogue appear neutral and helps condition the audience to favor the play.

Citing various issues related to the play's author and actresses, the epilogue asks the audience for mercy due to the handicaps of youth and age. A frequent theme in Restoration paratexts, its first claim recalls Congreve's lament in the prologue to *The Way of the World*: that success is difficult to retain. Yet by using a simile of epic proportions to compare fame to a mistress, Dryden displaces the play's faults onto women. Arguing that fame behaves like a mistress who jilts an older, well-paying lover for a younger and flightier one, the first twelve lines establish the playwright's simultaneous self-deprecation and displacement of responsibility.

The second twelve lines feature Dryden at his self-deprecating best.[43] After furthering the epic simile by comparing wits to older lovers for whom impotence accompanies passion, Dryden situates himself between youth and age. Declaring that he will retire at age forty, which he calls "[t]hat wretched, fumbling age of poetry," the thirty-nine-year-old playwright jokes at his own expense. This joke recalls his similar move in the *Tyrannick Love* epilogue when he has Gwyn mock him for miscasting her as a tragic heroine. Continuing the "fumbling" imagery of awkward and unsatisfying sex, he notes that "[w]ell he may please him self, but never you" and hopes that "you will not find him less a man."[44] Six years older than Dryden, Charles Hart's body may have reinforced these concerns.[45]

At this point, however, Dryden shifts the blame to actresses' sexuality. Whereas he worries about his own impotence, their functional reproductive systems breed his resentment because childbirth delays plays (the time lapse between the premieres of his previous play, *Tyrannick Love*, and *The Conquest of Granada* was an uncharacteristic seventeen months). Dryden tells the audience to

> Think him not duller for this years delay;
> He was prepar'd, the women were away;
> And men, without their parts, can hardly play.
> . . .
> Pity the virgins of each Theatre!
> For, at both houses, 'twas a sickly year!
> And pity us, your servants, to whose cost,
> In one such sickness, nine whole Mon'ths are lost.[46]

During her reproductive peak, Dryden complains, at least one actress has delayed the play through a nine-month "sickness." Evidence points to this actress being Gwyn, since she had starred in Dryden's most recent plays and gave birth to Charles II's son in May of 1670. But if Hart delivered the epilogue, then the actor–author relationship becomes strange. Hart both played Gwyn's lover in earlier Dryden plays like *Secret-Love* and *Tyrannick Love*, and was her off-stage lover until 1667. The audience was accustomed to seeing the two play opposite each other, and given that Pepys writes of Hart's hatred for her after she left him for another lover, many in that audience knew of their affair. There are thus all kinds of ironies present, since either Hart never impregnated her or their baby did not survive.

The speaker negotiates this balance by explicitly allying himself with neither Dryden nor the mistress/actress. In the second line, the speaker sets the merciful tone by referring to "our sad Poet." This pronoun represents the only time Hart refers to himself; after this early line, the text constructs his authority by not representing him as an individual but only Dryden through him.

While summarizing the epilogue's themes, the last four lines offer a final argument in favor of the play:

> Yet though he much has fail'd, he begs to day
> You will excuse his unperforming Play:
> Weakness sometimes great passion does express;
> He had pleas'd better, had he lov'd you less.

The most elegant statement about male impotence to appear during a period where the subject was often raised, the final couplet phrases the plea as an aphorism. The audience is reminded of their opportunity to judge, yet the lines, in displacing pleasure for love, may leave them weak-kneed—and, accordingly, passionate about the play. In letting Dryden speak through the neutral male informer, the cloaked epilogue conditions the audience to favor the play by interpreting its contentions as truth. This is a typical arrangement, where the male poet speaks through the mainstream male actor, and I suspect that the reason we know the identities of many more performers of exposed paratexts is due to the less visible relationship between the male author and the speaker of cloaked examples. Like Dryden's other 102 prologues and epilogues, then, the cloaked epilogue to *The Conquest of Granada, Part 1* merits attention for its poetic grace and its entwinement with the people and conventions of the London theater world.

The Female Cloaked Paratext

While sexual objectification usually prevented her from assuming a logical, impersonal voice, the actress sometimes did don a metaphorical black cloak to deliver a prologue or epilogue. In it she often discussed tendentious theatrical or domestic issues, and given the number of female cloaked paratexts, she must have received applause. The actresses who delivered these (minimum) fifty-one prologues and epilogues represent the earliest nonaristocratic female public speakers of collective viewpoints, and signify a key step in the democratization of speech in England. The quantity of female cloaked prologues and epilogues implies that audiences were receptive to women publicly commenting on cultural, political, and theatrical issues. Their proliferation indicates that actresses gave many performances where the text, at least, did not exploit their bodies. Either gender, it seems, could don a virtual cloak and perform these prologues and epilogues.

The great Restoration actress Elizabeth Barry delivered six of the fifty cloaked paratexts, three of which are discussed here. Commenting on various episodes during the volatile Popish Plot and Exclusion Crisis, Barry's examples demonstrate that women had license to speak out on political issues. Their impersonal style and lack of self-reference gave Barry the authority to comment on some of the Restoration's most heated political issues. And while we have no way of knowing whether the paratexts reflected her political beliefs, we need to recognize these moments as more than just authorial ventriloquism. As the arrest of Lady Slingsby attests, Barry would have been associated with, and perhaps even held responsible for, her paratexts.

While exposed paratexts offered possibilities for female self-expression yet often reinforced misogyny—sometimes simultaneously, as with breeches costumes—cloaked paratexts generated political clout by avoiding self-reference. Such is the situation in Barry's epilogue to Aphra Behn's 1679 melodrama, *The Young King,* where the epilogue overcomes attention to the actress's body and instead provides political commentary. Despite pointing out Barry's appearance—the introduction reads: "After a Dance of Shepherds and Shepherdesses, the Epilogue is spoken by Mrs. Bary, as Nymph, at his R. H. second exile into Flanders"—this cloaked epilogue idealizes pastoral joys by contrasting them to the frenzy of the Exclusion Crisis:

> Ambition is not known within our Groves;
> Here's no disputes for Empire, but for Loves:
> The humble Swain his Birthright here enjoys,
> And fears no danger from the publick Voyce.[47]

Both title and "humble Swain" allude to the Duke of York, whom Charles II had recently sent abroad after succumbing to pressure from the Whigs. Significantly, Barry uses the plural possessive "our" in these lines, something she does nine times in the epilogue without once singling herself out. The allusion continues with an even more direct reference:

> His Country and his Flocks enjoys with ease,
> Ranges his native Fields and Groves in peace:
> Not forc'd by Arbitrary Votes to fly
> To forein Shores for his security.[48]

This may read as another example of Behn's well-established Tory loyalties, and it adopts a stance also found in many male cloaked paratexts, where Barry's status complements Behn's political perspective, and the two serve as a united front. The notable element of this epilogue is its demonstration that a woman, Elizabeth Barry, had the authority to utter political commentary despite a number of objectifying events both on- and offstage. Unfortunately, no cast list for *The Young King* has survived, and because of the 1679 performance date it is hard to surmise which of the two leading female roles Barry would have played. The year 1679 falls midway between 1677's *The Rover,* in which Barry played the virginal Hellena, and 1681's *The Second Part of the Rover,* where she played the courtesan La Nuche. She could therefore have played either of the two leading female roles in *The Young King:* Urania, the virginal heroine who begs successfully for her lover to be released from prison, or Cleomena, the Amazonian future queen. Derek Hughes thinks that Barry might have played Cleomena, and as it is the meatiest role he could be right. I agree with *The London Stage,* however, in surmising that she might have played Urania, and suspect that a more experienced actress such as Mary Betterton might have played Cleomena instead. Why is the casting important? The titular "Young King" is Orsanes. At his birth, a herald predicted that as king he would rule tyrannically; in the draconian Oedipal logic of many Restoration tragedies, his mother accordingly locked him up for eighteen years with only an old tutor for company. At the beginning of the play, like Hippolito in Dryden and Davenant's *Tempest*, Orsanes has consequently never seen a woman. The honor of being his first glimpsed woman goes to Urania, and during this scene the young king is amazed at her breasts, narrating his impressions as he fondles each one. Had Barry played this role, it would have been especially remarkable for her to return and speak a cloaked epilogue, yet my suspicion is that she did.

Based on her high-profile affairs, Barry's sexual reputation might also appear to have precluded delivering such an authoritative paratext. By 1679 she had already engaged in affairs with Sir George Etherege and the Earl of Rochester, and had given birth to Rochester's baby. Her performance of Hellena in *The Rover* had made her famous, and she counted among her fans King Charles II and the Duke of York. Her cloaked paratexts demonstrate that she had fully entered the professional paradox of acting in the Restoration: one could be admired for one's skill, but not respected, due to the taint of the profession. For women, this contradiction was especially acute; Elizabeth Howe argues that actresses represented new voices brought to the public but had to endure exploitation by those enabling such exposure.[49] Yet this epilogue is a moment where a woman discusses a political issue within a setting structured to inspire applause. While it is not surprising that Behn would have given an actress the opportunity to speak politically, it is remarkable that Barry would possess the authority to do so in a general, non-self-referential way. By delivering this epilogue, she inspired others to produce political paratexts for her.

The second person to do so, Thomas Otway, wrote a prologue to Behn's *The City-Heiress* (1682) that enabled Barry to deliver political satire with a minimum of self-reference. Until the final couplet, this prologue is densely political and non-self-referential. Beginning with a customary chiding of the audience for treating the theater as a bordello and for not heeding playwrights' lessons, the prologue then concentrates its venom on the villain of the Popish Plot, Titus Oates, whose informing on others had caused their deaths. Oates is portrayed as a "Daemon" stalking London, where his accusations "at Random Halters flew / Round some unwary neck."[50] Barry also makes fun of Oates's lineage and falsified credentials (Oates padded his resumé by claiming, among other achievements, a doctorate of divinity from the University of Salamanca). Granted, by April of 1682 Oates was an easy target: His pension had been cut off, he had been thrown out of his lodgings in Whitehall, and he was eighteen months away from being arrested. But then Barry takes aim at a larger, present target: the Whigs. The Whigs had planned a great feast at Haberdasher's Hall on 21 April 1682 as a dinner to give thanks to God and to the "Loyal Protestant Nobility" for having protected the Protestant religion (in his edition of Otway, J. C. Ghosh reprints the text of the dinner ticket, which states these reasons).[51] Charles II cancelled the feast, however, and the prologue implies that steep ticket purchases of one guinea each went unrefunded. Barry adds insult to injury with the following lines:

> Who, but the most incorrigible Fops,
> For ever doom'd in dismal Cells, call'd Shops,
> To cheat and damn themselves to get their livings,
> Wou'd lay sweet Money out in Sham-Thanksgivings?
> Sham-Plots you may have paid for o'er and o'er;
> But who e'er paid for a Sham-Treat before?
> Had you not better sent your Offerings all
> Hither to us, than Sequestrators hall?[52]

In this passage Barry name-calls, levels class-based insults, and taunts the Whigs for financing both Oates's "Sham-Plots" and the failed feast. The punchline, however, is the one area where Barry does reference herself. The prologue ends directly following this passage with the couplet: "I being your Steward, Justice had been done ye; / I cou'd have entertain'd you worth your Money." This final couplet uncloaks the speaker and rehashes the old joke of actresses and whores providing similarly bawdy types of entertainment. Barry thus delivers offensive political material under a metaphorical cloak that the concluding couplet reverses, as in a Shakespearean sonnet, perhaps also absolving her from leveling the earlier satire.[53]

The third example of Barry's cloaked prologues and epilogues about the Exclusion Crisis demonstrates that she could affect authority even amid potentially demeaning circumstances. It accompanied a play by her former lover, the Earl of Rochester: *Valentinian*, first performed posthumously in 1684. This anonymous prologue, the third of three composed for the production, was "intended for *Valentinian*, to be spoken by Mrs. Barry," meaning that it probably was not spoken but was nevertheless published along with the play.[54] The prologue contains two parts; the first celebrates the Tories' domination of the Whigs, and the second part, in the same vein as the two previous prologues spoken by Sarah Cooke, mourns the deceased Rochester. (For an analysis of the first of Cooke's prologues, see chapter 3.) Given that Barry, like Cooke, had been Rochester's lover, one might expect the second part of the prologue to be sexually self-referential, but ironically, all self-references appear only in the political discussion. These references are also more general and not evocative of Barry per se. The first individual reference appears immersed in another stab at Titus Oates: "Shall I jeer Popish Plots that once did fright us, / And with most bitter Bobs taunt little *Titus?*" This is a fitting follow-up to her previous prologue; although *The City-Heiress* had appeared two years prior, that prologue was the most recent on record that Barry had spoken. Her two other self-references appear casually immersed in lines criticizing a Trimmer:

> No, even the worst of all yet I will spare,
> The nauseous Floater, changeable as Air,
> A nasty thing, which on the surface rides,
> Backward and forward with all turns of Tides.
> An Audience I will not so coursely use;
> 'Tis the lewd way of every common *Muse.*[55]

This passage reflects the course of the Exclusion Crisis. By 1684 the Popish Plot had been fully discounted, meaning that Barry and others could satirize less-threatening groups like the Trimmers. And in contrast to the numerous exposed prologues and epilogues where speakers objectify their own bodies, the repeated use of "I" merely advances the argument.

This paratext also exemplifies a key difference between prologues and epilogues: whereas the cloaked prologue allows Barry to hold forth about matters external to the play, the exposed epilogue, which Barry also delivered, displays betweenness. Barry speaks from the point of view of her character, Lucina, whom Valentinian has raped and who then dies of shame. In this "revived" epilogue, Barry/Lucina continues a trend that today we can find difficult to stomach, that of turning rape into a comic subject. To be sure, Barry/Lucina first protests the rape and the victim's resulting death. But then she facetiously observes that if such events transpired within Restoration society they would deplete theater audiences, and suggests that the rape inspires each female audience member to fantasize about having her own "Valentinian in her heart."[56] Such exposed epilogues are delivered by highly individualized character-actress amalgamations where the speaker's self-reference gives the audience a beguiling hint of who she might "really" be. They are, however, a far cry from Barry's political cloaked paratexts. As these three examples demonstrate, the genre allowed Elizabeth Barry and other actresses, including Charlotte Butler, Sarah Cooke, Betty Currer, Mary Lee (Lady Slingsby), and Mary Porter, to make political pronouncements, risk the audience's wrath, and potentially gain their applause.

More than twenty years later, in the epilogue to Mary Pix's 1703 comedy, *The Different Widows; or, Intrigue All-a-Mode*, actress Mary Porter wears a metaphorical cloak to declaim against continued criticism of the stage's immorality.[57] In presenting the actors as guilty but reformed, Porter uses the first-person plural referent to establish apparent objectiveness and to favor the play despite the potential resistance of antitheatricalists. The first stanza asserts that the play is the product of their self-cleansing:

> We own our Faults, and pardon crave to day,
> When we present you with a modest Play.
> Here no lewd Lines offend the chaster Ear,
> No Jests obscene raise Blushes in the Fair;
> This we cou'd wish *Collier* himself wou'd *hear*.[58]

Although Jeremy Collier was hardly alone in attacking the stage in the late 1690s, Porter facetiously wishes he were in the audience to confirm the play's morality. But Collier would likely find the play immoral. Before reforming the rake, the play first depicts his drinking, whoring, and cuckolding of other men. In fact, the play contains a hodge-podge of lewd plot devices. One man desires a woman he believes to be his sister, while another couple hides together in a closet. Lady Loveman not only nearly cuckolds her husband with two different men, but also, while cross-dressed, kicks and draws her sword on him. The epilogue, therefore, attempts to blanket licentiousness that might linger in the minds of spectators, while at the same time joking about the Restoration's most memorable antitheatricalist. This is one example of a number of post-Collier prologues and epilogues that functioned as decoys, I suggest, so that their plays could retain some risqué elements.[59]

In the remainder of the epilogue, Porter forcefully directs the audience in a disembodied fashion, lacking self-reference. Continuing from the "we" above, Porter speaks for a host of implied others: the author, other players, and theater producers. Ironizing her claim that the lewd characters have been punished, Porter urges that popular opinion override a few critical condemnations. The advancing of political opinion, and the placing of it within a cultural context, makes Porter a cloaked female speaker. Representing herself as both a female sympathizer and a moral authority, Porter positions the larger audience against Collier and the pamphleteers in a way that values the support of female spectators. First she employs a kind of moral peer pressure by telling the audience, "Since Virtue's then our only Theme to day, / 'Tis for your Honour, that you like the Play."[60] But then she offers women more power to determine the play's reception, advising them: "'Tis by your Eyes alone Mankind is aw'd, / They dare not disapprove when you applaud."[61] Although prologues and epilogues appealing to the female audience members for moral justification appeared more often toward the end of the Restoration, Porter does so without referencing herself as female.[62] Porter thus casts herself as judge of all concerned: Collier and the male and female audience. She achieves this high rank through direct address, broad statements about proper behavior, and above all, lack of self-reference. Porter became known as a moral actress, leading one scholar to speculate that her lack of a sensational offstage life has precluded biographical interest in her.[63] But it is her ability to generalize and speak authoritatively that makes the epilogue to *The Different Widows* an exemplar of the female cloaked style.

The Male Exposed Paratext

Whereas the cloaked style depended on the speaker's ability to be authoritative, the exposed style generated comedy from a character in the play or an actor's public persona. The most successful male exposed prologues and epilogues developed and nuanced a player's acting reputation. These played off an actor's comic role types, such as the rake, the conniver, and the fool. They presented a familiar persona to the audience, sometimes someone who did not appear in the play proper; accordingly, we are more likely to know the speaker's identity for an exposed paratext than for a cloaked one. We know more about speakers in the late Restoration in part because the exposed paratext grew in popularity. Often the way these paratexts appear in print indicates the dual vision that the theater audience would have witnessed: "Spoken by Mr Dogget, who acts Thorneback," for example, or "By Mr Nokes, Representing my Lady Beardsley."[64] In both spoken and written form they had the potential to disrupt the play. If, for example, an exposed epilogue followed a tragedy, then we have a case of the audience's potential tragic catharsis being interrupted (a condition discussed further in chapters 2 and 5). Since Restoration epilogues sometimes appeared in play quartos up front, between the prologue and the dramatis personae (a practice that became more frequent during the eighteenth century), this same effect might not take place for a reader. The paratext's location in print may not match its location in performance, so what disrupts the performance and the memory of the performance becomes both less and more intrusive in the printed text. That is, an epilogue following a tragedy disrupts the audience's experience of the play *qua* tragedy, but its repositioning in print between prologue and dramatis personae lessens this disruption. Yet for a reader who had attended the play's performance, the epilogue's move also interferes with the memory of the performance. Male exposed paratexts, which frequently disrupt tragedy, thus may either step out of the way of the narrative or continue to impede the reading experience of that tragedy through textual relocation.

The treatment of the actor as individual agent rather than disembodied authority typifies this category of paratext. Male exposed prologues and epilogues often employed a prop that symbolized the speaker's low-comic style. The first surviving examples include the prologue and epilogue to Richard Carpenter's (probably unacted) *The Pragmatical Jesuit New-leven'd* (c. 1660–1661), which features "Galen Junior, a Physitian" scrutinizing the contents of a urinal.[65] We have examples of exposed prologues and epilogues where the male speaker plays a character type, such as Cupid or an astrologer. Others feature famous personages, such as the ghosts of Shakespeare and Jonson. Comedians William Bowen, Thomas Doggett, Joseph (Jo) Haines, Thomas Jevon, John Lacy, Anthony Lee, James Nokes, and Will Pinkethman all specialized in this style.

Male exposed paratexts approach the author–actor relationship in two ways. The first type features one or more actors talking at a distance about the author. Such a text makes way for one of the first staged plays written by a woman; the prologue to Frances Boothby's *Marcelia* (1669) features three speakers who take turns relaying to the audience the playwright's orders and fears about reception. In the epilogue to *Injur'd Love* (1711), actors Thomas Doggett and Will Pinkethman speak "as themselves" about epilogues where a virgin actress "bribes" the audience. The actors refuse the playwright's request for this style of epilogue and instead the cross-dressed Doggett delivers a parody of one, featuring his "burning Blushes, and . . . down-cast Eyes" and taunting the audience that "all the Men on Earth shall ne'er debauch me."[66] In these examples the author is a figure to be referenced off-handedly. The second style consists of actors in character complaining about something—usually the author or audience. Spoken by James Nokes, the prologue to Thomas D'Urfey's *Squire Oldsapp* (1678) has Oldsapp complaining that playwrights "raise their Wits by making me an Ass"; likewise, the epilogue written by Jack Verbruggen for a 1700 revival of Charles Gildon's adaptation of Shakespeare's *Measure for Measure* features Verbruggen as Shakespeare's ghost, complaining that many lately have butchered his plays and from now on only stars like Betterton and Barry, or great writers like Congreve, Otway, and Wycherley should stage them. As opposed to the male cloaked paratext, the exposed types feature more pronounced characters who often complain (facetiously) about authors and place them at a greater distance.

The "drunken" prologue Dryden wrote for actor Joseph Williams to perform demonstrates how paratexts and actor reputations sustained a circular relationship, where each contributed to the success of the other. The play so introduced was actor-playwright Joseph Harris's tragicomedy, *The Mis-takes* (1690), the first of three plays he would write. It is a poor play; among other lowlights, it begins with a leading male reading an anonymous letter claiming that his lover has been unfaithful to him, before the audience has received any context about the man, his lover, or the letter-writer's motives. The editors of the *The Works of John Dryden* claim, justifiably, that Dryden had been commissioned to save the play with a prologue.[67] Yet some publications of the play feature two epilogues, each associated with a specific actor, suggesting that the play did not fail entirely but made it to at least two performances. To introduce a writer's first play, Williams was an atypical choice; while he acted in at least thirty-nine plays between 1673 and 1707, this example is the only paratext that records him as speaker, a detail consistent with the *Dictionary of National Biography*'s characterization of him as an actor "not quite of the first rank." Yet the prologue's emphasis on his drinking reflects two well-known theatrical personae used to comic effect: the drunkard and the teetotaler. It also stresses the importance of such paratexts for posterity; since information about Williams is scarce and it is the only apparent document that confirms his drinking, the prologue remains the only corroborating source for Colley Cibber's otherwise-suspicious alliterative claim, many years later, that Williams "lov'd his Bottle better than his Business."[68]

Featuring a total of three actors, the staggered entry of this prologue, which hypes Williams's "drunken" performance, attempts to create a desire to see the famed actor inebriated. Initially, actor George Bright claims that the play lacks a prologue, but then, shushing Bright, William Bowen announces the forthcoming Williams: "Here's honest Mr *Williams*, just come in, half mellow, from the *Rose-Tavern*. He swears he is inspir'd with Claret, and will come on, and that *Extempore* too, either with a Prologue of his own or something like one."[69] Bowen conditions the audience to associate drunkenness and unpredictability with Williams, thus setting the stage for an exposed prologue.

In Williams's subsequent lines, the consumed claret becomes a virtual prop. Playing with meter, Dryden has Williams versify drunkenness:

> I'le stick to my Friend the Authour, that I can tell ye,
> To the last drop of Claret, in my belly.
> So far I'me sure 'tis Rhyme—that needs no granting:
> And, if my verses feet stumble—you see my own are wanting.[70]

The claret exists only in retrospect, an imagined red glow in Williams's belly. Its supposed aftereffects appear in verse, most cleverly in the last line's extra metrical foot that augments Williams's drunken stumble. Typical of both an exposed paratext and a drunkard, Williams refers to himself sixteen times. In the middle of the prologue, he shifts briefly from his "fluster'd madness" and defends the playwright, extolling the value of actor-penned plays by reminding the audience that Shakespeare also acted. Williams concludes by adding an element of discernment to his boozy persona, extolling claret over beer in the couplet: "Peace and the Butt, is all our bus'ness here: / So much for that;—and the Devil take small beer."[71] The virtual prop and the emphasis on the actor's persona make Williams's prologue a typical example of the male exposed paratext. Subsequent "drinking prologues" recurred throughout the Restoration.[72]

Another example of the male exposed paratext, the so-called "ass epilogue," creates comedy from the actor's body. The body generates comedy not from its sexual aspects, as a female exposed paratext would, but from its location and movement. Spawning a series of epilogues where actors rode donkeys onstage, the concept, George Spencer Bower speculates, might have originated from the line in Hamlet, "Each actor upon his ass."[73] Although Thomas Doggett pioneered the ass epilogue when playing Sancho Panza in Thomas D'Urfey's Don Quixote Part I (May 1694), where the animal appeared throughout the play, comedian Jo Haines's self-authored ass epilogue for Thomas Scott's 1697 tragedy, The Unhappy Kindness (which featured only human actors), fixed him upon his ass as its icon, with two pictures immortalizing him in this stance.[74] Haines was one of Restoration theater's most colorful characters: a clown, a libertine, a strolling player, and an author, he could also be an incendiary presence.[75]

Like The Mistakes, The Unhappy Kindness bears no relation to its paratext. The play borrows a few characters and the primary conceit from George Powell's Alphonso, King of Naples (1691); as it happens, Jo Haines also contributed, but did not perform, the prologue to the earlier play. In The Unhappy Kindness, King Frederick has usurped his brother Alphonzo's throne, and while Alphonzo seeks revenge, Frederick desires the maiden Evadne, who instead loves Valerio (played by Joseph Williams, in a more typical role). By the play's end, Alphonzo, Frederick, and their mother have all been poisoned, leaving the kingdom to Valerio. The play is notable for a scene in Act III where Evadne looks forward to consummating her marriage with Valerio, to which several critics objected; Scott chides them in the preface. Otherwise, the play contains no levity, maintaining its serious tone throughout.

One of many examples where exposed epilogues follow Restoration tragedies, the epilogue's contrast in tone with the play is enormous. After the final scene of carnage, Haines, who did not act in the play, appears on his ass. While his lines and concepts resemble Doggett's, Haines creates a more satirically charged environment.[76] To begin with, he and the ass sport match-ing wigs, literalizing the epilogue's theme that the asinine lurks in everybody. The epilogue invests the environment with tension—like a modern-day comedy club, anybody could be picked on at any time—yet endears Haines because he appears as the satire's foremost subject. Lines such as the gallop-ing dactyls of "My Ass has *Relations*, and Great ones among ye" and the mis-chievous "Ladies, I'm sure you like his spruce Behaviour, / [*aside*] I ne'r knew ought but *Asses* in *Their favour*" exemplify his widely cast satire.[77] Haines also builds from his initial prop. Referring to the ass's "*Passive Obedience*," the epilogue gives a stage direction that locates the joke away from Haines's body: "[*Whips the Ass often, who, by reason of the innate Dullness of the Beast, never flinches for it*]."[78] Haines even treats as a prop the newly introduced type of currency; speaking to the ladies again about their propensity for asinine beaux, he says, "When his *Degree* a *Lover* does commence, / You *coin* an *Ass* out of a *Man of Sense*."[79] The epilogue thus capitalized on Haines's rakish persona and the live prop to deliver a bizarre conclusion to the tragedy.

Not only did the ass epilogue bolster Haines's comic reputation far beyond his death, but it and several spin-offs became central to the careers of other comedians. Will Pinkethman made it a centerpiece of his career, delivering either Haines's or a new ass epilogue after at least thirty-seven performances. The epilogue's publication record also indicates its popularity, since it ap-peared in two collections: *The Miscellaneous Works of . . . George, Late Duke of Buckingham* (1704), and *Pinkethman's Jests* (1721; reprinted 1735). Pink-ethman also one-upped Haines by delivering an epilogue atop an elephant, of which unfortunately there is no picture.[80] Thus the ass epilogue became a source of communication between actors. After Pinkethman performed ass epilogues on 5 June and 1 July 1704 at Drury Lane, Francis Leigh performed "A Prologue . . . in Answer to Will Pinkethman's *on an Ass*," which he deliv-ered atop a dray horse.[81] Other significant dates include another Pinkethman performance on 6 June 1719, accompanying Killigrew's play *Chit Chat*. With an ass standing next to him, Pinkethman delivered a prologue in a theater converted from an old barn where asses had previously lived. He points out that where the beaux now sit, twelve asses used to have their stables, and that the audience should support the play or else the theater will revert back to a place where cattle will eat. After he died in 1725, his son inherited the tradition and performed ass epilogues for many more years. Later actors capitalizing on the ass epilogue included Ned Shuter and Christopher Smart (as "Mrs Midnight").

The second wave of ass epilogues demonstrates Haines's continued influ-ence, as they frequently mention him by name and parody his earlier work.

As late as 1752, theater managers paid homage to Haines when advertising their performances. The following announcement is typical: A revival of *The Rehearsal* is followed by *The Parting Lovers*, by Carey, "With an Epilogue, written by Jo. Haines, Comedian of facetious Memory, to be spoke by Cibber, riding on an Ass."[82] The concept took a turn in 1732, when the ass epilogue was itself parodied. In an epilogue to Samuel Johnson of Cheshire's comedy, *The Blazing Comet*, the ass is ridden by the character "Mr Bays." The ass sports wings and is attended by several ragged women, to the sounds of drums and trumpets. Bays calls the ass "Pegasus," and when he gets tired of the character Lord Wildfire taunting him, he whips the ass and tries to get him to take flight: "Come, *Pegasus*—to shame these empty Boasters, / Let's soar—now mind—we'll reach th'Etherial Coasts, Sirs!"[83] Lord Wildfire then teases Bays, saying that the beast would fly except that he is carrying too heavy a load. In 1737 this concept reappears in an epilogue to the ballad-opera by Robert Baker, *The Mad-House*. Pinkethman Junior, who performed a small role as a servant in the play, leads his own "Pegasus" onstage and affectionately calls her "Old Peggy." Comparing her to Hudibras's horse and Sancho Panza's mule, he notes that his ass also knelt down for him to mount her, but boasts that Old Peggy outshines the other equines because she moves on wings. The contrast leads to eruptions: he says, "In Armour they fought, I in *Doggrel* to chuse, / And belch'd from my Breast the omnipotent Muse; / And thus my Belches began."[84] He then lets out a string of burps and then asks the ladies' pardon, but his burps return in subsequent lines and he ends by dancing a hornpipe. Other parodies of the ass epilogue included a performance on 29 May 1733 of Steele's *The Tender Husband*, with Pinkethman and two other actors all riding asses, and a "singing" three-ass performance of the Beaumont and Fletcher adaptation by Richard Brome, *The Royal Merchant*, on 15 April 1735. There were at least 124 performances of ass epilogues through 1759 and Danchin traces revivals of Haines' ass epilogue to 1797. As reflected by Haines's indelible association with the ass epilogue, this tradition demonstrates how the male exposed paratext exploited and increased an actor's celebrity, seemingly without regard for the play narrative.

Both cloaked and exposed prologues and epilogues capitalized on their speakers' personae. Cloaked paratexts created a reciprocal relationship between their speakers' reputations and authority; as the Betterton example demonstrates, a speaker would both bestow and receive authority from performing them. And agentive relations between author and actor vary from case to case. Yet despite their theoretically disembodied stance, cloaked paratexts were nevertheless delivered by actresses, representing a significant moment in the history of women's political engagement. Featuring levity often to the point of downright silliness, exposed paratexts, in contrast, fed off their speakers' personae and comic skill. The relocation of the audience's critical gaze away from the performer's body to the costume and prop (so successful in the ass epilogues, where the prop is another body) signifies the power of the male exposed prologue and epilogue to determine audience response. It also implies the difficulties of women assuming such a powerful stance, one that requires them at times to laugh at the audience. This is the position that Freud cannot imagine women holding, and for which Mahadev Apte has found scant cross-cultural evidence.[85] Yet as chapters 2 and 3 show, many female exposed paratexts capitalized on insulting the audience. Given its inherent risks, then, the female counterpart to the Hainesian paratext should be understood as a remarkable example of women's participation in the London theater world.

Notes

1. The offensive couplets were: "And of all Treasons, mine was most accurst; / Rebelling 'gainst a King and Father first" and "Not my Remorse, or Death, can expiate / With them a Treason 'gainst the King and State." Within the play, both couplets reference the point where Slingsby's character, Tarpeia, openly betrays her father, Spurius Tarpeius, as well as the Romans generally when she notifies Curtius of a way to storm the town through the west gate; here in the epilogue, Tarpeia atones for her sins. But in advance of the play, the lines appear to represent a repentant Duke of Monmouth. Also, the precirculated broadside epilogue names Behn as author and Lady Slingsby as speaker, in contrast to the 1683 play quarto, which omits both names from the epilogue and says only "Spoken by Tarpeia." The prologue is more virulent, singling out various Whig supporters; among other insults, it calls Henry Care, publisher of the Whiggish paper *The Weekly Packet of Advice from Rome*, a "Monkey," and it insinuates that members of the Green-Ribbon Club, the Whig society whose name refers to the supporters of Shaftesbury, perjured themselves during the Popish Plot proceedings. It also mocks the failure of the Whig feast at Haberdasher's Hall, which Charles II cancelled. But Monmouth was the most sensitive issue, and therefore the epilogue and not the prologue sparked the arrests.

The *True Protestant Mercury* reported that "Thursday last being Acted a Play called *The Tragedy of Romulus* at the Duke's Theatre and the *Epilogue* spoken by the Lady Slingsby and written by Mrs. Behn which reflected on the D. of *Monmouth* the Lord *Chamberlain* has ordered them both in custody to answer that affront for the same." Qtd. in Janet Todd, *The Works of Aphra Behn*, vol. 1 (Columbus: Ohio State University Press, 1992), 382.

2. LC 5/190: 178; qtd. in Pierre Danchin, *The Prologues and Epilogues of the Restoration, 1660–1700* (Nancy: Presses Universitaires de Nancy, 1981–1988), 2:152.

Danchin thinks this actually refers to the prologue Haines delivered to *Wits Led by the Nose*, by William Chamberlayne.

3. J. L. Austin, *How to Do Things with Words*, ed. J. O. Urmson and Marina Sbisà (Cambridge, MA: Harvard University Press, 1975), 22. Derrida, of course, pursues this further when responding to Austin and John Searle in *Limited, Inc*. See Jacques Derrida, *Limited, Inc*. Evanston, IL: Northwestern University Press, 1988.

4. In the introductions to each set of volumes, Danchin has suggested various patterns, including a few that I make use of later in this chapter. Emmett Avery, James Sutherland, David Vieth, and Autrey Nell Wiley have also located similarities within Restoration paratexts, but they worked with much smaller sample sizes. See Emmet Avery, "Rhetorical Patterns in Restoration Prologues and Epilogues," in *Essays in American and English Literature Presented to Bruce Robert McElderry, Jr.*, ed. Max Schulz, with William D. Templeman and Charles R. Metzger (Athens: Ohio University Press, 1967); David M. Vieth, "The Art of the Prologue and Epilogue: A New Approach Based on Dryden's Practice," *Genre* 5, no. 3 (1972): 271–92; James Sutherland, "Prologues, Epilogues, and Audience in the Restoration Theatre," in *Of Books and Humankind: Essays and Poems Presented to Bonamy Dobree*, ed. John Butt, J. M. Cameron, D. W. Jefferson, and Robin Skelton (London: Routledge and Kegan Paul, 1964); Autrey Nell Wiley, "Female Prologues and Epilogues in English Plays," *Publications of the Modern Language Association (PMLA)* 48 (1933): 1060–79; Autrey Nell Wiley, *Rare Prologues and Epilogues 1642–1700* (London: George Allen and Unwin, 1940; reprint, Port Washington, NY: Kennikat, 1970).

5. The figure of 40 percent concerns plays with prologues and comes from Douglas Bruster and Robert Weimann, *Prologues to Shakespeare's Theatre: Performance and Liminallity in Early Modern Drama* (London: Routledge, 2004), 4. The figure of 48 percent of plays between 1558 and 1642 having prologue, epilogue, or both comes from Wiley and is supported by Danchin, as is the figure that nine out of ten Restoration plays featured both prologue and epilogue. See Wiley, *Rare Prologues*, xxvii–xxviii; Danchin, *Restoration*, 1:xxv.

6. This number comes from Danchin's collections and follows his sometimes necessarily conjectural dating of plays. Because they occasionally use a character's name and thus indicate the gender of the speaker, closet dramas are included in this figure. There are also a few occasions where a paratext is reused for a different play; in those situations I have counted the paratext twice.

7. In a related issue, when dealing with paratexts whose speakers are unknown, it is tempting to assign these paratexts to male speakers, both because ungendered items have defaulted to the male side since time immemorial and because nearly all female paratexts indicate—indeed, exploit—their speakers' gender. I have opted, however, to avoid assigning gender to paratexts that do not possess clear gender markers, and for the most part I have chosen illustrative examples that feature named speakers.

8. For a discussion of Genette's term, see the introduction.

9. Autrey Nell Wiley provides a helpful chronology of prologues and epilogues, and my claims in this section are indebted to her research. See Wiley, *Rare Prologues*, xxiii–xlv. More recently, Douglas Bruster and Robert Weimann have provided ad-

ditional information about prologues' Greek and Roman origins, in Bruster and Weimann, *Prologues*, 13–14.

10. James William Gousseff, *The Staging of Prologues in Tudor and Stuart Plays* (Northwestern, 1962), 85.

11. Bruster and Weimann, *Prologues*, 25.

12. James Shirley, *The Coronation* (London, 1640), A2.

13. Danchin, *Restoration*, 1:88, 130. We do not know whether Davenant's prologue was performed.

14. Robert D. Hume and Harold Love, eds., *Plays, Poems, and Miscellaneous Writings Associated with George Villiers, Second Duke of Buckingham*, vol. 1 (Oxford: Oxford University Press, 2007), 404.

15. Pierre Danchin, *The Prologues and Epilogues of the Eighteenth Century* (Nancy: Presses Universitaires de Nancy, 1990), 1:431.

16. Danchin, *The Prologues and Epilogues of the Eighteenth Century: The Third Part, 1737–1760*, 2 vols. (Paris: Editions Messene, 1997), 2:544; *The Spouter's Companion; or, Theatrical Remembrancer* (London: c.1770), 33.

17. *The Spouter's Companion*, 8–9.

18. This can be contrasted to the "domino" costume. Worn to masquerades during the eighteenth century, the domino costume also signaled the cloak's expanded representation. Colorful or black cloaks that obscured the body, the domino costume symbolized not credibility and integrity, writes Terry Castle, but invisibility and muteness: a stage between quotidian dress and exhibitionistic masquerade. See Terry Castle, *Masquerade and Civilization* (Stanford, CA: Stanford University Press, 1986), 59. The shift in cultural perception from a cloak representing neutral bodily concealment to being worn as a costume expanded the range of subjects and viewpoints prologues and epilogues could adopt.

19. Danchin, *Restoration*, 1:372.

20. In one case, a paratext was used as a prologue to one play and an epilogue to another: Dryden's prologue to a c.1671–1672 performance of Fletcher and Massinger's *The Double Marriage* was recycled as both the prologue to Behn's *Abdelazer* (1676) and the epilogue to *The Widdow Ranter* (1689). For more examples of recycled prologues and epilogues, see the appendix.

21. Paul McCallum points out that such prologues and epilogues made their writers become important political figures; I would add that this same importance applies to their performers. See Paul McCallum, "Cozening the Pit: Prologues, Epilogues, and Poetic Authority in Restoration England," in *Prologues, Epilogues, Curtain-Raisers, and Afterpieces: The Rest of the Eighteenth-Century London Stage*, ed. Daniel J. Ennis and Judith Bailey Slagle (Newark: University of Delaware Press, 2007), 61.

22. John Harold Wilson has located breeches costumes in 89 of 375 Restoration plays; see John Harold Wilson, *All the King's Ladies; Actresses of the Restoration* (Chicago: University of Chicago Press, 1958), 73. The prologue/epilogue estimate is mine; as always, more may have been lost.

23. For an example, see my discussion of Congreve's *Love for Love* in chapter 4.

24. Danchin, *Restoration*, 3:224–25.

25. From Ravenscroft, *The English Lawyer* (1677); Settle, *Fatal Love, or, the Forc'd Inconstancy* (c.1680); and D'Urfey, *The Banditti; or, A Ladies Distress* (1686).

26. Many paratexts begin or end with singular self-referential pronouns but otherwise use the plural; because these only acknowledge but do not distinguish the speaker, the paratexts should be considered cloaked. This is not, however, an exact science, and the unclarity is most acute at the beginning of the Restoration, when prologues and epilogues were still developing as genres.

27. John Dryden, "Prologue," in John Banks, *The Unhappy Favourite, or, The Earl of Essex* (London: Lintot, 1699), 63. I cite the 1699 edition because it fixes a spelling error present in the first edition of 1682. The misspelling remains in Gardner, Danchin, and the California *Works of John Dryden*.

28. Avery, "Rhetorical Patterns."

29. Marta Straznicky uses this term to describe how authors represent themselves onstage. See Marta Straznicky, "Restoration Women Playwrights and the Limits of Professionalism," *English Literary History* 64, no. 3 (1997): 708.

30. Danchin, *Restoration*, 3:383.

31. Danchin, *Restoration*, 2:91, 92.

32. Danchin, *Eighteenth*, 1:354–56.

33. Danchin, *Eighteenth*, 1:444.

34. Colley Cibber, *An Apology for the Life of Colley Cibber*, ed. B. R. S. Fone (New York: Dover, 1968; reprint, 2000), 150. Between 1660 and 1709, Betterton delivered a minimum of thirty-seven prologues and nine or ten epilogues; Anne Bracegirdle is the second most prolific, with a minimum of thirteen prologues and twenty-seven epilogues.

35. William Congreve, *The Way of the World*, 1st ed. (London: Tonson, 1700), A3r.

36. Ibid.

37. Betterton only delivered two each of exposed prologues and epilogues, and these were among the earliest of his career.

38. William Van Lennep, ed. *The London Stage, 1660–1800*, 5 vols. (Carbondale: Southern Illinois University Press, 1965), 1:525.

39. Dryden's editors, John Loftis and David Stuart Rodes, think that this costume refers to Nokes's performance of the character Sir Arthur Addell in John Caryll's *Sir Salomon; or, the Cautious Coxcomb*. They cite John Downes's eyewitness report: "The *French* Court wearing then Excessive short Lac'd Coats; some Scarlet, some Blew, with Broad wast Belts; Mr. *Nokes* having at that time one shorter than the *French* Fashion, to Act Sir *Arthur Addle* in; the Duke of *Monmouth* gave Mr. *Nokes* his Sword and Belt from his Side, and Buckled it on himself, on purpose to Ape the *French*: That Mr. *Nokes* lookt more like a Drest up Ape, than a Sir *Arthur*: Which upon his first Entrance on the Stage, put the King and Court to an Excessive Laughter; at which the *French* look'd very Shaggrin." John Loftis and David Stuart Rodes, eds., *The Works of John Dryden*, 20 vols., vol. 11 (1978), 445.

40. Hume and Love, *Plays, Poems, and Miscellaneous Writings*, 404.

41. Regarding the speaker's identity, in "Some notes on Dryden," G. Thorn-Drury writes of finding in the diary of Sir William Haward a reference to *Granada*'s prologue and epilogue speakers. The text reads, "the Prologue to the first part of the Conquest of Granada, spoken by Mohun, and the Epilogue to the second part of the Seige of Granada, spoken by Hart." Since we know that the prologue to Part 1 was spoken by Nell Gwyn, the first attribution is incorrect. Thorn-Drury writes, "By a slip the words *first* and *second* have been interchanged." Gardner and the editors of *The Works of John Dryden* (University of California Press) cite Thorn-Drury. My own consultation of the Haward manuscript confirms that the text of what Haward calls the epilogue to the second part of Granada is actually the epilogue to the first part. The other suggested actor is Michael Mohun, but this comes from an unjustified attribution by James Winn. See William Bradford Gardner, *The Prologues and Epilogues of John Dryden* (New York: Columbia University Press, 1951); Sir William Haward, "Ms. Don. b. 8," (Bodleian Library), 249; Loftis and Rodes, *Dryden*, 11: 451; G. Thorn-Drury, "Some Notes on Dryden," *Review of English Studies* 1, no. 3 (1925): 325; James Anderson Winn, *John Dryden and His World* (New Haven, CT: Yale University Press, 1987), 208.

42. Before the play was printed, however, the character had already morphed into the ridiculous Drawcansir in *The Rehearsal*, and accusations of plagiarism named Almanzor as a hero stolen from other texts.

43. Vieth finds that Dryden specializes in "humorous self-deprecation" in his prologues and epilogues, listing, among others, the prologue to a 1667 revival of *The Wild Gallant*. In this prologue, Dryden compares himself to a "raw Squire" who has remained a virgin until age twenty-one due to the pleasures of masturbation, a "Sport" he thinks he has invented. See Danchin, *Restoration*, 1:239; Vieth, "Art of the Prologue and Epilogue," 278.

44. Danchin, *Restoration*, 1:383.

45. If by chance the speaker was Mohun, then his fifty-four-year-old body would also have emphasized these lines.

46. Danchin, *Restoration*, 1:383. According to Haward, the second couplet was not performed. Haward, "Ms. Don. b. 8," 249.

47. Danchin, *Restoration*, 2:198.

48. Ibid.

49. Elizabeth Howe, *The First English Actresses: Women and Drama, 1660–1700* (Cambridge: Cambridge University Press, 1992), 26, 37.

50. Danchin, *Restoration*, 2:402.

51. Thomas Otway, *The Works of Thomas Otway*, ed. J. C. Ghosh, 2 vols. (Oxford: Clarendon, 1968), 2:540. Many more prologues and epilogues referred to the Exclusion Crisis and Oates in particular; see James Thorson, "The Dialogue between the Stage and the Audience: Prologues and Epilogues in the Era of the Popish Plot," in *Compendious Conversations: The Method of Dialogue in the Early Enlightenment*, ed. Kevin L. Cope (Frankfurt: Peter Lang, 1992).

52. Danchin, *Restoration*, 1:403.

53. It should be noted that Thomas Shadwell directly responded to this prologue in "The Tory-poets, a Satyr," which attacks Behn and Otway but spares Barry. Given the many lines of the prologue that Shadwell mimicks, it is likely that he had access to a copy of the prologue and therefore would have focused on its authorship rather than Barry's performance.

54. John Wilmot, 2nd Earl of Rochester, *Valentinian*, 1st ed. (London: Timothy Goodwin, 1685), [A3r].

55. Danchin, *Restoration*, 2:516. The Trimmers, political moderates during the Exclusion Crisis, were headed by the first Marquess of Halifax, who embraced the label in his political analysis of contemporary government, *The Character of a Trimmer* (1684).

56. Ibid.; See chapters 2 and 4 for further discussion of this issue.

57. Other prologues and epilogues where women discuss theatrical politics include Mrs. Cooke's epilogue to Behn's *The Emperour of the Moon* (1687), and the female epilogue (the speaker is unknown) to Dryden's adaptation of Beaumont and Fletcher's *The Prophetess; or, The History of Dioclesian* (1690).

58. Danchin, *Eighteenth*, 1:166.

59. Others within the decade following Collier include Jane Rogers's epilogue to D'Urfey's *The Famous History of the Rise and Fall of Massaniello Part 1* (1699), Porter's prologue to William Walker's *Marry or Do Worse*, (1703); Mrs. Babb's prologue to Farquhar's *The Recruiting Officer* (1706); and, of course, Betterton's prologue to Congreve's *The Way of the World*.

60. Danchin, *Restoration*, 1:167.

61. Ibid.

62. For a discussion on the techniques actresses used to address female audiences, see chapter 3.

63. Edward A. Langhans, "Tough Actresses to Follow," in *Curtain Calls: British and American Women and the Theater, 1660–1820*, ed. Mary Anne Schofield and Cecilia Macheski (Athens: Ohio University Press, 1991), 12.

64. Epilogues to John Crowne's *The Married Beau* (1694) and Thomas D'Urfey's *The Virtuous Wife* (1679).

65. Danchin, *Restoration*, 1:46–48.

66. Danchin, *Eighteenth*, 1:480–81.

67. John Dryden, *The Works of John Dryden*, ed. Earl Miner and Vinton Dearling, vol. 3 (Berkeley: University of California Press, 1969), 510.

68. Cibber, *Apology*, 111.

69. Danchin, *Restoration*, 2:854.

70. Ibid.

71. Ibid., 855.

72. Other "drunken" paratexts include Joseph Haines's "Reformation Prologue" (1692), George Powell's prologue (written by Haines) to Farquhar's *Love and a Bottle* (1698), Bowen's prologue to Thomas Dilke's *The Pretenders* (1698), and Will Pinkethman's epilogue to David Crauford's *Courtship a la Mode* (1700).

73. George Spencer Bower, *A Study of the Prologue and Epilogue in English Literature from Shakespeare to Dryden* (London: Kegan, Paul, Trench, 1884), 28.

74. John Russell Brown, ed. *The Oxford Illustrated History of Theatre* (Oxford: Oxford University Press, 2001), 217.

75. For additional information on Haines's life, see Kenneth M. Cameron, "Jo Haynes, Infamis," *Theatre Notebook* 24, no. 2 (1969): 56–67; Philip H. Highfill, Kalman A. Burnim, and Edward A. Langhans, *A Biographical Dictionary of Actors, Actresses, Musicians, Dancers, Managers and Other Stage Personnel in London, 1660–1800*, 16 vols. (Carbondale: Southern Illinois University Press, 1973), 7:7–17; J. W. Robinson, "Elegy on the Death of Joseph Haines," *Theatre Notebook* 35, no. 3 (1981): 99–100; Cheryl Wanko, *Roles of Authority: Thespian Biography and Celebrity in Eighteenth-Century Britain* (Lubbock: Texas Tech University Press, 2003), 26–28, 30–38. For more on the ass epilogue, see Danchin, *Restoration*, xv–xvi.

76. Although the only recorded performances of *Don Quixote Part I* took place in 1694 and 1700, the many references in this epilogue to the previous one lead me to concur with Danchin's speculation that a revival of D'Urfey's play took place around 1697; see Danchin, *Restoration*, 3:306.

77. Thomas Scott, *The Unhappy Kindness: or a Fruitless Revenge* (London: H. Rhodes, S. Briscoe, and R. Parker, 1697), [A3v], [A4r].

78. Ibid., [A4r].

79. Danchin, *Eighteenth*, 3:309. "[A]n allusion to the new coinage which was then taking place, replacing the old clipped money by new coins." Ibid., 3:307.

80. Danchin documents the various performances of ass epilogues throughout the century; see Danchin, "Le Développement du Spectaculaire sur le Theatre Anglais (1660–1800): le Role des Prologues et Épilogues," *Medieval English Theater* 16 (1994).

81. Danchin, *Eighteenth*, 1:217.

82. Qtd. in Danchin, *Eighteenth*, 3:100.

83. *The Honey-Suckle; Consisting of Original Poems, Epigrams, Songs, Tales, Odes, and Translations*, ed. "A Society of Gentlemen" (London: Charles Corbett, 1734), 182. Danchin provides a helpful trace of the epilogue's performances in Danchin, *Eighteenth*, 2:490. Eliza Haywood also performs (sans ass) in this epilogue.

84. Danchin, *Restoration*, 2:801.

85. Sigmund Freud, *Jokes and Their Relation to the Unconscious* (New York: Atheneum, 1966), 117–20; Mahadev Apte, *Humor and Laughter: An Anthropological Approach* (Ithaca, NY: Cornell University Press, 1985), 69.

CHAPTER TWO

~

Female Exposed Paratexts, Part One: Actress as Joker and Target

Contemporary Irish comedian Mary Bourke performs a joke about the stigma attached to female comedians: in an effort to obscure her real profession, her father "tells the neighbors I'm a crack-head whore."[1] Given the continued social resistance to women performing comedy, Bourke's words enable us to appreciate the transgressions of female stand-up comedians over three hundred years earlier. In the Restoration, for a woman to perform onstage was itself a political act, with antitheatricalists decrying their profession and satirists slandering their behavior as whorish. Performing comedy was even more political, because it meant that the actress could control the theatrical environment. That women possessed the attributes required to perform stand-up—the aggressiveness, the potential to mock any member of the audience as needed, and the strength necessary to make oneself vulnerable and plumb the body as joke fodder—made these performers the real locus of power and represented an advance in the English theater world. This is all the more reason why we must consider prologues and epilogues, and more largely Restoration drama, in performance: otherwise we miss the chance to examine the figure of the female comedian, previously an unheard-of public figure in Britain.

The content of what I am calling female exposed prologues and epilogues varies widely but rests upon the cultural assumption of actresses' sexual expertise. Each individual prologue and epilogue contains differing proportions of two elements: sexual stereotypes about female players and actresses' outspokenness. The tone is often murky; some feminist-sounding statements seem tailored to provoke ridicule and thus reinforce female objectification. Occasionally, misogyny plays out word for word, as in a prologue where a woman complains of men's physical censorship, only to have a man prove her point by upstaging her.[2] More often, however, the speaker would use either absurd or wishful diction to imagine greater agency or talk herself into accepting a misogynist point of view; there are many of these would-be outspoken female prologues and epilogues. Others, however, genuinely questioned the strictures on women. Particularly in the 1690s, epilogues interrogated the female repression that the play had just presented. Many prologues and epilogues celebrated women and subverted misogyny.

In this chapter and the next, I identify six types of female exposed paratexts.[3] The first four types, which form the basis of this chapter, are: revived, breeches, virgin, and tendentious. Of these four, the first three types are readily recognizable. It is easy to categorize epilogues that feature a woman arising from lying "dead" on the floor, wearing breeches, or offering up her virginity. But I have grouped the less immediately discernible category of the tendentious with the other three because it shares with them many features. As opposed to their male exposed counterparts, all four use props and stances not to attract and then disperse the audience's gaze but to retain it so that the audience perceives the performer as both joke-teller and target. All create comedy from the actress's body. And many female paratexts inhabit more than one category; Letitia Cross's series of "virgin" paratexts (discussed later in this chapter), for example, also qualify as tendentious.

How can such exploitative paratexts give actresses agency? After all, the revived epilogue capitalizes upon associating women with orgasm, the breeches expose her calves and ankles, the virgin corporeally represents young girls' naiveté, and the tendentious sexualize women, sometimes violently. These types would seem to emphasize the author's agency, particularly if the author is male, since for women to play these roles might seem demeaning or self-destructive. This raises the question of self-deprecating comedy: is it demeaning for women to deliver comedy that is self-deprecating or misogynist? As Joanne Gilbert points out, "To some, the very fact that women got up onstage alone and took up time and space makes this a 'feminist' act. To others, only humor in which patriarchal norms are overtly attacked qualifies as 'feminist.'"[4] These four categories form an uneasy amalgamation of the protofeminist female comedian and the objectifying, and sometimes downright misogynist, content. From examining the archive, I contend that the sheer fact of women controlling hundreds of audience members through performing comedy, arguably the most powerful form of speech, counterbalances the often disturbing content of their prologues and epilogues. As misogynist as the content might be, the author depends on the actress to perform, and the two are implicitly complicit in granting the actress the authority necessary to perform comedy. Discussed in chapter 3, the two additional types—female solidarity and social critique—center less on a physical gimmick and more on verbal content. In contrast to the prior categories, these two types range from creating female community to critiquing marriage and male infidelity.

Revived Epilogues

No epilogue, I pray you; for your play needs no excuse. Never excuse; for when the players are all dead, there need none to be blam'd.

—Theseus to Bottom, A Midsummer Night's Dream[5]

Many authors of epilogues to Restoration tragedies must have disagreed with Theseus's statement to the "Pyramus and Thisbe" performers, because they composed revived epilogues, spoken by actresses whose characters had died in the play.[6] The revived epilogue converts the body of its female speaker from a source of pathos (in its prone or supine "dead" state) into a sexual spectacle. Not only does the revived epilogue literally reverse the character's life cycle, but it also potentially curtails the tragedy's potential for catharsis. Since the audience has known the character for five acts, the sudden betweenness of character and actress necessitates a jarring reinterpretation of the role. The audience's attention thus shifts from the heroine's plight to the epilogue's critique of such a plight.

The revived epilogue is one example of the Restoration convention of concluding a tragedy with a bawdy epilogue; chapter 5 devotes significant space to examining the popularity of and resistance to this practice, but a few words here help contextualize the phenomenon and its critical reception. While the history of following English tragedies with comic material is found as early as the Elizabethan jig, the practice of selecting a character from the tragic main piece and making her over as a comedian in the epilogue, either by having the actress speak through her public persona, or by creating a betweenness of the actress and character, was pioneered during the Restoration era. Among modern critics, Allardyce Nicoll first observes its presence in early eighteenth-century plays; Autrey Nell Wiley then terms it the "merry epilogue" and locates resistance to it in Restoration documents such as Buckingham's The Rehearsal, which mocks actors for standing up and walking offstage after their characters have died.[7] Mary Knapp traces the continuation of this Restoration phenomenon through the eighteenth century and finds that in the early part of the century, tragedy and sentimental comedy featured prologues that trumpeted their plays as teachers of morality, and epilogues that countered this function. Renaming them "indecent" epilogues, calling them "the most convincing evidence of wide-spread corruption," and singling out such epilogues to tragedies as a "vicious practice," however, Knapp takes a less exploratory, more punitive approach to these epilogues.[8] Tragedies with bawdy epilogues are thus ripe for reconsideration.

The number of revived epilogues and references to them speak to the influence of this favored form. There were at least eighteen revived epilogues between 1669 and 1714. Authors included Behn, Lee, Otway, and Rowe, while star actresses Elizabeth Barry and Anne Bracegirdle delivered four and three such epilogues, respectively. Variations on the practice include Edmund Waller's epilogue for The Maid's Tragedy Alter'd, where the character Aspasia delivers the epilogue while dying. There is even a revived prologue, delivered at a private performance at Belvoir Castle in 1675, where the speaker, a Mrs. P. L., begins by "starting up, as rising from the dead."[9] The revived epilogue's prominence in the theater world is also evident through other texts' references to it, such as the epilogue to John Banks's 1696 tragedy, Cyrus the Great, delivered by a boy and a girl who mention two female characters' deaths and ask, with tongues in cheeks, "wou'd you have dead Bodies rise again?"[10]

The most celebrated example of a revived epilogue appears in Dryden's 1669 heroic tragedy, Tyrannick Love, performed by Nell Gwyn. Here I want to extend the introduction's intermittent discussion of this epilogue into a wider context, arguing that it places audience desire for bawdy comedy ahead of character development and genre fidelity. More famous for epilogue than plot, the play derives its tragedy from featuring multiple characters who love the wrong people. The play's tyrant is the ruthless Roman emperor Maximin, who returns home from a successful run of empire building to find that his appointed successor and designated future son-in-law, Porphyrius, is instead smitten with Maximin's own wife, Queen Berenice. Meanwhile, Maximin's attractive Christian prisoner of war, St. Catherine, opts to martyr herself rather than marry him, in part because she knows he would slay his current wife. While ultimately Porphyrius does get to marry Queen Berenice, the play closes with the deaths of five characters, the bodies of Valeria and two others remaining strewn across the stage.

Gwyn's character, Maximin's daughter Valeria, combines ardent love with crafty strategy. Upon discovering that her love for Porphyrius is unrequited, she breaks their engagement, a move Porphyrius has difficulty understanding. This maneuver communicates the depth of her love to Porphyrius, because not only does she free him to woo the queen, but she also suffers imprisonment for her filial disobedience. Later, she also saves the imprisoned Porphyrius by convincing her own suitor, Placidus, to release him. Valeria's strategic love also informs her mode of death, where she cunningly distracts Placidus by taking his hand in a suggestion that she will marry him, but then stabs herself with a dagger in her other hand before he can intervene:

> Let me be just before I go away.
> Placidus, I have vow'd to be your Wife;
> Take then my hand, 'tis yours while I have life.
> One moment here, I must anothers be:
> But this, *Porphyrius*, gives me back to thee.
> *Stabs her self twice, and then* Placidus *wrests the Dagger from her.*[11]

In this scene, Valeria negotiates a difficult circumstance and manages to please everybody, even if only momentarily. She comes across as both noble and assertive, as evidenced by her sleight of hand, and the ambiguity of her position is also empowering, though fatal.

In a hallmark example of comic incongruity—laughter in the face of death—the epilogue begins with Valeria snapping back to life. She inaugurates this transformation, moreover, by adding to her character of a self-sacrificing virgin lover the comic turns of a sassy wench. Much of the wit comes from this alteration: Gwyn interrupts Valeria's quiet complexity with her first couplet, directed to her pallbearer: "Hold, are you mad? you damn'd confounded Dog, / I am to rise, and speak the Epilogue."[12] These lines launch what the epilogue sustains: a challenge to the play's high drama. While she continues to speak in heroic couplets, the first line of the epilogue interrupts the former stately progress of her earlier lines. The imposition of a question mark, the rising intonation required to pose it, and the insulting canine comparison that follows signal a comic change in her character. Valeria also jokes by using the word "mad." Despite Dryden's curiously sympathetic preface to the play, where he defends the antagonist King Maximin, the word "mad" suits this bloodthirsty dictator. Yet none of the other characters consider him mad, and many remain loyal to him even as he calls for their deaths. That Valeria directs this epithet not at her sadistic father but at an unnamed pallbearer just doing his job undercuts the high tragedy and the consistency of her character.

The second line sustains the arrest of the tragic catharsis, this time interrupting the audience's willing suspension of disbelief by drawing their attention to the actress function. When Gwyn says, "I am to rise, and speak the

Epilogue," she alters the audience's sense of who the "I" represents, returning them to their prior conception of "Nell-ness." The role Gwyn has performed is just an occupation, one of many with which the audience was acquainted. Gwyn's progress from a server of "strong-Waters," to orange-seller/prostitute, to actress, to mistress of Charles II, was well known to London theatergoers. This line thus represents just another case of Gwyn getting up for work.

When Gwyn declares in line four, "I am the Ghost of poor departed Nelly," she exploits the betweenness of character and actress for comic effect.[13] That the dead Valeria would have a ghost makes sense in the world of theater, but in the liminal epilogue space it explains how Valeria might again appear in an upright position while connected to the name of the very much alive actress. The word "poor" and the use of a nickname remind the audience of their familiarity with and affection for Gwyn. "Departed" increases the joke, since the would-be departed person is in fact physically present and speaking in the first person. Combined with the allusions to Gwyn's reputation, the joke of Valeria's death and ghostly reappearance comically blur the character/actress divide.

The rest of the epilogue plays off of the disjunction of character and actress in a way that both mocks the preceding tragedy for comic effect and advances Gwyn's career. Dryden frequently pokes fun at himself in prologues and epilogues, and here he has Gwyn critique his play's composition and casting:

> To tell you true, I walk because I dye
> Out of my Calling in a Tragedy.
> O Poet, damn'd dull Poet, who could prove
> So sensless! to make *Nelly* dye for Love;
> Nay, what's yet worse, to kill me in the prime
> Of *Easter*-Term, in Tart and Cheese-cake time![14]

In the same way that "mad" adopts a comic meaning in the epilogue, here the words denoting death turn comic in their new contexts. In addition to the late seventeenth century's association of death with orgasm, the first instance of the word "dye" suggests the contextual denotation "to be miscast." For a lesser-known actress, this situation could in fact result in the demise of her acting career, but here instead it suggests Dryden laughing at himself through Gwyn because he understands that her talent lies in performing comedy.[15] The second appearance of the word trades on Gwyn's lengthy and well-known sexual history, while the third reference to death reflects Gwyn's zest for life through gluttony. This joke undercuts the play's religious undertone—the martyrdom of St. Catherine—by restyling the holiest Christian day as instead a time to enjoy sweets. The Gwyn/Valeria amalgam parodies Jesus's rebirth by coming back to life herself and then reducing the Easter holiday to an opportunity to nosh.

The final four lines of the epilogue wrap up earlier comic threads and challenges to the tragedy:

> As for my Epitaph when I am gone,
> I'le trust no Poet, but will write my own.
> Here *Nelly* lies, who, though she liv'd a Slater'n,
> Yet dy'd a Princess, acting in S. *Cathar'n*.[16]

In this selection, the first couplet furthers Dryden's joke on himself through Gwyn, that he so poorly understands her acting style that she is forced to take pen in hand (despite being semiliterate herself) and script her own epitaph. Often quoted in biographies of both author and actress, the epitaph underscores the betweenness of character and actress. Gwyn seems to suggest, not altogether facetiously, that acting has elevated her to the level of princess, not only in the role she has just performed, but also in her social status. Underlying these lines are cultural anxieties about actresses using the stage for social advancement. Sumptuary laws forbade actresses to wear costumes outside the theater, for fear that they would be mistaken for aristocrats; and Charles II already had elevated actresses Mary Davys and Elizabeth Farley to the rank of royal mistress.[17] But because Gwyn was so well known and beloved, these lines represented a pleasing rise in stature, not a threat.

Not only does the epilogue disrupt Gwyn's characterization, but it also challenges Dryden's stated vision of the play. While his *Essay on Dramatic Poesy* (1667) and *A Defense of an Essay on Dramatic Poesy* (1668) contain more sustained statements about drama that define Dryden's early years as a literary critic, including his identification and modulation of the neoclassical unities, *Tyrannick Love*'s own preface—due to its proximity and specificity—must predominate this discussion.[18] The preface shows Dryden defining the genre of the heroic play and defending the treatment of religious subjects in blank verse, arguing that "By the Harmony of words we elevate the mind to a sense of Devotion, as our solemn Musick, which is inarticulate Poesie, does in Churches."[19] Dryden also defends the play by asserting its piety, its punishment of evil, and its accordance with the neoclassical unities of time, place, and action. Michael Gelber has stated that although the epilogue represents Dryden satirizing his own work, it does not undo the preface; but like Wiley and others, he supports this latter point merely by quoting twelve lines of the epilogue.[20] While these statements make it seem clear that Dryden views the play and epilogue as separate entities, the reconception of a play's character cannot help but suddenly deflate the earlier elevation of the mind.

The reception of Gwyn's epilogue is as famous as the epilogue itself, attesting to the importance of prologues and epilogues to an actress's career. It is difficult to determine when Gwyn's affair with Charles II actually began; Derek Parker claims that Gwyn and the king were on "extremely familiar terms" by spring 1668, a year before the premiere of *Tyrannick Love*, and defends this by quoting the lines Dryden writes for Gwyn to perform as Donna Jacintha in *An Evening's Love*, on June 12 of that year, about sexual trading-up. According to her character, an ordinary lover was only good "to be admitted to pass my time with while a better comes: to be the lowest step in my Stair-case, for a Knight to mount upon him, and a Lord upon him, and a Marquess upon him, and a Duke upon him, till I get as high as I can climb."[21] Peter Cunningham points out the contradiction between Pepys, who on 11 January 1668 noted that the king sent for Gwyn several times; and Edmund Curll, who may have started the *Tyrannick Love* epilogue legend.[22] Yet many sources either maintain or cite as one possibility the fable that Charles II took Gwyn to supper and then to bed for the first time after witnessing her deliver the *Tyrannick Love* epilogue. As mentioned in the introductory chapter, the legend remains current in academic circles and often substitutes for fact. Gwyn remains best known for her liaison with the king, and that the epilogue is either viewed as the catalyst or celebrated in conjunction with their mutual good humor confirms the association of prologues and epilogues with stardom.

The epilogue/royal mating story prompts speculation on Dryden as "royal matchmaker." Percy Fitzgerald, the late nineteenth-century author of *A New History of the English Stage*, offers the following interpretation:

> The marvel really is to think of Dryden, a poet of the first rank and dignity, thus degrading himself to supply a creature of this kind with rhymes, the aim and intent of which was only too obvious. Indeed, these prologues and epilogues, which form a series, could only have been spoken by persons of the character and profession to whom they were entrusted. The "glorious John" must have been flattered when he learned that his lines had proved so piquant, that the King that very evening came behind the scenes and carried away the speaker to sup with him.[23]

While Fitzgerald correctly records the theater practice of tailoring prologues and epilogues to specific players, he mistakenly places the agency entirely with the playwright. According to Fitzgerald, Dryden debases himself in composing this material but then finds happiness when his epilogue pimps royally for Gwyn, enhancing his status with Charles II by supplying a woman made attractive through language. He emphasizes Gwyn's lack of agency in attracting the king by terming her "a creature of this kind" instead of naming her. But it is precisely the fact that Gwyn is more than just such a creature—that her persona attracts first-rate dramatists to write for her—that gives her agency and influence with her theater audience. Gwyn's ability to trade on her sexual reputation provides Dryden with joke fodder, meaning that the actress–author combination together creates a comedy all the more uproarious for violating the preceding neoclassical unities and tragic deaths. Fitzgerald's conception of the actress as the empty vessel for the author's words is precisely the critical approach I am arguing against. It considers the author function too narrowly—in such a personalized epilogue, Gwyn must be considered a cocreator—and it conceptualizes performance only in terms of the actual lines uttered onstage, failing to consider the figure from whose mouth they emanate. Gwyn's reputation, both as a whore who trades upon this epithet to win audience adulation and as a skilled actress who exploits her body and persona for comic effect, joins with Dryden's lines to make this epilogue deservedly famous. More widely cited than *Tyrannick Love* itself, it represents a collaborative coauthorship between actress and playwright, it successfully challenges the play's genre, and it exemplifies the need for a performance-based approach in order to consider prologues' and epilogues' relationship to their orators and audiences in conjunction with the plays they frame. Gerard Genette notes the ability of paratexts to both frame and challenge the texts they accompany. In this case, the epilogue as paratext both throws the play out of balance and, through retroactive metalepsis, fosters a new narrative that many writers during the intervening centuries have superimposed on Gwyn and Charles II's history.[24]

As Gwyn's example illustrates, concluding a tragedy with a revived epilogue challenges the integrity of character and genre. It also demonstrates the radical agency of the epilogue speaker. A primary character such as Valeria, who had exhibited single-minded, noble behavior, now fuses with her performer's public persona. This union of character and persona retroactively undoes the audience's investment in the coherence and morality of character and plot. In extending their theatrical exposure by choosing to remain for the epilogue, the audience members countenanced this practice. The tragic genre experienced a concomitant disruption: Revived epilogues curtailed and possibly unraveled audience's cathartic responses to tragedies. Building on the work of Eric Rothstein, Christopher Wheatley discusses two competing theories of tragedy in the Restoration: the Horatian belief that literature should both delight and inspire (as Thomas

Rymer articulates, that Restoration tragedies should convey a useful moral lesson) and the Aristotelian emphasis on the audience experiencing tragic catharsis.[25] The rise of she-tragedy in the second half of the Restoration indicates an expansion of the latter mode, with its emphasis on what Jean Marsden calls "the spectator's vicarious enjoyment of suffering woman-hood."[26] Staged female suffering frequently stemmed from rape, and rape meant the victim's death. The revived epilogue thus made a protofeminist intervention, albeit a bizarre one, into the high seriousness of tragedy and the prescribed deaths of tragic heroines.

These combinations of character and persona, tragedy and comedy, both enlivened spectators and sparked debates about decorum that themselves in-fluenced the authorship and reception of character and genre. The case study of Nell Gwyn indicates that London authors, theater managers, and publish-ers frequently brushed aside the integrity of role and genre to accommodate audience desire for actresses' sex comedy. The public's enthusiasm demon-strates, moreover, that whereas female performance of comedy was (and is) often discouraged, such was not the case for Gwyn and many other actresses.

Because Gwyn's is the most famous Restoration epilogue, it can over-whelm the revived category, and therefore, a brief look at another example is in order. Trading on the popularity of the form, Thomas Otway wrote a revived epilogue for his debut, *Alcibiades* (1675). The tragedy is a formulaic instance of a hero fighting corrupt villains; the lovers Alcibiades and Timan-dra, played by Thomas and Mary Betterton, are persecuted by jealous rivals, including Deidama, the Queen of Sparta, who loves Alcibiades, and Ther-amnes, who attempts to rape Timandra. Having been kicked out of Athens but made the ruler of Sparta, Alcibiades has driven Tissaphernes, the former Spartan leader, to murderous rage. The play contains events typical of Res-toration tragedies, including poisonings, stabbings, suicides, and a visit from Theramnes's ghost. By the end of the play, the body count is six: Theramnes, the king, Tissaphernes, Alcibiades, Timandra, and finally the queen. This last death leads straight into the revived epilogue.

Mary Lee's performance of the epilogue interrupts her characterization of the vengeful Queen of Sparta, which itself had already discontinued her usual line of virgin characters.[27] While throughout most of the play Tissa-phernes is the primary villain, in the final act the queen supersedes him and kills five. She does so, moreover, in ways sadistic to both victims and survi-vors; she emasculates Tissaphernes by seizing the dagger out of his hands to kill the king, and her poisoning of Timandra also inspires Alcibiades's suicide because she makes him watch his lover die. The target that the queen pursues in the epilogue is by comparison much milder and changes the mood from grim to facetious. The epilogue does contain emasculating insinuations, this time directed at the playwright, but the stakes are so low that comedy is the clear result.

In parodying the play, the epilogue undoes some of its power. Whereas in the main text the ghost that menaces Tissaphernes is meant to be frightening, Mary Lee's return as the ghost of the queen creates comedy. Her actions recall Gwyn's star turn as "the Ghost of poor departed Nelly," so one wonders whether this trend led audiences to associate any ghosts that appeared in the play proper with subsequent facetious incarnations in the epilogue.[28] This is also a clear moment of contrast between male- and female-orated paratexts. In male cloaked paratexts, such as the prologue to *The Way of the World* and the epilogue to *The Conquest of Granada* (discussed in chapter 1), the speaker often bids the audience blame the author if the play fails to please. And in male exposed epilogues the speaker, subsumed in the character, does so as well. But neither of these speakers exhibits betweenness as a gendered way of facetiously countering the author. Lee, in contrast, combines her character's condition with a coquettish persona, where she bonds with the audience by mocking the playwright. The epilogue begins with her implying that playwrights are cowards who themselves avoid fighting but fill their plays with bloodshed. In merely sixteen lines she uses four epithets—two for the weakling poets and two for Otway—and invites the audience to help her damn him to hell:

> Ours made such Havock, that the silly Rogue
> Was forc't to make me rise for th'Epilogue.
> The fop damn'd me, but e're to hell I go,
> I'd very fain be satisfy'd, if you
> Think it not just that he were serv'd so too.[29]

These lines capture the same sentiment as the prologue to *The Way of the World*, where Betterton bids the audience to "Save or Damn" Congreve, "after your own Discretion."[30] But the content is much different. In five lines she makes four self-references and calls Otway a rogue and a fop, so that he comes across as a mocked lover. Lee also makes blasphemous references to hell and damnation, begging the audience to send Otway to hell because "You've been in Purgatory all this while."[31] The flirtatious and bathetic transmutation of hell from literal location to comic metaphor curtails any tragic catharsis the audience experienced during this overblown play. Together, Otway and Lee create this gendered rivalry that belies their cooperative agency.

This example also shows the range of revived epilogues; whereas the prior one featured sympathetic characters restored to life, this one reincarnates a murderous, unrepentant queen. But here, as in *Tyrannick Love*, the speaker likewise taunts the playwright, thereby theoretically neutralizing any hostile responses by the audience. If the audience boos the play, the epilogue construes their disapprobation as in concert with its speaker. If the audience does not favor the play but enjoys the epilogue, their favorable response to the paratext may sweeten their overall sentiments about the theatrical evening. By positioning the epilogue speaker against the playwright, Otway, like many authors before him, strategizes that this maneuver will prevent the audience from responding unfavorably. Otway thus understands the paratext as a device that can condition the audience's response to the main piece. More than one revived epilogue features the speaker punning on the fact that she has "died," and another showcases a bleeding heroine who claims that only audience applause will restore her to life.[32] Such epilogues therefore deflect blame in a way contrary to Theseus's strategy of "when the players are all dead, there need none to be blam'd." In so doing, they birthed the careers of many Restoration actresses, elevating their comic skill and fame within and beyond the theater.

Gender Confirmation and Transformation through Breeches

One of the most enduring exposed styles, the breeches paratext explores the betweenness of the actress's persona and her embodiment of pseudo-maleness. Although the *Oxford Encyclopedia of Theatre and Performance* gives the traditional definition of the breeches role as indicating parts written for men but performed by women, a definition that explicitly excludes female characters who adopt male disguise midplay, it also cites the term's reclaiming by feminist critics and thereby leaves the door open for such an application.[33] Such is the way the Restoration breeches role is discussed today; it is defined by costume rather than duration. While the breeches costume was not designed as an authentic disguise, but rather as an excuse to accentuate the female body, when actresses wore breeches to deliver prologues and epilogues the costume also enabled a comedy of possibility, one that both confirmed and challenged gender regulations.

While the objectifying aspects of the breeches costume have garnered much critical attention, I extend Kirsten Pullen's argument that the breeches costume is customized to its inhabitant, to prologues and epilogues, which capitalize on such personalization.[34] Certainly there is no denying that with its separation of the legs and its exposure of the ankles and calves, the breeches role exploits the female body, and that this aspect accounts at least in part for its appearance in nearly one-quarter of all new Restoration plays.[35] And as Pat Rogers has claimed, characters adopting the costume do not unconditionally enter a Forest of Arden that enables gender exploration; Pullen points out that when they do access permissive environments, they are wrenched away through others unceremoniously exposing their breasts.[36] And yet, stopping here is too reductive, too inclined to see Restoration theater as prohibitive. Better to support the more expansive possibilities that Micheline Wandor sees in cross-dressing: that it can either contain rebellion or represent the rebellion itself.[37] Despite its exploitation of the female body, the breeches part automatically gives actresses a comic role to perform, in plays and in paratexts. Recognizable within the breeches part is the female character, the new male figure she is attempting, and the actress herself. The performativity present in the mingling of gendered attire and behavior makes space for a comedy of possibility, one that confirms gender regulations yet also challenges them through the fact of the woman performing comedy.

Some of the forty breeches paratexts minimize the structural differences between prologue and epilogue. Earlier I argued that because the audience had not yet met the actress's character, exposed prologues more often concentrated on her persona, while epilogues created a betweenness involving the actress's persona and her character. This general formula assumes that most epilogue speakers also appeared in the play. But within our surviving records, more epilogues than prologues employed what I consider a gratuitous use of the costume: breeches-wearing actresses who did not otherwise appear in the play. There are two such prologues, George Powell's to *The Treacherous Brothers* (1690) and the anonymous prologue to Congreve's *Love for Love* (1695), and at least four epilogues: Catharine Trotter's to *Agnes de Castro*, Thomas Dilke's to *The Lover's Luck* (both 1695), Settle's to *The World in the Moon* (1697), and the 1703 revival of Sir John Vanbrugh's to *The Pilgrim* (1700). The latter three double as "virgin" epilogues and indicate an experimental looseness between plays and epilogues during this time period, as also evidenced by the male exposed "ass epilogues" described in chapter 1. There are also two prologues "proposed" to be spoken by actresses wearing breeches whose characters do not do so during the play: one for Susannah Mountfort in Dryden's *Don Sebastian* (1689) and one for Anne Bracegirdle in Congreve's *Love for Love* (1695).[38] Our incomplete records preclude general statements about the frequency of these gratuitous breeches appearances, but the extant examples suggest that many breeches paratexts were more "occasional," less relevant to the play.

For Hester Santlow, the new epilogue to a 4 February 1710 revival of Thomas D'Urfey's *Don Quixote Part II* furthered a sequence of breeches performances that launched her career. A professionally trained dancer who debuted at Drury Lane in 1706 at age twelve or thirteen, Santlow made a name for herself within eighteen months and began acting three years later.[39] She countered early scandals (she bore a child out of wedlock in 1712, and she may have been the mistress simultaneously of James Craggs and the Duke of Marlborough, the former having arranged the latter liaison), with what seems to have been a remarkably compatible marriage to the tragedian and theater manager Barton Booth. Her early-career epilogue to *Don Quixote Part II* capitalized on Santlow's recent forays into cross-dressed roles. In *The Incomparable Hester Santlow*, Moira Goff identifies Santlow's acting debut, where she cross-dressed to play the eunuch Lycias in Rochester's *Valentinian*, as occurring a mere seven days before this epilogue. She must have been well received, because an advertisement for the second performance singled out Santlow as "being the second Time of her appearing in Boys Cloaths."[40] Following *Valentinian*, Santlow delivered two breeches epilogues, the other adjoining a revival three days later of Centlivre's *The Gamester*.[41] Her part in Rochester's play therefore began a metatheatrical narrative that continued in the bawdy breeches epilogue to *Don Quixote Part II*.

The comedy of this epilogue centers on Santlow's gender performances, where the actress calls attention to her masquerade as a man. Unfortunately, we know neither the part that Santlow played in *Don Quixote Part II* nor the author of the new epilogue. But our inability to deduce this knowledge also demonstrates the independence of the breeches epilogue and the agency of its speaker. The epic simile in the first eight lines, where the speaker compares herself to a brave soldier, signals a mock-heroic tone. Toying with gender roles, she acts jingoistic, asserts physical strength, and emphasizes certain words to demonstrate her unyielding battle-time commands. Yet she also combines gender-coded elements in the lines where she claims to exemplify bullying female behavior: "A woman's reason, is her yes, or no; / All things are this, or that, because we'll have them so."[42] The use of the first person plural and the declamatory statement suggests her authority in speaking for women, even as she masquerades as a man.

Her multigendered performances are most pronounced during two moments of gest (to use Brecht's term), where she invites any unsatisfied audience members to duel. Here, the gest indicates the comic clash of gender codes:

> Thus, then, I Draw, and Frowning, thus Decree,
> To Night our *Quixot* SHALL applauded be:
> I say't, and what I say, who dares Deny?
> If any Dares—let him come out and Dye:

He who refuses to Obey my Will,
And dang'rously resolves to try my Skill,
I Challenge by this Pledge,*—which He who takes,
   (*Throws down a glove.)
All Hopes of Safety, nay of Life, forsakes:
Weak as I am, that Wretch had better tarry:
For I can make such *Thrusts*—as no Man here can Parry.[43]

In these five couplets her facetious performance of masculinity comically contrasts with Santlow's girlish appearance. The act of throwing down the gauntlet connotes in male terms a masculine anger and an eagerness to duel, but in female terms it continues the action of disrobing that the breeches costume implicitly began. And the thrusts described in the alexandrine ridicule the notion that she could ever perform combatively or sexually as a man, yet her portrayal of a man must have satisfied her "masculine" order that the play shall be applauded. The whirl of sartorial and gestured communication relies on recognizably gendered behavior, but when combined with Santlow's persona and performance history, allows additional meanings to coax the audience's laughter.

The breeches paratext thus eroticizes the actress's body yet also permits comic experimentation and control over the theatrical environment. The duality of physical exposure yet verbal command enables the actress to challenge parts of the playtext, performance, or extratheatrical subjects. As an example, during the 1672 fad for reviving plays using all-female casts, in Dryden's *Secret-Love* the breeches-clad Anne Reeves says in the epilogue that since women have performed male characters so well, there should be a new theater just for all-female plays, which appears to argue against the prospect of the two companies uniting.[44] In 1692, Anne Bracegirdle in breeches says that women should enjoy the forthcoming play, Thomas D'Urfey's *The Marriage-Hater Match'd*, because the titular figure is punished. As exploitative of the body as they are, breeches paratexts may also contain progressive ideas, even if facetiously presented. Santlow's sassy epilogue thus affirms that there were sometimes liberating aspects to a Restoration actress shedding her clothes.

The Virgin's Self-Marketing

One of the most lurid types of exposed prologues and epilogues featured the hymen as its virtual prop. By flaunting their presumed virginity and intimating their developing sexuality, fledgling actresses under the age of fifteen titillated the audience. Contrasting sexually precocious language with their speakers' slight bodies, virgin paratexts created a comedy of incongruity. The first surviving example featuring a girl calling attention to her virginity is Dryden's epilogue to *The Indian Emperour* (1674–1675); the first where the girl barters her virginity for audience approval is Otway's epilogue to *Don Carlos* (1676).[45] Several stars got their start this way. Anne Bracegirdle likely delivered the epilogue to D'Urfey's 1685 play, *A Commonwealth of Women*, when she was approximately thirteen years old.[46] Delivering virgin paratexts also brought fame to Mary Porter. Authors of the fifty-eight surviving examples include Behn, D'Urfey, Farquhar, Finch, Manley, Otway, Settle, and Vanbrugh. The late 1690s marked their heyday, when they were frequently performed by Christopher Rich's company; Danchin has observed that, lacking the star-caliber actors of Betterton's company, Rich made that weakness a strength through employing young girls in this capacity, professionalizing them in the process.[47] The paratexts' level of obscenity fluctuates; before 1695, most use distant temporality to suggest that the girls were growing ready for later sexual partnerships—such as the epilogue for Charlotte Butler in Otway's *The Orphan* (1680), where she asks for audience protection while she matures, and the epilogue for Lady Dorothy Burk in Tate and Purcell's *Dido and Aeneas* (1689), which requests audience patience because "in few years we shall be all in Tune."[48] That approach changes, however, with the epilogue to *Bonduca*, when six-year-old Miss Denny Chock refers to her "Rose-bud."[49] Both male and female playwrights employ the metaphor of flora blooming; Delarivier Manley in particular uses much innuendo in her epilogue to *The Royal Mischief*, where Miss Bradshaw calls the playhouse "a Hot-Bed to young plants."[50] The age difference between playwright and actress tilts agency toward the former, especially as the appeal of these suggestive paratexts is rooted in the young girls' vulnerability and apparent ignorance about the barter they are proposing. Breeches and other paratexts written for presumably nonvirgin actresses offer their performers a comparatively higher level of agency.

Virgin paratexts contradicted the Marian association between divinity and virginity, where the perfection and inviolability of the condition casts the woman as a godly representative. As an entity poised at transition, Marie Loughlin claims, the virgin's unstable body evokes the common male fear of marrying a nonvirgin.[51] Helen Hackett's description of the virgin gaining power from resisting "the tyranny of others" also suggests the male challenge contained therein.[52] The combination of virginity and veracity represented a long-standing cultural anxiety about the purity and ownership of the female body, with which the virgin paratext interfered.[53]

Part of their appeal to Restoration audiences may have been that virgin paratexts presented such issues comically. While virgin prologues and epilogues represented new opportunities for girls to enter the profession, they also pandered to male desires to chart the course of virgin bodies, especially since actresses' chances of marrying were much lower than those of the total female population. Kristina Straub points out that these prologues and epilogues allude to not only prostitution but also, implicitly, rape.[54] The open call to male patrons suggests a gang mentality and implies that the speaker might be in danger when she steps offstage. And these paratexts made transparent the difference between virgin characters and presumed nonvirgin actresses. Here, virginity itself becomes comically tainted.

For actress Letitia Cross, virgin prologues and epilogues chronicled her sexual development. During the mid-1690s, audiences saw "Miss Cross" grow up onstage from ages twelve to sixteen and deliver ten such paratexts, more than any other actress.[55] The following two examples demonstrate how the virgin paratext called for performers to exploit their sexuality both verbally and visually.

Cross's prologue to Mary Pix's she-tragedy, *Ibrahim, the Thirteenth Emperour of the Turks* (late spring 1696), clashes with the play's heroic genre. Ibrahim, who already has a full harem, orders his head mistress, Sheker Para, to pimp for him. Because Amurat, the man Sheker Para loves, does not reciprocate her feelings, she gets revenge by presenting the woman he loves, the virginal Morena, to Ibrahim, who rapes her. This act leads to the deaths of Ibrahim, Sheker Para, Morena, and four other characters. The play provides some levity through the casting of Susannah Verbruggen in a breeches role as Achmet, chief of the eunuchs. But Achmet also ends up dead, and in 1699 Charles Gildon wrote that "the Distress of Morena never fail'd to bring Tears into the Eyes of the Audience."[56] Cross herself did not play a named role but sang in a dialogue "between a Eunuch Boy and a Virgin."

In contrast to the play's sympathetic treatment of Morena, the prologue markets Cross for sexual consumption. Probably composed by Thomas D'Urfey, this example differs from the prologue Cross delivered at the play's premiere in late May, where she simply apologized for the "dull Heroick Play" to come.[57] While in the earlier prologue she refers to herself only once, and not sexually, in the later prologue (which, astonishingly, she delivered at a command performance for Princess Anne) she promotes herself as a fourteen-year-old nearly ready for sexual intercourse. She speaks suggestively as having progressed to the next stage of performing, and she calls her two earlier prologues "Childish" and "simp'ring," despite having delivered both within the past nine months. In her performance of naiveté, she reconfigures sexual maturity and its accompanying cultural stereotypes as sites of mock female agency. First, as Danchin points out, she alludes to venereal disease in the line: "I am not now so fond of being clapt."[58] She then personalizes and embraces the actress-whore conflation by describing her sexual ambitions:

> Look to't, ye Beaus, my Fifteen is a coming.
> That happy Age, which you so dearly prize,
> I'm pleas'd to think, how I shall Tyrannize;
> For I intend to Murder—Kill and Slay,
> An Army of Young Coxcombs every Day.[59]

These lines satirize the virgin's power by facetiously transferring it to the realm of combat. Rather than maintaining the virgin's passive steadfastness, Cross attempts to extend power into her nonvirginal future by dictating the number and passion of her lovers. Her allusions to sex and murder advance this imaginative sexual agency. First she implies that her young coxcombs will be so enamored that she will have to fight them off to the death, creating, like Hester Santlow, a comic image of a women performing physical violence. Second, Cross becomes the dominant sexual partner; she will not only engage in but also initiate orgasm (she not only "dies" but also "murders"). The comic combination of murder and sex clashes with the genre of the ensuing tragedy; the memory of Miss Cross joking about orgasm may complicate the play's subsequent depiction of military combat. The virgin paratext aimed to focus male attention on the speaker, rewarding sexually exploitative behavior yet also advancing stardom. The vision of Cross controlling her future lovers may appear wishful thinking, but as a young woman she also controls the theatrical environment through comedy. For a time, she does in fact control her sexuality while building her reputation.

Another virgin paratext by Letitia Cross should inform discussions of Colley Cibber's comedy, *Love's Last Shift* (January 1696), which from its first performance has generated a debate about its morality. Considered the first sentimental comedy, and famous also for inspiring Vanbrugh's dramatic retort, *The Relapse* (December 1696), *Love's Last Shift* features a rake tricked back into marital fidelity. Having abandoned his wife, Amanda, ten years earlier for a life of dissipation, Loveless has become sick and destitute. Through masquerading as another woman, allowing him to think he seduces her, and then revealing her identity, Amanda gets Loveless to renounce his rakish ways and commit to marital fidelity. In its day, the play was considered moral; the anonymous *A Comparison between the Two Stages* (1702), a text more likely to lampoon than praise, lauded the play as possessing "purity of Plot, Manners and Moral."[60] Modern critics, however, have questioned this judgment, calling attention to the scene where Loveless's servant rapes Amanda's maid, and claiming that Cibber at times out-lewds even Wycherley and Etherege.[61] (Along these lines, I would point out that for Loveless to renounce all other women after having sex with his wife must mean that his wife performed ingenious maneuvers in bed, a skill at odds with her character and class.) While recently Aparna Gollapudi has argued that a performance-based approach to the play makes its depiction of moral reform more visible to today's readers, the virgin epilogue accompanied at least one of those performances, and when considered in context it provides visual evidence *against* a moral reading.[62] Like so many other examples, considering this epilogue alongside the text leads to different interpretive possibilities.

While on the page this epilogue is less explicitly of the virgin category—Cross does not make the familiar offer of her virginity to the loudest clapper—its situation in the play and its presentation of Cross both trade on her virginity and augment the play's lewdness. The emphasis on virginity originates in the prologue, spoken by Jack Verbruggen, which uses the familiar metaphor of a playwright's "virgin" debut. In this construction, the virgin play is like "the Tender Plant, that Ripens but for you." It continues:

> Nature in all her Works requires Time,
> Kindness, and Years, 'tis makes the Virgin Climb,
> And shoot, and hasten to the expected Prime;
> And then, if untaught Fancy fail to Please,
> Y'instruct the willing Pupil by Degrees;
> By Gentle Lessons you your Joys improve,
> And Mold her Awkward Passion into Love.[63]

In describing the process of instructing a virgin in the art of sex, the extended double metaphor foreshadows the epilogue by Miss Cross, who had delivered her first virgin prologue four months prior.[64] And the initial editions and issues of the play made this connection more overt, because they published the prologue and epilogue back to back, placing both early in the volume, before the play.[65] The majority of plays' first editions printed during the Restoration emulate the performance order, printing first prologue, then play, then epilogue. In performance, but especially in print, then, the prologue anticipates the virgin epilogue.

The epilogue bids the audience remember the lewd parts of the play, a message all the more powerful because conveyed by a woman barely old enough to perform onstage, and costumed to show off her nubile body.

Not only does it showcase Cross at approximately fourteen years old, but it also features her in a breeches part: "Spoken by Miss Cross, who Sung CUPID."[66] Act 5 concludes with her performance, so the epilogue features a young girl revealing the erotic divide of her legs. In her bid for the play, Cross addresses several different segments of the audience, trying to enliven their attentions in turn. First, she addresses the "Citty-Gentlemen" in the middle row, whom she facetiously comforts by boasting, "There's not one Cuckold made in all his Play." In mock-reassuring them with lines such as "For he declares to day, he meerly strives / To maul the Beaux—because they maul your Wives," Cross converts this section of the audience into her comic victims.[67] The longest part of the epilogue appeals to the rakishly minded:

> Now Sirs, to you, whose sole Religion's Drinking,
> Whoring, Roaring, without the Pain of Thinking;
> He fears h'as made a fault, you'll ne'er forgive,
> A Crime, beyond the hopes of a Reprieve;
> An Honest Rake forego the Joys of life!
> His Whores, and Wine! t'Embrace a Dull Cast Wife;
> Such out of fashion stuff! But then agen!
> He's Lewd for above four Acts, Gentlemen!
> For Faith he knew, when once he'd chang'd his Fortune,
> And reform'd his Vice, 'twas Time—to drop the Curtain.[68]

The youth of their speaker further enlivens these witty lines. A young girl describing alcohol and prostitution courts the audience by excusing Loveless's turn toward morality. Magnifying the tone in both performance and publication, the four exclamation points within five couplets demonstrate that their speaker's naiveté is perhaps even more garish than Loveless's infractions against his wife. And in the line "He's Lewd for above four Acts, Gentlemen!" Cross courts the rakes by encouraging them to think of the play as over 80 percent lewd. Although the epilogue ends with Cross reminding the ladies of Amanda's virtue and gesturing for them to convince the men of the play's worth, it is an anticlimactic afterthought, as Cross refers offhandedly to the ladies in the third person. Considered in performance, therefore, this epilogue curtails act 5's moral reform.

As three subsequent epilogues make apparent, by the time of her elopement to France in 1698, Cross had left her mark on the London theater world. Jo Haines's epilogue to Farquhar's *Love and a Bottle* (1698) joined the backlash against Jeremy Collier's *A Short View of the Immorality, and Profaneness of the English Stage* by, of all things, blaming Collier for her elopement. In the epilogue to Thomas D'Urfey's *The Famous History of the Rise and Fall of Massaniello, Part 2* (1699), twelve-year-old Mary Ann Campion first insinuates that Cross was a whore, and then threatens, if the audience does not like the play, to elope to France herself. In her absence, Congreve even wrote an epilogue for Cross, meant to accompany *The Way of the World* (1700). From 1698 to 1704, Cross performed at Dublin's Smock Alley, and from 1704–1732 acted intermittently at several theaters. She performed at the Haymarket under Owen Swiney's management between 1709 and November 1710, but when Swiney was transferred back to Drury Lane, his comanagers—Cibber, Robert Wilks, and Thomas Dogget—refused to extend her contract.[69] When Cross returned for the third time to London theater in 1716 and delivered her first epilogue in eighteen years, to Aaron Hill's *The Fatal Vision*, she asserted that she had changed but that men's desire to see young actresses had not:

> We've young, fresh Actresses, whom we don't show;
> Because, of late, your Practice seems to own,
> You like *That* best, which you have *longest known;*
> Then certainly you'll ease *Us* of our Fears,
> For, by our Tell-Tale Records, it appears,
> That you've known some of us these *Twenty Years:*
> Won't that do neither?—Hang me if it will:
> No, no, I find you'll be for *changing* still. . .[70]

Although the epilogue subsequently directs the audience to change by not patronizing the rival theater company at Drury Lane, it nevertheless speaks feelingly about the plight of the aging actress. Initially joking with the audience that they prefer familiarity to novelty, Cross concedes her age and culturally diminished desirability but still protests against the fad for change and youth. She subsequently delivered three more epilogues from the point of view of a sexually experienced woman making protofeminist remarks to men.[71] Across the arc of her long career, Cross's prologues and epilogues began with the virgin type that generically interfered with the plays and ended with such statements that implicitly countered that earliest form. As such, Cross loses the desirability that virgin paratexts amplified in young actresses, but graduates to more empowering statements. To view or read a play with a virgin prologue or epilogue is thus to receive an unusual commentary from someone who is currently too young to participate in the play's depictions of sex or violence. She may be an unreliable narrator, but she may also inspire a metatheatrical fanship, drawn to future plays by wanting to see her develop as a woman.

The Tendentious Paratext

Many misogynist paratexts can be called tendentious. Frequently these prologues and epilogues foster an allure of sexual self-reference, as if actresses are confessing lurid details of their offstage lives, even if the confessions have no apparent basis in fact. Anne Bracegirdle's epilogue to Dryden's *King Arthur* (1691), for example, features her reading and mocking several billets-doux that the actress has supposedly received.[72] Their apparent sexual gratuitousness make these paratexts tend toward misogyny. My argument that the sheer act of Restoration actresses performing stand-up comedy represents a major protofeminist gain is perhaps least defensible here, but I maintain that in significance, female performance of comedy outweighs the paratexts' often-disturbing content.

Freud's description of tendentiousness befits this category. In a way that aligns with the construction of agency in prologues and epilogues, Freud describes tendentious jokes as requiring three people: a joke-teller, the object of hostility, and an audience for whom an instinct has been satisfied.[73] (One of the many feminist criticisms of Freud is that he sees women inhabiting only the object role.) In tendentious paratexts, the joke-teller and the audience align directly with the actress and the theater or reading audience, but the actress also frequently becomes the object of hostility.

The subjects of tendentious prologues and epilogues range widely. Admittedly something of a catch-all, this populous category highlights gags such as the recurrent puns on "clap," "die," and "member." Many speakers of tendentious paratexts barter with the audience: sex for approval of the play. Usually the actress advertises her own body, but in the tendentious (and breeches) epilogue to Catharine Trotter's *Agnes de Castro*, Susannah Verbruggen advertises that if the audience applauds, the author will "lay aside her Modesty and Fear."[74] Not all examples are sexual; the epilogue delivered at Oxon in 1686 makes fun of Catholics. Many trade on cultural beliefs, such as the belief that widows are sex-crazed (epilogue to Richard Brome's *The Northern Lass*) or that women pretend to be virgins in order to get married (epilogue to Henry Higdon's *The Wary Widow*). Perhaps the strangest example is when, in the epilogue to John Smith's *Cytherea, or, The Enamoring Girdle*, the character of Venus throws her girdle into the pit.

Frequently the most tendentious paratexts appear alongside tragedies that might otherwise represent progressive gains. In tracing the development of English tragedy, Laura Brown has found that during the Restoration, plays gradually recentered the tragic action around the heroine.[75] This situation is particularly clear regarding rape; in the 1680s, the advent of what Nicholas Rowe would later term she-tragedy converted rape from a secondary and often comic plot to the primary and pitiable action of the play. As Brown establishes, the centrality of the rape emphasizes the importance of this crime and depicts the heroine as sympathetic. But whereas the violated woman was portrayed sympathetically, she was also eroticized through the display of her loose hair and torn clothes. Brown and Jean Marsden concur that such circumstances reinforce the male/active–female/passive dichotomy, especially since afterward the greatest agency permitted to the heroine is suicide.[76] Despite its disturbing conclusion, the rape's primary status and the emotionally gratifying aftermath—often the victim's lover exacts vigilante justice on the rapist—represent improvements from the casual depictions of rape in comedies.

The tendentious epilogue, however, perversely challenges this trend. One strain features a secondary female character praising rape or wishing that she could be raped too; Vanbrugh's epilogue for Anne Oldfield in *The False Friend* (1702) is an example. This comic turn luridly reenvisions the event, and thus compromises possible gains derived from the rape's centrality. And yet, many she-tragedies feature revived epilogues, where the reincarnated heroine treats her death flippantly. If a heroine is raped, kills herself, and subsequently reappears in a revived epilogue, one implication is that, contrary to the rules of high tragedy, a rape victim does not necessarily have to treat herself as damaged goods. In this environment, she may die, but she does not need to remain dead. Epilogues such as Dryden's for Bracegirdle in *Cleomenes* (1692) may treat rape garishly, but by reviving Bracegirdle to read her will they also challenge the idea that the only possible fate for a raped heroine is death.[77]

Charles Hopkins's she-tragedy, *Boadicea, Queen of Britain* (1697), contains some progressive qualities but juxtaposes them with an epilogue that from a modern sensibility may be difficult to stomach. A vehicle for showcasing Bracegirdle, *Boadicea* centers the plot around her character Camilla's rape, eliciting much grief and regret from male characters. One of a number of seventeenth- and eighteenth-century dramatizations about the first-century warrior-queen of the Iceni, an early Celtic tribe, the play depicts Boadicea (a bastardization of Boudica, her Celtic name) defending her dead husband's kingdom against the invading Roman army. The Britons and the Romans are at war, so the play features an interracial couple—the British Venutia (Queen Boadicea's daughter) and the Roman Paulinus—wrestling with issues of love and patriotism. When the Romans gain ground, their commander, Decius, rapes the play's central figure, Boadicea's older daughter, Camilla. When she tells her lover, Cassibelan, of the rape, his anger changes the course of the war; his army gains ground against the Romans, and he tortures and kills the repentant Decius. At last the warrior Paulinus surrenders and Boadicea gains Roman land. Grieving over Camilla's rape, however, Boadicea, Camilla, and Cassibelan drink poison. Only Paulinus and Venutia survive.

Especially when compared to other dramatizations of the Boudica story, Hopkins's play is relatively progressive. In *The Legacy of Boadicea: Gender and Nation in Early Modern England*, Jodi Mikalachki finds that most early modern interpretations of the Boudica legend reinforce masculine governmental domination by depicting women as inept or cruel leaders. According to Mikalachki, although some dramatists, such as Thomas Heywood, find Boudica praiseworthy, most writers before Hopkins emphasize her barbarism, such as Raphael Holinshed, who claims that her troops cut off the breasts of their female victims and sewed them to their mouths.[78] As Wendy C. Nielsen shows, most pre-1800 adaptations emphasize the character's barbarity to the point where they sympathize with the Romans instead of the British.[79] John Fletcher's 1612 play, *The Tragedie of Bonduca*, sets the stage for vicious portrayals, which recur in Richard Glover's 1753 *Boadicea* and George Colman's revival of Fletcher's version in 1778. But as Nielsen points out, Hopkins switches allegiance to the Britons against the Romans and accordingly projects more sympathy onto its female characters, albeit at the price of portraying them as lovers and not fighters.[80] One paratext from Hopkins's 1697 quarto presents a rarity: for once, the *Dramatis Personae* lists actresses before actors. And compared to many other late-Restoration she-tragedies, Hopkins grants his rape victim a longer afterlife. After Camilla is raped, she does not kill herself immediately but instead rallies Cassibelan to seek revenge against the Romans and celebrates his victory before committing suicide.[81] And despite her rape, the victim's lover does not reject her.[82] Mikalachki finds that Hopkins's emphasis of love over warfare, and his domestication of the female characters, reflects the belief that Restoration women were similarly domesticated, no longer possessing a threatening access to the public sphere.[83] (As Katherine Eisaman Maus points out, actresses represent the great exception to the Restoration's increased restrictions on women's public presence.[84]) This aspect notwithstanding, through the realignment of audience sympathy with the Britons and the treatment of the rape victim as untainted, Hopkins introduces more progressive aspects into his adaptation.

But that changes in the epilogue. Rather than mourning her sister Camilla's death, Venutia (played by Elizabeth Bowman) reimagines rape as good sex and complains that she was left out of the action. She makes comedy out of her audience's knowledge of Boadicea as a historical figure when she says:

> You Sparks, who knew the Story of this Play,
> Thought to have seen two Ravish'd Maids to day.
> But by our Bashful Youth one half is stifl'd,
> My Sister only (to my sorrow) rifl'd.
> Pray, tell me, Gentlemen, and tell me true,
> Might not I well have claim'd that kindness too?[85]

Like the virgin type, the tendentious paratext often derives comedy from flirting with cultural gray areas. This passage certainly takes a euphemistic approach to rape, calling it "rifl'd" and a "kindness." In *Boadicea*, rape is the most important plot point and precipitates the victim's suicide. But in the metaleptic epilogue, rape represents the putative pleasure for the epilogue's speaker. Using this language, the actress endangers herself by pre-absolving any would-be assaulter in the audience of committing a crime. This may also absolve the male author, who helps perpetuate the idea that women like rape. And yet, at this strange moment, the figure of betweenness uses her agency to divide sex from violence and express desire. The incongruity of her approach, moreover, both following the play's sober ending and rewriting the gravity with which the play treated rape, creates a highly tendentious joke. Even though the prospect of joking about rape may nauseate the modern reader, we can nonetheless recognize that these lines contain both misogynist and what might be called "sex-positive" implications. As with the revived and breeches forms, the comedy of tendentious paratexts can contain both protofeminist and retrogressive elements.

The audience's familiarity with the speaker makes the moment more acceptable and comic. Elizabeth Bowman was a well-known actress. Raised in the Betterton family after her father died, she married the actor-singer John Bowman in 1692 and performed many famous roles, including Silvia in Congreve's *The Old Bachelor* (1693) and Mrs. Foresight in his *Love for Love* (1695), with her husband playing Tattle. The couplets that follow Venutia's complaint, therefore, temper the misogyny through establishing a betweenness of character and actress:

> Maids may indeed in such a case Miscarry,
> But what are Rapes to us wise Folks that Marry?
> Thieves may bolt easily into open Houses,
> And Force will still excuse us to our Spouses.[86]

Bowman turns the rape joke into a cuckold joke, complicating her perspective to comic effect. In recalling her spouse, something Venutia does not have (although at play's end she and Paulinus appear headed to the altar),

Bowman reminds the audience of her husband, whom they know very well, and teases them with the prospect of cuckolding him. The audience then receives the supposed opportunity to rape her: "on my Conscience now, our Author knew, / The way to please, was to save one for you."[87] Again the implications are tendentious, but the prospect of meting out rapes is consistent with the typical paratextual move of promising something sexual to the audience. Here the joke plays on the more customary move typical of virgin paratexts—an actress offering herself to the loudest clapper. Hence the epilogue threatens to undercut the play's otherwise serious treatment of the crime, yet reconnects with the audience through their knowledge of Bowman's persona and marital status.

Tendentious paratexts may thus possess the potential to interfere with their plays' portrayal of women. Their degree of tendentiousness varies, and with Restoration plays their level is, in part, indicated by how little or how much they interfere with their main texts. For epilogues following rape, many of which are discussed further in chapter 4, the level of tendentiousness is so great because the play *has* made protofeminist interventions, through creating a sympathetic heroine, subjecting her to male tyranny, and emphasizing rape as a crime. Perhaps tendentious paratexts confirm more than any other variety that comedy, misogyny, and protofeminism can coexist within comic performance and print.

The revived, breeches, virgin, and tendentious paratexts combine the protofeminist figure of the female comedian with often-misogynist content. Most challenging to character and genre, revived epilogues graduate the performance from tragic action to a retroactively metaleptic comic critique of such action. Both breeches and virgin paratexts combine bodily objectification with a degree of agency, where the actress may plumb (and thus control) her body for comic effect. Recent treatment of self-deprecating humor has found it less masochistic and more celebratory, and such is the case with these paratexts.[88] And the tendentious reaffirms misogyny yet also challenges certain subjects, including the typical portrayal of the rape victim's self-hatred. These four categories of prologues and epilogues thus provide opportunities for individual actresses to deliver stand-up comedy, albeit often objectifying and exploitative. Alongside such degradations of female bodies and glorifications of rape, however, exist more straightforward complaints about marital inequities and male mistreatment of women, as well as jokes at men's expense. Those are the subjects of the next chapter.

Notes

1. Mary Bourke, "Comedy Cabaret: Downstairs at the King's Head" (Crouch End, London, 2002).

2. Performed in 1670, this play (the title of which is unknown) was probably authored by Shadwell; see Pierre Danchin, *The Prologues and Epilogues of the Restoration 1660–1700* (Nancy: Presses Universitaires de Nancy, 1981–1988), 1:349–50. Another example is Charlotte Butler's epilogue to the 1684 revival of Richard Brome's 1662 play, *The Northern Lass*, where a widow in general is considered a "rank *Egyptian* Flesh-pot"; see ibid., 2:525.

3. The appendix contains a category, "other exposed." This category consists of examples that most resemble the male exposed style: an actress performs her character or her own persona.

4. Joanne Gilbert, *Performing Marginality: Humor, Gender, and Cultural Critique* (Detroit: Wayne State University Press, 2004), 32.

5. *The Riverside Shakespeare*, ed. Herschel Baker et al. (Boston: Houghton Mifflin, 1997), 280.

6. All known speakers of revived epilogues are female, but Danchin has identified an epilogue where the speaker is unknown and therefore could have been male. This is the epilogue to Sir John Denham's *The Sophy* (12 January 1670). See Danchin, *Restoration*, 1:352. A satire on the form confirms the dominance of the female speaker: In the epilogue to *Woman's Revenge; or, A Match in Newgate* by Christopher Bullock (performed 24 October 1715), actor Benjamin Griffin dresses up as "Mother Griffin" and satirizes the practice: "Some beauteous Nymph has from the Grave ascended, / With Epilogue of Smut."

7. Allardyce Nicoll, *A History of Early Eighteenth Century Drama, 1700–1750*, 2nd ed. (Cambridge: Cambridge University Press, 1929), 64–66; Autrey Nell Wiley, "Female Prologues and Epilogues in English Plays," *Publications of the Modern Language Association (PMLA)* 48 (1933): 1075–78. "Merry" is the term used in Spectator No. 341; see chapter 5.

8. Mary Etta Knapp, *Prologues and Epilogues of the Eighteenth Century* (New Haven, CT: Yale University Press, 1961), 103, 291, 297.

9. Danchin, *Restoration*, 4:25.

10. John Banks, *Cyrus the Great: or, the Tragedy of Love*, 1st ed. (London: Richard Bentley, 1696), 58.

11. Maximillian E. Novak and George R. Guffey, *The Works of John Dryden*, 10 vols. (Berkeley: University of California Press, 1970), 10:186-87.

12. Ibid., 10:192.

13. Ibid.

14. Ibid.

15. One aspect of Dryden deserving greater study is his differing approaches to paratexts written for his own versus others' plays. When introducing or concluding

others' plays, he avoided holding the author responsible for any problems with the play, often looking for sources of blame far beyond the author. In many paratexts, including the prologues to Lee's *Caesar Borgia* (1679) and Tate's *The Loyal General* (1679), for example, Dryden blames the audience for their poor reception, while in others, such as the epilogue to Etherege's *The Man of Mode* (1676), Dryden praises the author's keen writing. In his prologue to Vanbrugh's 1700 adaptation of Fletcher's *The Pilgrim*, Dryden compares playwrights to bears "Brought muzled to the Stage, for fear they bite" (Danchin, *Restoration*, 3:663). But in numerous paratexts to his own plays, Dryden makes fun of himself. See also my discussion, in chapter 3, of Dryden's prologue to Lee's *The Princess of Cleves*, where he suggests that a Jew has tampered with the text, and in chapter 1, on the epilogue to *The Conquest of Granada, Part I*.

16. Novak and Guffey, *The Works of John Dryden*, 10:193.

17. For more on the application of sumptuary laws to Restoration actresses, see Cynthia Lowenthal, "Sticks and Rags, Bodies and Brocade: Essentializing Discourses and the Late Restoration Playhouse," in *Broken Boundaries: Women and Feminism in Restoration Drama*, ed. Katherine M. Quinsey (Lexington: University of Kentucky Press, 1996), 228. Mark Dawson posits that the sexualization of actors and actresses also combats the fear that they will attain gentility. See Mark S. Dawson, *Gentility and the Comic Theatre of Late Stuart London* (Cambridge: Cambridge University Press, 2005), chapter 11.

18. The first edition of *An Essay on Dramatic Poesy* was entered into the Stationers' Registrar on 7 August 1667, but its title page says 1668.

19. Novak and Guffey, *The Works of John Dryden*, 10:109.

20. Michael Werth Gelber, *The Just and the Lively: The Literary Criticism of John Dryden* (Manchester: Manchester University Press, 1999), 29–30. For more on the phenomenon of critics quoting this epilogue in lieu of analyzing it, see the introduction, footnote 3.

21. Derek Parker, *Nell Gwyn* (Phoenix Mill, Britain: Sutton, 2000), 90; Novak and Guffey, *The Works of John Dryden*, 10:273.

22. Peter Cunningham, *The Story of Nell Gwyn and the Sayings of Charles II* (New York: F. P. Harper, 1896), xxviii. Curll describes the beginning of the Charles II–Nell Gwyn affair in William Oldys and Edmund Curll, *The History of the English stage, from the Restauration to the present time* (London: E. Curll, 1741), 56–57.

23. Percy Fitzgerald, *A New History of the English Stage* (London: Tinsley Bros., 1882), 1:113.

24. Genette defines metalepsis as "any intrusion by the extradiegetic narrator or narratee into the diegetic universe (or by diegetic characters into a metadiegetic universe, etc.), or the inverse (as in Cortazar), produces an effect of strangeness that is either comical (when, as in Sterne or Diderot, it is presented in a joking tone) or fantastic." Gerard Genette, *Narrative Discourse: An Essay in Method*, trans. Jane E. Lewin (Ithaca, NY: Cornell University Press, 1980), 234. For further discussion, see the introduction, xiv–xvii.

25. Christopher J. Wheatley, "Tragedy," in *The Cambridge Companion to Restoration Theatre*, ed. Deborah Payne Fisk (Cambridge: Cambridge University Press, 2000), 72.

26. Jean I. Marsden, *Fatal Desire: Women, Sexuality, and the English Stage, 1660–1720* (Ithaca, NY: Cornell University Press, 2006), 65.

27. This line began with her premiere as Olinda in Behn's *The Forc'd Marriage* (1670); it was interrupted once before *Alcibiades*, when Lee played the vindictive role of Salome in Samuel Pordage's *Herod and Mariamne* (1673). Lee becomes "Lady Slingsby" after her second (but unconfirmed) marriage in 1680 to the baronet Sir Charles Slingsby.

28. The play also debuted just one month following the revived epilogue to the anonymous *Piso's Conspiracy*, so as Danchin points out, the spectral expectation would be stronger. Audiences at subsequent performances would already have these expectations in mind. See Danchin, *Restoration*, 1:685.

29. Danchin, *Restoration*, 1:686.

30. Danchin, *Restoration*, 3:49.

31. Danchin, *Restoration*, 1:687.

32. Other revived epilogues punning on dying include Samuel Pordage's epilogue for the character Mariamne in *Herod and Mariamne* (1673), Behn's for Mary Lee, Lady Slingsby, in *Romulus and Hersilia* (1682), Dryden's epilogue for Bracegirdle in *Cleomenes* (1692), and Rowe's epilogue for Bracegirdle in *The Ambitious Step-Mother* (1700), the latter two discussed further in chapter 4. The epilogue to Edmund Waller's *The Maid's Tragedy Alter'd* (1690) features "Aspasia bleeding" and saying "Now if I dye, 'tis want of your Applause." See Danchin, *Restoration*, 2:746. J. M. Barrie, in his creation of Tinkerbell in *Peter Pan*, would adopt the strategy of clapping as restoring a character to life. Thanks to Scott MacKenzie for this reference.

33. Gilli Bush-Bailey, "Breeches Role," in *Oxford Encyclopedia of Theatre and Performance*, ed. Dennis Kennedy (Oxford: Oxford University Press, 2003; reprint, 2005).

34. Kirsten Pullen, *Actresses and Whores: On Stage and in Society* (Cambridge: Cambridge University Press, 2005), 50.

35. John Harold Wilson counts 89 of 375 plays as featuring breeches roles. See John Harold Wilson, *All the King's Ladies; Actresses of the Restoration* (Chicago: University of Chicago Press, 1958), 73.

36. Pat Rogers, "The Breeches Part," in *Sexuality in the Eighteenth Century*, ed. Paul-Gabriel Boucé (Manchester: Manchester University Press, 1982), 257; Pullen, *Actresses and Whores*, 48–49. For more on the discussion of Restoration breeches roles as exploitative, see Laurence Senelick, *The Changing Room: Sex, Drag, and Theatre* (London: Routledge, 2000), 211.

37. Michelene Wandor, "Cross-Dressing, Sexual Representation and the Sexual Division of Labour in Theatre," in *The Routledge Reader in Gender and Performance*, ed. Lisbeth Goodman and Jane de Gay (New York: Routledge, 1998), 172.

38. For an extended reading of Bracegirdle's prologue, see chapter 4.

39. Moira Goff identifies an advertisement for "dancing by Miss Santlow and others" on 10 January 1708. See Moira Goff, "The Incomparable Hester Santlow," in

Performance in the Long Eighteenth Century: Theatre, Music, Dance, ed. Jane Milling and Kathryn Lowerre (Burlington, VT: Ashgate, 2007), 11.

40. Goff, "The Incomparable Hester Santlow," 26.

41. The text of Centlivre's epilogue has not been found; Danchin speculates that it might be the same as the Don Quixote Part II epilogue.

42. Pierre Danchin, The Prologues and Epilogues of the Eighteenth Century, 8 vols. (Nancy: Presses Universitaire de Nancy, 1990), 1:455.

43. Ibid.

44. Danchin points to the couplet about the merits of an all-female theater company as alluding to a possible discussion of union: "This would prevent the houses joyning two, / At which we are as much displeas'd as you." Danchin, Restoration, 1:491. Amy Scott-Douglass reads this epilogue as challenging men to acknowledge actresses' successes in male roles. See Amy Scott-Douglass, "Aphra Behn's Covent Garden Drollery: The First History of Women in the Restoration Theatre," in The Public's Open to Us All: Essays on Women and Performance in Eighteenth-Century England, ed. Laura Engel (Newcastle: Cambridge Scholars, 2009), 105.

45. Danchin first notices this trend, which he calls the "young girl" category. He restricts the category to prologues and counts twenty-nine examples, but there is no apparent reason to exclude the epilogues. See also Michel Adam, "L'Utilisation des actrices dans les prologues et epilogues sur la scene anglaise de 1668 a 1689," in De William Shakespeare a William Golding: Melanges dedies a la memoire de Jean-Pierre Vernier, ed. Sylvere Monod (Rouen: Rouen University Press, 1984).

46. Lucyle Hook, "Anne Bracegirdle's First Appearance," Theatre Notebook 13 (1959). The epilogue speaker is identified as "Miss Nanny."

47. Danchin, Restoration, 3:xxii.

48. Danchin, Restoration, 2:773.

49. Danchin, Restoration, 3:205.

50. Danchin, Restoration, 3:284.

51. Marie H. Loughlin, Hymeneutics: Interpreting Virginity on the Early Modern Stage (Lewisburg, PA: Bucknell University Press, 1997), 47.

52. Helen Hackett, Virgin Mother, Maiden Queen: Elizabeth I and the Cult of the Virgin Mary (New York: St. Martins, 1995), 240.

53. For further discussion of this issue, see chapter 4.

54. Kristina Straub, Sexual Suspects: Eighteenth-Century Players and Sexual Ideology (Princeton, NJ: Princeton University Press, 1992), 102.

55. In his prefatory section, "Training and Exploiting Young Girls as Prologue Speakers," Danchin argues persuasively against Highfill et al. that, in line with the era's perception of sexual maturity, Cross began her career at age twelve rather than eighteen. See Danchin, Restoration, 3:xviii; Philip H. Highfill, Kalman A. Burnim, and Edward A, Langhans, A Biographical Dictionary of Actors, Actresses, Musicians, Dancers, Managers and Other Stage Personnel in London, 1660–1800, 16 vols. (Carbondale: Southern Illinois University Press, 1973), 4:62–64.

56. Charles Gildon, The Lives and Characters of the English Dramatick Poets (London: Nick Cox and William Turner, 1699), 111.

57. Danchin, *Restoration*, 3:286. Because the prologue appears in Thomas D'Urfey's *Songs Compleat, Pleasant and Divertive* and in his *Wit and Mirth; or, Pills to Purge Melancholy*, he may be the author.

58. Ibid., 289.

59. Ibid.

60. Charles Gildon, *A Comparison between the Two Stages* (London, 1702), 25.

61. Robert Hume calls attention to the "parallel seduction": While Amanda seduces Loveless, his servant rapes her maid, although in the Restoration version of retribution he is made to marry her afterward. And editor David Womersley writes that "Wycherley and Etherege never dramatized a scene as lubricious as what passes in Act IV, Scene iii between Loveless and the disguised Amanda, where the fact that she is actually his wife is a mere technicality of no relevance to the nature of Loveless's emotions in the scene." See Robert D. Hume, *The Development of English Drama in the Late Seventeenth Century* (Oxford: Clarendon, 1976), 412; David Womersley, *Restoration Drama: An Anthology* (Oxford: Blackwell, 2000), 554.

62. Gollapudi's argument rests on attire; she points, for example, to Loveless's wig, which is either ratty or absent, as symbolizing his physical and moral decrepitude. See Aparna Gollapudi, "Seeing Is Believing: Performing Reform in Colley Cibber's *Love's Last Shift*," *Restoration and Eighteenth-Century Theatre Research* 19, no. 1 (2004): 1–21.

63. Danchin, *Restoration*, 3:250.

64. Cross delivered the prologue to Thomas Scott's *The Mock-Marriage*, which Danchin convincingly dates as premiering in September 1695.

65. This publishing sequence applies to the first six editions—the 1696, 1702, 1711, 1717, 1720, and 1721 quartos—as well as the 1721 *Plays written by Mr. Cibber*, a two-volume collection published by Jacob Tonson. The 1725 quarto, the first printed outside of London, is also the first to feature the epilogue following the play. The first London publication to do so is the 1735 duodecimo. Thanks to Jacqueline Dean of the Bodleian Library for her assistance with this issue.

66. Colley Cibber, *Love's Last Shift, or, the Fool in Fashion*, 1st ed. (London: H. Rhodes, R. Parker, S. Briscoe, 1696), B1r. There is precedent for a young girl playing Cupid: the epilogue to Elkanah Settle's *The Heir of Morocco* (1682) was "Spoken by Mrs. Coysh's Girl, as CUPID."

67. Danchin, *Restoration*, 3:251.

68. Ibid.

69. For more details, see Judith Milhous and Robert D. Hume, "Theatrical Politics at Drury Lane: New Light on Letitia Cross, Jane Rogers, and Anne Oldfield," *Bulletin of Research in the Humanities* 85, no. 4 (1982): 412–14.

70. Danchin, *Eighteenth*, 1:625.

71. These were the epilogues to Louis Theobald's *The Perfidious Brother* (12 February 1716), the revival of Vanbrugh's *The Provok'd Wife* (22 March 1716), and Christopher Bullock's *Love Is a Riddle* (4 December 1716). *The London Stage* also lists Cross as having delivered a new, no longer extant epilogue in her benefit performance of *Hamlet*, 18 April 1723.

72. For further discussion of this epilogue, see chapter 4.

73. Sigmund Freud, *Jokes and Their Relation to the Unconscious* (New York: Atheneum, 1966), 118.

74. Danchin, *Restoration*, 3:225.

75. Laura Brown, "The Defenseless Woman and the Development of English Tragedy," *Studies in English Literature* 22 (1982): 430.

76. Jean I. Marsden, "Rape, Voyeurism, and the Restoration Stage," in *Broken Boundaries: Women and Feminism in Restoration Drama*, ed. Katherine M. Quinsey (Lexington: University Press of Kentucky, 1996), 190.

77. For an extended discussion of the agency of raped heroines, see chapter 4.

78. Jodi Mikalachki, *The Legacy of Boadicea: Gender and Nation in Early Modern England* (London: Routledge, 1998), 123, 14.

79. Wendy C. Nielsen, "Boadicea Onstage before 1800, a Theatrical and Colonial History," *Studies in English Literature* 49, no. 3 (2009): 595–614.

80. Ibid., 601.

81. This is also historically consistent; Boudica and her daughters rode among the Celtic soldiers, inciting the Romans to battle.

82. Jean Marsden has also located this lack of rejection of the rape victim in Pix's *Ibrahim*. Marsden, *Fatal Desire*, 111.

83. Mikalachki, *Legacy of Boadicea*, 147–48.

84. Katharine Eisaman Maus, "'Playhouse Flesh and Blood': Sexual Ideology and the Restoration Actress," *English Literary History* 46 (1979): 600.

85. Danchin, *Restoration*, 3:449.

86. Ibid.

87. Charles Hopkins, *Boadicea Queen of Britain* (London: Tonson, 1697).

88. See, for example, Christie Davies, "Exploring the Thesis of the Self-Deprecating Jewish Sense of Humor," *Humor* 4, no. 2 (1991): 189–209.

CHAPTER THREE

~

Female Exposed Paratexts, Part Two: Solidarity and Social Critique

Chapter 2 argued that the act of women performing comedy outweighs the often-disturbing content of their prologues and epilogues. In those breeches, virgin, and tendentious prologues and epilogues, however, some of the material, most notably the promotion of rape in *Boadicea's* epilogue, contains a misogynist undertone. In the present chapter, happily, the argument can be more strident, the disclaimer less stringent. These final two categories of female exposed paratexts, called "female solidarity," and "social critique," represent the genre's strongest assertions of protofeminism.

For actresses to single out and speak to female audience members is a fundamentally protofeminist move. The topic of women addressing women presents opportunities to observe gender connections that exist despite class differences and to widen our perception of the female audience beyond critical portrayals of them as embodying morality. In the two examples of female solidarity discussed below—the prologues by Behn to Rochester's *Valentinian* and by Dryden to Lee's *The Princess of Cleve*—actresses directly address female audience members. These two prologues represent an archive of paratexts where either in passing or throughout, female–female connections take place. The subsequent trio of examples—the epilogues to Behn's *The City-Heiress* and Wycherley's *The Country Wife* and the prologue to the anonymous pastoral *The Constant Nymph*—demonstrate actresses critiquing men. Sometimes the paratexts further their plays' social critiques, while at other times they feature female rejoinders to the plays' misogynist events. Such examples represent a series of paratexts that interrupt the male homosocial relationships dominant in Restoration comedies and tragedies, from Nell Gwyn's epilogue to *Tyrannick Love* (1669), which reanimated the victim of competing men, to Hester Santlow's epilogue to Susannah Centlivre's *The Wonder: A Woman Keeps a Secret* (1714), which responds to the title's incredulity by saying that of course women can keep secrets—otherwise London Society would know of many more illegitimate men. All five examples demonstrate the need to examine prologues and epilogues alongside their texts, because by doing so we can grasp the agency they gave to their performers, the liberties they took with play themes, and the connections they fostered between actresses and audiences. One argument of this book is that prologues and epilogues gave actresses a sanctioned space to perform comedy and receive applause; this chapter considers the most contentious of those ideas about gender. Protesting the customary abuses of women in Restoration culture, the prologues and epilogues in this chapter thus best illustrate Philip Auslander's declaration that female stand-up comedy is a political act.[1]

And yet, does the nature of these particular paratexts vest their speakers with agency? Of the five examples, two are written by men, one by a woman, and two are anonymous. What does it mean for men to write protofeminist prologues and epilogues for women to deliver? At the very least, it gives the lie to the concept of the actress as the empty vessel for the male playwright's words. Instead the playwright imagines women addressing women, or women critiquing misogynist social practices, thus having been inspired by the idea of either writing for a woman or of investing in a specific actress. Here is a point where the author imbues the female speaker's voice with extra agency, especially when the speaker addresses other women or portrays women's plight.

Female Solidarity

Studies of Restoration theater's relationships between women have focused on the oeuvre of Aphra Behn, the triumvirate of Manley, Pix, and Trotter, and the 1690s sympathetic comedies by Southerne and Vanbrugh, but there is more to the story. Stimulated by Gayle Rubin's "The Traffic in Women" and Laura Mulvey's "Visual Pleasure and Narrative Cinema," in recent years critical interest in cross-cultural female audiences has grown, but thus far discussion of the connections between Restoration theater audiences and actresses has just begun.[2] The most sustained treatment of Restoration female audiences remains David Roberts's pioneering *The Ladies: Female Patronage of Restoration Drama* (1989), but it is due for an update. Roberts argues that theaters were largely hostile to and objectifying of female spectators, and that prologues and epilogues contributed to this environment.[3] In making the second claim Roberts overlooks evidence to the contrary. A subset of his argument, that prologues and epilogues rarely addressed female audiences, becomes problematic when we consider that many paratexts addressed neither sex directly. Roberts's assertion also forfeits the opportunity to understand players' direct communication with female audience members. And although Roberts cites ten prologues and epilogues that do directly address women, his list is far from complete—by my count, between 1660 and 1714 there are eighty-six such paratexts spoken by actresses.[4] It must be conceded that since prologues and epilogues were first and foremost advertisements to attract and retain customers, they needed to please those holding the purse strings first and their female companions only incidentally. But there are many instances of paratexts that court women. What I want to suggest is that players' direct addresses to women indicated the value of female audiences, and that such moments occurred more frequently when the players themselves were female. It is also another first—a time when women spoke to other women in a public forum. Here the fact that such texts were written for rather than by them is trumped by actresses' physical embodiment of the paratext and resultant connection with women in the audience. I want to stress the air of possibility largely absent from Roberts's argument: prologues and epilogues provided avenues for women to communicate in public.

The other major treatment of Restoration female audiences limits its scope to plays proper rather than considering all performances taking place in a theatrical afternoon. In a fascinating and counterintuitive argument, Jean Marsden finds that by complaining about staged carnality, theater moralists ironically activated female spectators; by reining in such performances, playwrights sought to contain those audiences.[5] Marsden finds that the few plays that focus on female sexuality ultimately curtail that sexuality, even Vanbrugh's *The Provok'd Wife* (1697), which presents adultery as a marital salve. Prologues and epilogues spoken by women to women, however, provide their recipients with stimulating material. Sometimes they encourage female fantasy; often, they critique male sexual performance. These woman-to-woman paratexts represent collusion, a sense that the female speaker and audience are perpetuating, not curtailing, sexuality.

Although settling on a definitive number is difficult because of ambiguity about what constitutes direct address, by my count, between 1660 and 1714 a total of 115 prologues and epilogues feature actresses either addressing female spectators or voicing universal statements about the sex. This total is conservative; applying Roberts's methodology would increase the number because he also includes paratexts that refer to women in the third person. By comparison, male actors address female audiences twenty-one times, while fifteen paratexts where women are addressed do not specify the speaker's gender. Within this category, addresses to women occupy varying amounts of text, with those earlier in the period usually devoting more space to female address. Examples of paratexts primarily addressing women include a prologue to Thomas Killigrew's *Selindra* (1662–1663), advising ladies that they had better like the play because their money will not be refunded; and an epilogue written by R. Boyle, possibly to *Mr Anthony* (c.1671–1672), claiming that poets try but fail to craft male characters whom women find admirable. In later years, the only male paratexts to devote so much time to female audience members are those accompanying the annual "musick speeches" held at Oxford and Cambridge, which were often considered obscene and thus consequential for women to hear.[6] The 115 paratexts addressing women encompassed many perspectives during this time period, and, as I show, varied according to the sex of their speaker.

When looking at male- and female-orated paratexts that address women, it becomes apparent that the critical commonplace about female audiences favoring virtue requires modification. Prologues and epilogues often raise the subject of virtue, but when addressing female audience members they are just as likely to extol the play's lack of virtue as a selling point. Certainly some do promote virtue, including the prologue to Killigrew's *The Siege of Urbin* (1663), where the speaker claims that due to ladies' virtue their approbation counts more than that of their male counterparts; and the epilogue spoken by Jane Rogers to the anonymous *The Triumphs of Virtue* (1697), where she credits the ladies for inspiring Bellamira, her virtuous character. But many others appeal to women by demoting virtue, including the epilogue to Ravenscroft's *The Citizen Turn'd Gentleman* (1672), where the speaker says that to win the ladies' favor Ravenscroft will become "the greatest debauchee"; and the epilogue to Thomas Wright's 1693 comedy, *The Female Vertuoso's*, where Susannah Mountfort sneers that older ladies "boast of Virtue, 'cause unfit for Vice."[7] It is these latter examples Jeremy Collier has in mind when, describing actresses' prologues and epilogues, he fears that they will corrupt female spectators:

> Here are such Strains as would turn the Stomach of an ordinary Debauchee, and be almost nauseous in the *Stews*. And to make it the more agreeable, Women are Commonly pick'd out for this Service. Thus the *Poet* Courts the good opinion of the Audience. This is the Desert he regales the Ladys with at the Close of the Entertainment: It seems He thinks They have admirable

Palats! Nothing can be a greater Breach of Manners then such Liberties as these. If a Man would study to Outrage *Quality* and Vertue, he could not do it more Effectually.[8]

His sarcastic description of the ladies' "admirable Palats" reflects Collier's belief that women appreciate obscene performances. Restoration textual treatment of the female spectator thus goes well beyond conceiving her as only appreciating morality. Virtue was just one strategy used to court women; other tactics took an antithetical approach.

When addressing women, male- and female-orated paratexts share a few strategies. Both distinguish women by social class. While the majority address "the ladies," several paratexts during the late Restoration acknowledge city-wives and prostitutes, confirming Gilli Bush-Bailey's observation that by the 1690s female spectators had grown more diverse.[9] Another shared tactic is an appeal to the higher-class female audience, claiming that their approval will influence men. The prologue spoken by Mr. Mills to Centlivre's *The Wonder* (1714) informs women that since they excel at winning men's hearts, by applauding the play they inspire the same in men; the epilogue spoken by "Imperia" to John Wilson's *Belphegor* (1690) likewise asserts that men will copy ladies' approving behavior.[10] And some late Restoration paratexts claim that compared to women in other countries (usually Spain), English women possess more liberties, are better behaved, or enjoy happier lives. Examples include the epilogue to Francis Manning's *All for the Better* (1702), which claims English women have superior breeding over those from Madrid, and Anne Bracegirdle's epilogue to Shadwell's *The Amorous Bigotte* (1690), which states that although their Spanish counterparts are wiser, English women are happier because they need not fear their husbands finding out about their lovers.[11] There is thus some tactical overlap in male and female-orated paratexts that address women.

But the paratexts spoken by men often belittle their female audiences. When male paratexts distinguish between ladies, city-wives, and prostitutes, they praise the first at the latters' expense. Prologues spoken by John Hodgson to Thomas Dilke's *The Lovers' Luck* (1695) and by William Bowen to Dilke's *The Pretenders* (1698) exemplify this treatment; in the former, Hodgson courts the ladies while denigrating city-wives, whose progeny will "still supply the Stage, / And furnish Scandal for th' ensuing Age," while in the latter prologue, having toasted "sound Masks" only to declare that there are no such beings, a "drunken" Bowen drops to his knees and begs only the ladies for mercy.[12] Several paratexts mock women to their faces, such as the prologue delivered by Betterton to Nicholas Rowe's *Ulysses* (1705), which sarcastically suggests that "our English wives" are just as chaste as Penelope. The highest number of paratexts—ten—simply spend a few lines at the end saying they would take pride in the ladies' approbation. Compared to these limited and often demeaning options, when it comes to female speakers addressing women, opportunities expand.

The distinguishing feature in paratexts spoken by women to women is mutuality. In twelve paratexts, actresses ask women for support because male spectators "dare not disapprove when you applaud."[13] While several appeal to their virtue, others instead court women's wit or charm, or simply assume that women can control men. Forty-one paratexts feature the actress representing her gender collectively, perhaps most famously the epilogue to Wycherley's *The Country Wife* (1675), where Mrs. Knep concludes by declaring, "But then we Women,—there's no coz'ning us."[14] Seven others court women by encouraging heterosexual lust, including two exhortations for women to like the play because the male playwright is sexy, and one homoerotic address by Miss Howard in breeches, telling women to indulge in their sexual desires and saying that upon returning from military service "he" will "Conquest gain."[15] These 115 prologues and epilogues encouraged an active and varied female spectatorship, offering women many more ways of experiencing theater than has been thought. And the fact that so many of these were authored by men means that the authors had to imagine themselves in the role of actress colluding with other women. In such cases the actress is less impacted by the author's words than the author is by the actress's direct address of other women.[16]

Rochester's *Valentinian* and Female Sexual Fantasy

When the Earl of Rochester's tragedy *Valentinian* finally premiered in February 1684, it featured a prologue of admiration for the dead playwright. Written by his friend Aphra Behn for actress Sarah Cooke to perform, the prologue capitalizes on a collective memory of Rochester's sex appeal, courting female favor by encouraging women to fantasize about sex with the dead poet.[17] An early example of so-called female bonding, this first prologue to *Valentinian* activates the female audience as both fans and imagined sexual agents: a sex-positive appeal.

As one might expect from the author of "A Ramble in St James's Park," the play centers around the enormous sexual appetite of the Roman emperor Valentinian, whose quotidian promiscuity has melded into a single destructive lust for Lucina, wife of his friend Maximus. The play has a complex origin: Rochester first adapted John Fletcher's *Valentinian* into *Lucina's Rape* in the early 1670s, but then reworked his own adaptation into the more performance-oriented *Valentinian*. While *Lucina's Rape* never saw public performance, three extant manuscripts contain dramatis personae that correspond to King's Company personnel in 1675. The first print publication of Rochester's *Valentinian* in 1685 features the cast of the 1684 United Company production. In adapting Fletcher's play, Rochester reshapes it around the rape, making it an antecedent of the she-tragedy genre. After Lucina rejects him in the play's first scene, Valentinian enlists his servants to eroticize her environment, stimulating her sexual visions and dreams. Summoning her to the castle under false pretenses, Valentinian rapes Lucina, prompting her suicide. A bloodbath ensues when the emperor's own army turns on him. Criticism of the play has centered on Valentinian the character, with many likening him to Charles II. In an ingenious line of criticism, Harold Love draws parallels between the scene settings within *Lucina's Rape* and the architecture of Whitehall palace— with the rape occurring in Rochester's own apartment.[18] While such rich scholarship distinguishes the play, its three published prologues and one epilogue have not entered the discussion until now.

Spoken by Sarah Cooke, Behn's prologue to *Valentinian* rewards audiences in the know about an affair between the actress and the playwright. The (probably apocryphal) story of Rochester teaching Elizabeth Barry her craft remains well known; the remarkably similar story of him repeating these lessons to Cooke is not.[19] According to the sensationalist *Memoirs of the Life of Count de Grammont*, Cooke, then a maid of honor to the Duchess of York, became involved with Rochester when her aunt complained to him that Miss Hobart, a maid known for her lesbian tendencies, had made advances on her niece. Rochester interjected himself: "he thereupon advised her to take [Cooke] out of Miss *Hobart's* Hands, and managed Matters so well, that she fell into his."[20] A stanza in the several versions of the anonymous lampoon "Satyr on the Players" also mocked Cooke:

> Impudent *Sarah* thinks she's prais'd by all
> Mistaken Drab back to thy Mother's Stall,
> And let true Savin whom thou hast prov'd so well
> 'Tis a rare Thing that belly will not swell
> Tho' fuck't & fuck't and as debauch'd as Hell.[21]

The reference to savin implies her "talent" for promiscuity without pregnancy: "Savin is strongly poisonous; it possesses emmenagogic properties, and hence was a common means of procuring abortion."[22] The lampoon circulated in 1684, the same year Cooke performed both prologues to *Valentinian*.[23]

Behn's prologue courts male and female audiences in different ways: it deflects men and promotes solidarity with women.[24] The prologue immediately establishes Cooke's authority as speaker; as Danchin observes, the opening couplet—"With that assurance we to day address, / As standar'd Beauty certain of success"—acknowledges her beauty and fitness to introduce the play.[25] It also establishes a pattern of revision and collusion; Rochester's domination over women, both factual and fictional, gets revised by Behn's adoring prologue, which in turn is revised by Cooke's idiosyncratic delivery and authority as his former lover. Next, the prologue endeavors to pacify critics, encouraging them to gossip instead of watching the play, so that they cannot slander it afterward. Included are topical references to events like the "Blanket Fair," a festival held on the frozen Thames during the winter of 1683–1684; men are encouraged to gossip about how cheap the rates of prostitution were during that event.[26]

During the second half of the prologue, when attention turns to the late great playwright, the gender-customized advertising strategies become apparent. At first there are five couplets extolling the poet's wit, wherein Rochester is celebrated as mending Fletcher's already great play; these lines might appeal to men or women. But with the words "Listen ye Virgins," the prologue promotes solidarity among author, speaker, and female audience. The audience is invited to watch the play while enveloped in the aura of its sexy playwright. Then the prologue evokes an appealing vision of him that for some audiences becomes more powerful because of their knowledge of Cooke's affair with Rochester, as well as Behn's own allegiance to the dead poet. Here described is a shared fantasy: female admirers promote remembrance of Rochester. Cooke, via Behn, creates such a vision with the female audience. The following ten lines about the poet urge female spectators to circumvent behavioral restraints and indulge in fantasy:

> Listen ye Virgins to his Charming Song,
> Eternal Musick dwelt upon his Tongue:
> The Gods of Love and Wit inspir'd his Pen,
> And Love and Beauty was his Glorious Theam;
> Now Lady you may Celebrate his Name,
> Without a Scandal on your spotless Fame:
> With sighs his dear lov'd Memory pursue,
> And pay his Wit, what to his Eyes was due,
> 'Twill please his Ghost even in th'Elizian shade,
> To find his Power has such a Conquest made.[27]

The first four lines envision Rochester as a siren. Beginning as sexual agents, women then fall under the spell of the man's eternal song, where "eternal" refers to both the siren's ongoing music and Rochester's posthumous poetic, sexual, and theatrical successes. Returning to the present, lines five and six restore women's sexual agency; women may now imagine scandal-free liaisons with the poet. The final two couplets advise women to transfer their lust for Rochester into appreciation for his play, enabling for him a new type of conquest. Converting the author's male body into a virtual prop, this passage courts female approval by volleying sexual agency back and forth between man and woman, and dangling the fantasy of intimacy with the poet. Cheri Langdell's comment that Behn's paratexts are "a forum for the assessment of relations between the sexes" applies to this example as well as many others.[28] For those who knew of Cooke's affair, these lines may have been even more striking, since the actress extolling his abilities as a lover was speaking from experience.[29]

The prologue's approach is further illuminated when contrasted to Behn's "On the Death of the late Earl of Rochester," which voices hostility to women. A performance-oriented poem, the elegy addresses several audiences in turn: muses, young men, "Beauties," and "little Gods of Love," telling each to "Mourn, mourn." Composing it shortly after Rochester's death on 26 July 1680 and not needing to court their instant approval, Behn blames her female readers; Rochester is "your victim'd Slave" who was "Too sad a Triumph of your Victories."[30] But by the time of *Valentinian*'s premiere, Behn reanimates Rochester so that he seduces from the grave, presenting one such conquest in Cooke and uniting author, actress, and female audience in shared fantasies of Rochester as lover. And as the actress delivering the prologue, Cooke in turn appears as the authority on such matters; while not written by her, this prologue is resolutely hers. Such situations confirm that prologues and epilogues addressed female spectators and offered them a wide range of responses. At a time before regular moral appeals to the ladies, this prologue suggests an opportunity for authors to win women's approval by appealing to their erotic desires.

The Princess of Cleve and Female Conspiracy
Dryden's prologue to Lee's *The Princess of Cleve* (1682) demonstrates an actress pleasing the entire audience while reaching out to female patrons.[31] The play centers on the heroine, who confesses to her bridegroom, the Prince of Cleve, that she instead loves the play's rakish and sinister protagonist, Nemours; after said prince dies of grief, she remains faithful to his memory and spurns her lover. While in its portrayal of doomed love the plot accords with much of Restoration heroic tragedy, its subplots differ, featuring one female lover of Nemours pimping other women for him, as well as various men attempting to cuckold each other. Given the play's misogynist content, the prologue conditions the audience to receive Nemours more tolerantly.

Critical reception details the play's lewdness but not its conditioning of the audience to receive such content. Scholars have focused on one of three topics: its overload of smut, its representation of the recently deceased Rochester in one or more characters, and its lack of fidelity to Lee's source, Marie-Madeleine de Lafayette's novel *La Princesse de Cleve* (1678). Robert Hume, for example, has called the play "a rotting dung heap," although arguing that that was in fact Lee's purpose.[32] Editor Michael Cordner has found much to appreciate yet still acknowledges the play's "abrasive frankness."[33] Cordner argues that the play treats Rochester in a mixed fashion by representing him as both the deceased, witty Rosidore that other characters mourn and also, perhaps, as the libertine Nemours who seduces women with every breath.[34] While Tara and Philip Collington find that Lee inherits most of the "smut" from the adapted source, they concur that the play is "quite offensive" even by Restoration standards.[35] They point out, however, that the audience would have been familiar with both the English translation of Lafayette's novel and the characters' real-life counterparts from the Valois court, and thus may have brought tolerance with them to the theater. Whether or not the audience knew these sources, however, the prologue suggests a way for the female audience to deal with the smut and this more sinister portrayal of the Rochester character. By having a female speaker address women directly and men implicitly, preparing them for what lies ahead, the prologue promotes the entire audience's acceptance of the play.

Distinguishing the female audience is the prologue's first strategy toward winning approval. With the first word, "Ladies!" and the following lines, the prologue immediately sets up a mock-adversarial relationship between female and male audience members:

> I long to whisper something in your Ear:
> A Secret, which does much my Mind perplex,
> There's Treason in the Play against our Sex.[36]

Here the actress flirts with both genders; she teases women by invoking secrecy, and in the process she piques male curiosity about the data she wants to conceal from them. Thus, she activates the female audience, turning the men into their spectators. Her tone is far from complaint—declaring treason only works if played for laughs—but its boldness advances comedy customized to the gender of each audience member. It comically prepares women to meet a cad, Nemours, while it establishes for male consumption an attractive allegiance between women. By stating an apparent resemblance between the villain and other men, she then advances the joke:

A Man that's false to Love, that Vows and cheats,
And kisses every living thing he meets!
. . .
Out on him, Traytor, for a filthy Beast,
Nay, and he's like the pack of all the rest;
None of 'em stick at mark: They all deceive.[37]

This joke allows the women to share a groan over male treachery while striking a mere glancing blow at the male audience. In rhyming about male treachery, though, the prologue prepares women to meet Nemours while making them feel that their complaints about treacherous male behavior have been anticipated.

The rest of the prologue maintains parallel gendered jokes. Discussing male deceit, the speaker says: "To hide their faults they rap out Oaths and tear: / Now tho' we Lye, we're too well bred to Swear." Casually asserting sexual transgression, double entendres on "Lye" and "Swear" comically advance female superiority of manners, implying that their socialization makes their extramarital affairs only half as bad as men's. Declaring "*perjuria ridet Amantum*," the speaker flatters educated men as she furthers the joke of women identifying unsatisfactory male behavior: "I'm not Book Learn'd, to know that word in vogue, / But I suspect 'tis Latin for a Rogue."[38] Her displayed ignorance of Latin makes clear that the speaker does not threaten male status, but there is some irony here, since although its etymology is unknown, the word "rogue" itself probably has Latin origins. Women's recourse, then, is to reject marriage: "To trump their Diamonds, as they trump our Hearts."[39] Through a double-voiced discourse, the prologue fosters female bonding, packaged attractively for the benefit of all audiences.

This prologue can also be distinguished from the paratexts Dryden wrote for his own plays, because as it activates the female speaker, there is no curse against the "damn'd dull Poet."[40] As demonstrated in *Tyrannick Love* and *The Conquest of Granada Part I* epilogues, Dryden enjoyed having a laugh at his own expense. But in this case, Dryden adopts the same strategy that he later uses for Joseph Williams's "drunken" prologue to Joseph Harris's *The Mistakes* and diverts any possible blame from Lee.[41] He even has the actress offer an alternative target, with the line: "Some *Jew* has chang'd the Text, I half believe."[42] Investing the actress with agency thus implicitly shields the playwright from blame while ensuring that Dryden does not threaten his friendship with Lee.

Conditioning the audience to receive Nemours, who seduces women up until his very last speech, the prologue provides something absent from the play—a sympathy between women. This connection returns in the epilogue, also penned by Dryden, where the same (unknown) female speaker discusses how women cope with their many types of lovers. "We Women Love like Cats, that hide their Joys," she explains, and then complains about men's sneaky and limp methods of courting.[43] Considered alongside the play, then, and despite having a male author, the prologue and epilogue offer the audience an experience counter to the plot: a female agent cracking jokes to other women at males' expense.

The prologues to *Valentinian* and *The Princess of Cleve* showcase varied textual and performance techniques employed to win female favor. In doing so, they remind us to treat plays as performances. Envisioning actresses addressing female audiences thus leads to a fuller understanding of women's roles in Restoration theater.

Social Critique

The combination of social critique and brazen flippancy makes the prologues and epilogues in this category both progressive and popular. And as with speeches inducing female solidarity, authors of this type are mostly male, meaning that they effectively effaced themselves for the sake of the female voice: a testament to the high demand for actresses to deliver prologues and, especially, epilogues. The many prologues and epilogues in this category critique at least one of three subjects: marriage, masculinity, and male mistreatment of women. Of the surviving paratexts, Dryden and D'Urfey wrote the greatest number of them (eight), followed by William Burnaby with six, Congreve with five, and Behn with four. Barry and Bracegirdle delivered the greatest number, with eleven each. Among the subcategories, the most numerous and expansive is mocking masculinity, with George Etherege inaugurating the trend in his epilogue to *Love in a Tub* (1664). Of the forty-one prologues and epilogues that critique love and marriage, only three occur during the first two decades of the Restoration, while on the other hand, ten of the nineteen paratexts that critique male mistreatment of women originated in the 1670s. And as with female solidarity, these paratexts may also feature bonuses for men in the audience, as some complaints transmit as facetious. But to my argument in chapter 2, that the sheer fact of women controlling the audience through comedy is a protofeminist act, is added the bold subject matter. Together, the three subcategories join with "female solidarity" as representing the most progressive examples of Restoration prologues and epilogues.

Critiques of Love and Marriage: *The City-Heiress*

In this first category, paratexts fault both individual and institution: men receive criticism for their poor service as lovers and husbands, while marriage is treated as a limitation and a curse. Sometimes these paratexts are consonant with their plays when the latter portray marriage negatively; other times they accompany comedies that end happily with marriage, or tragedies that center on lovers' inability to marry or to remain so. Some paratexts draw analogies between marriage and negative scenarios, such as the epilogue to Thomas Shipman's *Henry III of France, Stabbed by a Fryer* (1672), which compares the dullness of patronizing only one theater to marrying only one man. In an example of retroactive metalepsis, the breeches epilogue to Settle's *Love and Revenge* (1674) criticizes marriage by disabusing the audience of the idea that anyone today would die for love, as happens in the play; speaker Mary Lee promotes marriage as being solely for economic gain. Written by Congreve for Susannah Verbruggen, the epilogue to Southerne's *Oroonoko* (1696) works in conjunction with the play's comic plot to echo this materialistic view of marriage. Several paratexts present marriage as a penalty; in her epilogue to Nahum Tate's *The Sicilian Usurper* (1680), Sarah Cooke denounces play critics by wishing them "The Curse of Curses—*Marriage* Take ye all."[44] While such a "curse" transmits as facetious, the simple fact that a woman voices a negative comment about marriage in public indicates the freedoms that prologues and epilogues extend to female performers. Another subset complains of husbands abusing wives, such as the prologue to D'Urfey's *The Banditti* (1686), which chides husbands for treating their wives poorly, and the political epilogue to Charles Gildon's *Love's Victim* (1701), written by William Burnaby for Mary Porter, which alludes to contemporary cases where supposed cuckolds sued their wives for divorce and complains that society would never permit the reverse. Still others justify wives cuckolding their husbands, such as the epilogue to Southerne's *The Wives' Excuse* (1691), where Elizabeth Barry says that many women have straying husbands like that of her character, and therefore "Women ne'er want cause for what they do."[45] Critiques of love and marriage run the gamut but tend to stress male unfitness for the position of husband.

How is it that women were allowed to register such complaints? The actresses' beauty and charm certainly helped, as did the willingness of male authors to envision inhabiting a female body amid oppressive cultural foundations, as well as the audience's knowledge of male authorship; but a major aspect is simply the phenomenon of joke reception. When a self-deprecating joke is performed in public, social pressure and the need for the listener to demonstrate a sense of humor discourage responding immediately with outrage, whatever retaliation might happen later. An additional reason, as Joanne Gilbert explains, is that when hearing a gender, ethnic, or other group to which we belong become the object of comedy, we tend to recognize our affiliation with that group yet disassociate from the group's stereotypical qualities.[46] Some of us may inhabit the role of mother-in-law, for example, yet when we hear a mother-in-law joke we normally do not take it personally. In discussing jokes about older women, Ruth Shade, borrowing from Bakhtin, argues that such jokes should not be taken seriously because they inhabit a performance setting, not a daily reality.[47] In order to tolerate such criticism, Restoration audiences must have recognized the performance space as liminal and unreal. And yet within such spaces, social critique found audiences, leading to subsequent prologue and epilogue writers and speakers who perpetuated the trend and to spectators whose delight in this social critique couched in entertainment prompted return trips to the theater.

The epilogue to Aphra Behn's 1682 comedy, The City-Heiress, portrays marriage as a derelict institution against which women can rebel. Written by a "person of quality," the epilogue itself actually suits all three branches of the "social critique" category—infidelity provides a primary source of marital complaint, and husbands' masculinity becomes a subject of public scrutiny when the heroine describes the physical signs of cuckoldry. An adaptation of Middleton's A Mad World My Masters (performed 1605, published 1608), the play traces a rake's progress with three women; staged during the Exclusion Crisis, it affirms Behn's Tory inclinations by satirizing Whigs, particularly Shaftesbury. First, the rake-hero Wilding disposes of a former mistress, Diana, by disguising her as an heiress and marrying her off to his uncle Sir Timothy Treat-all. Then Wilding seduces the widow Lady Galliard, who afterward feels she must marry the automaton Sir Charles to preserve her respectability. Naturally, Wilding saves the virgin heiress, Charlot, for himself.

Recent discussion of the play has concentrated on two subjects: politics and protofeminism. Concerning the former, the ungenerous Sir Timothy Treat-all is widely seen as parodying the first Earl of Shaftesbury, so several critics read the battle between uncle and nephew as analogous to Whig versus Tory. Robert Markley, for example, finds that the play portrays "Toryism triumphant," while Susan Owen writes that compared to the play's Whigs, "the Tory rakes are more refined, more sexy and more fun."[48] Considering his treatment of women, many critics view Wilding as a rougher rake than

The Rover's Willmore; as Derek Hughes points out, he had and may still have syphilis, and he seduces Lady Galliard after having negotiated marriage with Charlot, meaning that he is unfaithful to the woman whom Restoration culture would have recognized as his wife, before they consummate their marriage.[49] Marriage to Charlot elevates his social standing, demotes his Whiggish uncle's status, and punishes Diana and Lady Galliard. Within the play's economy, Wilding has captured the grand prize.

Attempting to square the popularity of Behn's plays with her protofeminism and cynicism, recently Markley has written compellingly of the play's "profound skepticism about love and marriage."[50] Applying Peter Sloterdijk's term "cynical reason" to the play, Markley shows how Lady Galliard knowingly reifies antifeminist social practice when she allows Wilding to seduce her without further commitment. Charlot similarly knows about Wilding's sexual infractions but disregards this knowledge and marries him anyway. Markley's is an important reading of *The City-Heiress*, but it should be noted that many epilogues by Behn and others have promoted such cynicism through the process of retroactive metalepsis.

The epilogue demonstrates that Wilding's success is itself tainted and offers a female rebuttal. Whereas during the play men control marriage, in the epilogue the woman both determines her own union and satirizes marriage as an institution. Because Charlotte Butler is no longer playing the heroine, Charlot, but instead performing her own persona, the comedy stems from the incongruity between the character's naiveté and the actress's own apparent savoir faire. By the epilogue's end, her critique of marriage has advanced to the point that the only uncertainty left is whether marriage sustains prior infidelities or provokes new ones.

While Charlot represents the prized conquest on the marriage market, Butler questions the felicity of Charlot's marriage to Wilding and, more generally, marriage as an institution. Like Letitia Cross's epilogue to Pix's *Ibrahim* (discussed in chapter 2), Butler's epilogue immediately reorients our view of the heroine. Butler no longer plays the passive prize but instead appears as a figure who satirizes marriage. To do this, she first expresses incredulity at the character she plays: "My Part, I fear, will take with but a few, / A Rich young Heiress to her first Love true!"[51] Skepticism is a mode actresses use frequently to reflect on their idealistic characters; recall, in her epilogue to *Love's Last Shift*, Cross's incredulity that Loveless has renounced the libertine lifestyle: "An Honest Rake forego the Joys of life!"[52] Referencing elements of the play, Butler then frames them as more insidious. Early in the play, for example, her character poses as the niece of a Puritan lady to investigate

Lady Galliard's relationship with Wilding. But in the epilogue she conceives of marriage as a more significant masquerade:

> Marrying's the Mask, which Modesty assures,
> Helps to get new, and covers old Amours

and then suggests the beginnings of cuckoldry:

> In the gay spring of Love, when free from doubts,
> With early shoots his Velvet Forehead sprouts.[53]

The "Velvet Forehead" indicates the downy skin that covers a deer's horns during the growing stage, and this reference to the development of a cuckold's horns suggests the difference between play and epilogue. While in the play Charlot betrays a doe-like naiveté, ultimately awarding herself to Wilding despite his liaisons with two other women, here Butler possesses a more seasoned view of marriage. The "gay Spring" of love refers to Charlot and Wilding's newly wedded state, and since text after text portray love in the Restoration as lasting for a mere three months, the current time represents the lone season for fidelity. That Butler locates sprouts on the husband's forehead during this earliest time suggests that their marriage contains no honeymoon period; the wife never planned to be faithful, not even for a season.

Besides insinuating marriage's sexual permeability, the epilogue complains that men like Wilding possess unreasonably high standards for their brides. Concluding in a darker tone, Butler curses would-be bridegrooms who hold out for heiresses:

> But if at best our hopefull Sport and Trade is,
> And nothing now will serve you but great Ladies;
> May question'd Marriages your Fortune be,
> And Lawyers drain your Pockets more than we:
> May Judges puzzle a clear Case with Laws,
> And Musquetoons at last decide the Cause.[54]

Whereas the play portrays marriage to a rake with a sense of foreboding, the epilogue is even more direct. For men who refuse to marry any but "great ladies," Butler dispenses marital instability, lawsuits, and even murder.[55] As Danchin notes, the play's release date coincides with a notorious divorce case that resulted in the husband's murder.[56] The customary facetiousness behind paratextual threats may instead give way to a more insidious tone, giving bite to this marital critique. With its satire on marriage from the wife's point of view, Butler's epilogue to *The City-Heiress* joins other female paratexts in demonstrating that love and marriage in their idealized forms do not survive beyond act 5, and that therefore we might question the value of them as heroic rewards.

Mocking Masculinity: *The Country Wife*

The second category contains perhaps the most strident paratexts. Filled with insulting jokes, the examples that mock masculinity reverse the gender power hierarchy and call men incompetent, powerless, insecure, cuckolded, or impotent. Containing fifty-six examples, this populous category features five different strategies of actresses castigating men. They couch criticism in comedy, but the criticism nonetheless transmits.

In the first style, women assert their power at males' expense. The epilogue to John Crowne's *Juliana, or the Princess of Poland* (1671) features "Paulina and Landlord" bickering over issues of gender and power; Paulina elevates women by proclaiming a "Senate of Ladies, lower House of Men."[57] Inaugurated by Gwyn's epilogue to Dryden's *Tyrannick Love* (1669), a second type features male playwrights making fun of themselves. In the epilogue to *A Very Good Wife* (1693), for example, Mrs. Knight hurls insults at playwright George Powell, calling him "our puny Whisler" and referencing "His Pigmey Muses."[58] The audience must have enjoyed laughing at the insults themselves, at a woman making fun of a man, and at Powell's self-excoriation as a defensive strategy.

By far the most numerous strategy within all female paratexts is the straightforward insult. Women call men incompetent or superfluous. Frequently composed by Behn or Dryden, these paratexts imply that men depend on women for basic needs. In Dryden's prologue and epilogue to *Don Sebastian* (1689), Susannah Mountfort mocks men who cannot fight; in a lighter mode, in the epilogue to the 1672 all-female revival of *Secret-Love*, Dryden's breeches-wearing mistress, Anne Reeves, says that this performance shows that men are superfluous and that in the future women will be able to please each other. In the prologue to *The Counterfeit Bridegroom* (1677), possibly a collaboration between Behn and Thomas Betterton, the speaker mocks men who have remained in town over the summer and facetiously advises them that tradesmen's wives await them in the country. And while Behn's epilogue to *Sir Patient Fancy* (1678) has garnered much critical attention for her self-defense against charges of plagiarism, it also provocatively reverses gendered descriptors, referencing women's "valour" and men's "worse than womanish affectation."[59] Finally, in the epilogue to *The False Count* (c. 1681), she mocks men's fickleness and frivolity.[60]

The final two subcategories of paratexts that mock masculinity relate to male sexual failure: they either mock men's impotence or insinuate cuckoldry due to men's failure to please their wives. Together these two subcategories span some of the most popular Restoration plays, including *The Country Wife, Lucius Junius Brutus, The Double Dealer,* and *Love's Last Shift*. Exemplifying accusations of male impotence are: Mary Lee's epilogue to Otway's *Titus and Berenice* (1676), which bans from the theater men who have lost their "stings," and Barry's epilogue to Nathaniel Lee's *Lucius Junius Brutus* (1680), which teases men for "your all talking, and your noe performing"[61] Cuckolds get called out in such paratexts as Miss Cross's virgin epilogue to Cibber's *Love's Last Shift*, which mock-reassures men sitting in "the middle row" that they should approve of the play because no character was cuckolded, and Bracegirdle's epilogue written by Thomas Baker for Centlivre's *The Platonick Lady* (1706), which refers to the many characteristics men hide about themselves, including cuckoldry, wearing false calves, and having sex with little boys. These paratexts have range.

A discussion of Wycherley's *The Country Wife* (1675) demonstrates how the epilogue, which insinuates male impotence, can influence an interpretation of the play. In her seminal discussion of the play, Eve Kosofsky Sedgwick claims that pairs of men communicate (hostilely) through their shared female vessel, which does not have a significant voice.[62] This analysis, however, succeeds only when the play is defined as narrowly as possible: as five acts. When the play is considered alongside its original prologue and epilogue, with which it premiered in performance and print, her theory only partially illustrates the play's female–male relationships. The prologue, and particularly the epilogue, turn the "which" back into a "who." They give the speaker a chance to joke publicly about her experiences and satirize male sexual inadequacy.

Paratextual discussions of male sexual dysfunction reinforce the image of powerful actresses. The epilogue to *The Country Wife*, performed by Mrs. Knep (the play's sexually self-indulgent Lady Fidget) calls men impotent; but because the play featured the rake-hero Horner posing as a eunuch so that he may have sex with unsuspecting husbands' wives, the male audience may have also received these jabs as compliments. Nevertheless, the epilogue's undermining of male sexual function is not an isolated occurrence, and the thirteen paratexts that make fun of male impotence almost equal the fifteen that mock Restoration men's greatest sexual fear: cuckoldry.

In *The Country Wife*, Horner's scheme and the china scene may be read alongside the epilogue as a tripartite consideration of the social consequences of impotence. Whereas the play turns on Horner's masquerade as a eunuch so that he may seduce his unsuspecting friends' wives, the china scene shows him to be not as virile as his scheme would imply. Before they have sex, Horner displaces his performance anxiety onto Lady Fidget's concern for her reputation:

> *Horner.* If you talk a word more of your honour, you'll make me incapable to wrong it. To talk of honour in the mysteries of love is like talking of heaven or the deity in an operation of witchcraft, just when you are employing the devil; it makes the charm impotent.[63]

By concealing his fears through the double negative and the abstract simile, Horner retains control of the sexual arena. But after they have successfully had sex, Lady Fidget invokes their recent and (for him) depleting intercourse in order to control his other affairs. Realizing after the fact that Horner has many sexual targets, she reduces him to empty promises: he guarantees Mrs. Squeamish a future "roll-wagon," only to be pitied by the apparently sexually irrelevant Old Lady Squeamish. Sedgwick's theory of the homosocial triangle, which interprets Lady Fidget as one of the objects shared between men, fails to account for the character's own sexual struggles with Horner. Deriving her theory from René Girard, who says that another person's desire for an object awakens our instinct to desire it too, Sedgwick further activates the (here, male) desiring beings by claiming that they communicate through the passive female vessel.[64] Her theory applies to Horner sharing Margery with the unwitting Pinchwife but not to his sharing of Lady Fidget with Sir Jasper, nor to Lady Fidget refusing to share Horner with Mrs. Squeamish.[65] Instead, the china scene portrays Horner as the object that Lady Fidget (unlike Pinchwife with Margery) successfully keeps to herself.

The epilogue increases Lady Fidget's mastery of male sexuality. Here Lady Fidget/Mrs. Knep, the figure of betweenness, controls a wider range of men yet also indicates that men should not feel threatened. In doing so, she proves an astute yet frustrated critic. In the first thirteen lines, she portrays actresses sympathetically as women who must endure men's loud solicitations and soft performances. She satirizes the supposedly "vigorous" men who ardently woo, then reject, whores in the audience so passionately as to frighten the actresses onstage. The critique of men's talk without action treats both the women on stage and those in the audience as spectators, even as both groups present their bodies for show. Lady Fidget/Mrs. Knep then mocks older men whose attempts to signify sexual prowess through cuckolding do not hurt the husbands so much as the wives, who must endure their impotence. This series of jokes deflates an idea that the play takes as a given: that women's reputations suffer through extramarital sex.

The general knowledge of Mrs. Knep's sexual behavior doubles the joke of the epilogue's last line, "But then we women—there's no coz'ning us!"[66] The knowledgeable cynicism accords with Knep's public persona to actively promote her offstage sexuality.[67] Peter Holland's observation that her less-sexual part as Eliza in Wycherley's *The Plain Dealer* "deliberately inverts Mrs. Knep's status in Wycherley's plays" confirms the linkage of her roles and reputation.[68] When Knep played other prominent parts, including Beatrix in Dryden's *An Evening's Love*, the common knowledge of her affairs with Samuel Pepys and Jo Haines made her lines resonate with betweenness. Entries in Pepys's diary from the late 1660s record his public interactions with Knep. Escorting home his new acquaintance, Pepys "got her upon my knee (the coach being full) and played with her breasts and sung."[69] Subsequent entries also suggest that their alliance was not a secret; these include his descriptions of Knep's ill-natured and surly husband, their carnal activities (more fondling, intercourse, and monetary transactions), and his wife's public outrage upon discovering Pepys appearing publicly with Knep (a scene repeated with others of his dozen mistresses). Given the public nature of their relationship, in-the-know patrons might savor the possibility that Knep speaks autobiographically. Insinuations like this build public intimacy, where the audience can enjoy the titillating events it thinks that it knows about.[70]

Lady Fidget does, however, argue that women govern sexual intercourse itself and its (usually) private setting. The suggestion here is that since intimacy forces them to share their secrets with lovers, men with sexual issues like Horner empower women. Lady Fidget complains against the would-be cuckolder, who, represented by Horner, has been celebrated for his ingenuity. She outdoes Horner's cunning by establishing, as editor James Ogden points out, that women too feign virtue, and she criticizes his selection of Margery Pinchwife for an urban affair.[71] Anthony Kaufman observes that during the play, the audience identifies with Horner, but in the epilogue, suddenly they are treated like Sparkish.[72] Lady Fidget's establishment of female sexual agency enables this condition in the male audience.

A triplet demonstrates Lady Fidget's agency in the homosocial triangle:

> In fine, you essenced boys, both old and young,
> Who would be thought so eager, brisk, and strong,
> Yet do the ladies, not their husbands, wrong.[73]

By identifying her collective gender as the injured party, Lady Fidget again resists the objectification of the woman within the triangular exchange. She insinuates that, whereas Horner's affairs depended on the ladies maintaining secrecy out of self-interest, liaisons with impotent men might license disappointed women to make this knowledge public. Women also can make the private public, and Lady Fidget's epilogue achieves that on a broader scale.

The epilogue suggests that there is a private sexual truth only women can access. The Lady Fidget/Mrs. Knep amalgam cynically reminds the male audience that they are not Horners and that extramarital sex may also bear public consequences that damage rather than establish their virile reputation. It furthermore names women as the repositories of sexual knowledge in a play where sex dominates every sphere. Lady Fidget is the first lover to understand Horner's scheme, and Mrs. Knep is the only one who knew the truth about her own affairs. When read in concert with its paratexts, the play invests women with sexual knowledge that extends beyond the stage. Whom they have "known" is what they alone know.

Complaints of Male Mistreatment: *The Constant Nymph*

Although the content of this final category of socially critical paratexts overlaps with the other two types, the difference is tone: complaint. This mode may be the least empowering of the speaker, as critique often occurs in a less plaintive fashion and mockery implies establishing superiority over the taunted object; but it may also represent the most direct approach. While sometimes the male mistreatment described in these paratexts is men's absence, the majority criticize men or the institutions that award them control over women. Several additional prologues complain of men abusing their lovers; the tone remains fairly lighthearted but their subject matter is more consequential, as the speakers protest male infidelity, public condemnation, or desertion. One of these, an epilogue spoken by Mrs. Moyle at Oxford in 1682, finds the university audience attractive as contrasted with unfaithful Londoners, while another, Bracegirdle's epilogue to John Crowne's *Regulus* (1692), complains of men's habitual seduction, then desertion of women. Two paratexts feature actresses protesting male audience members' abuse: one, "a prologue to an unknown play" (c. 1670), complains of men discussing actresses' physical blemishes, while "an epilogue spoken by a woman leaving the stage" (late 1680s) protests male audience members in Dublin failing to support the stage and in particular the women, and threatens that all actresses will depart for Britain, leaving them again with only male players.[74] Ranging from debauchery to infidelity to desertion, male mistreatment of women in general and actresses in particular receives critique in these paratexts.

The title of the anonymous play *The Constant Nymph, or, The Rambling Shepherd* (c. July 1677) establishes the leading female and male characters' divergent sexual practices that the prologue and play subsequently protest.

The play centers on the impending marriage between Astrea, one of two nymphs, and Astatius, the rambling shepherd, Mary Lee's breeches role. Not only did Astatius love and leave all of Astrea's bridal attendants before the start of the play, but on the way to his wedding he meets and courts another woman. This new target, Euplaste, is actually the male Philisides in disguise, played as a breeches role by Elizabeth Barry. The interrogation of Astatius's infidelity—he sees himself not so much as inconstant to each lover but instead as "One Constanter to Love"—comes across as absurd because of his number of past lovers, the "funny thing" that happens to him on his way to the wedding (his profession of love for Euplaste), and the fact that he is played by a she.[75] An unsuccessful play, in the dedication the male author attributes its failure partially to its premiere during the summer season: both its smaller audiences and the unwillingness of the Duke's Company managers to fund decent costumes, scenery, and other staging accoutrements. The author notes that many scenes and lines were cut, out of "decorum, as was pretended," but insinuates that the actual reason was because the women could not memorize all of their lines.[76] Nevertheless, simply the casting of two primary male roles as breeches parts must have put a comic spin on the portrayal of infidelity, something that worked against the author's conception of the play as a pastoral.

By staging three dialogues in which she plays both the male and the female roles, Mary Lee's prologue interrogates male infidelity and mistreatment of women. Spoken by Lee before she became Lady Slingsby, the prologue introduces one of the primary features of the play: its cross-dressed parts. After first explaining that she will appear as a man throughout the performance, she then adopts the pose of a man and imagines encounters with three past lovers (whom she also portrays), enjoyed by none of the women. The dialogues are set off from the text with long dashes and seven sets of marginal brackets, the first of which features a note next to it that says "In a Womans Voyce" and the rest of which alternately indicate "In his voice" and "In her voyce."[77]

The dialogues feature the man attempting to make light of his past affairs while the three female characters upbraid him for abandoning them. After introducing himself to the audience as a man who has "Been kind to all the Sex, but true to none," in the first dialogue he encounters an "old cast Citty Mistress" and falls back upon niceties.[78] When he asks after her husband she expresses astonishment that he inquires after someone he abused; and when he wonders about his "little Godson" she complains that the boy too closely resembles his delinquent father. After such admonishment, the man happily escapes his "Thunder clap" of an ex-mistress.[79]

In the second dialogue, a young woman berates him for having seduced and abandoned her, forcing her into prostitution. Describing her as a "*Covent-garden*-Friend," the man accuses her of profligacy, but she retorts:

> Well, if I am: the greater Villain you,
> You are the first my frailty ever knew.
> And when
> Her honour's lost, her Fortunes, mind too.
> What would you have a poor weak Woman do?[80]

There is no room for his retort as the third dialogue—really a one-sided harangue—begins. The third paramour, an old lover, says she no longer trusts men in the wake of his courtship. He swore fidelity, followed her "from Park to th' Plays," and "kept me up whole Nights twixt sleep and waking."[81] She then slants the criticism toward the men in the audience, remarking how easy it would be to enumerate their crimes against women, but conceding that if she complains, there is no way that men can find the play diverting, since "That's your old constant Musick every day." By the end, the female has subsumed the male voice, but the prologue has also catered to the male audience's presumed desire for more pleasant entertainment. Instead of exclusively providing such entertainment, however, the play features many women complaining about Astasius's profligacy. The prologue, therefore, inaugurates the play's interrogation of male infidelity and extends it to the Restoration audience's own environment.

The prologues and epilogues featured in this chapter represent the most protofeminist categories of the genre. Their performers express sexual desire, create gender solidarity, and protest inequities. For an actress to address female audience members can itself be threatening to men, whether she does so to evoke a sexual fantasy or a collaborative resistance. Female prologues and epilogues contained within these categories also protest domestic abuse, male infidelity, debauchery, and desertion. Perhaps most threatening are the paratexts featuring women mocking masculinity, which go beyond identifying gender inequities and actually attack men. The recurring themes of male incompetence and impotence represent some of the genre's most inventive language. And both female and male writers (here Behn, Dryden, and Wycherley, as well as two unknowns) wrote these strident roles for women, meaning that they were able to conceive of actresses' spheres far beyond that of sexual availability. Prologues and epilogues represent the first sanctioned spaces for English women to receive applause for voicing ideas that in other circumstances many audience members would find unpalatable. That is the benefit of the comic structure, permitting through this rhetorical mode more tendentious ideas than would otherwise be acceptable. In *Performing Marginality*, Joanne Gilbert writes of how women, marginalized by their gender, perform social critique within the palatable framework of stand-up comedy.[82] That actresses' prologues and epilogues couch within comedy such solidarities, critiques, mockeries, and complaints about gender inequities makes these paratexts both pleasurable and consequential.

Notes

1. Philip Auslander, "Comedy about the Failure of Comedy: Stand-Up Comedy and Postmodernism," in *Critical Theory and Performance*, ed. Janelle G. Reinelt and Joseph R. Roach (Ann Arbor: University of Michigan Press, 1992), 204.

2. Gayle Rubin, "The Traffic in Women: Notes on the 'Political Economy' of Sex," in *The Second Wave: A Reader in Feminist Theory*, ed. Linda Nicholson (New York: Routledge, 1997); Laura Mulvey, "Visual Pleasure and Narrative Cinema," *Screen* 16, no. 3 (1975).

3. David Roberts, *The Ladies: Female Patronage of Restoration Drama, 1660–1700* (Oxford: Clarendon, 1989), 28.

4. See appendix, part 5. Recently Fiona Ritchie has also questioned Roberts's findings. Looking for all mentions of women in prologues and epilogues without regard to their speakers' gender, she finds that 54 percent of those paratexts refer to women, as opposed to Roberts's 40 percent. See Fiona Ritchie, "'Jilting Jades'? Perceptions of Female Playgoers in the Restoration, 1660–1700," in *Theatre and Culture in Early Modern England, 1650–1737*, ed. Catie Gill (Surrey, UK: Ashgate, 2010), 132.

5. Jean I. Marsden, *Fatal Desire: Women, Sexuality, and the English Stage, 1660–1720* (Ithaca, NY: Cornell University Press, 2006), chapters 1 and 2.

6. As Roberts has argued, women had to feign ignorance of obscenity; if they acknowledged it even in protest, they placed their reputations at risk. See Roberts, *The Ladies*, 38.

7. Pierre Danchin, *The Prologues and Epilogues of the Restoration 1660–1700*, 4 vols. (Nancy: Presses Universitaires de Nancy, 1981–1988), 3:115.

8. Jeremy Collier, *A Short View of the Immorality, and Profaneness of the English Stage*, 1st ed. (London: S. Keble, 1698. Reprint, 1996), 13–14.

9. Gilli Bush-Bailey, *Treading the Bawds: Actresses and Playwrights on the Late-Stuart Stage* (Manchester: Manchester University Press, 2006), 83.

10. Pierre Danchin, *The Prologues and Epilogues of the Eighteenth Century*, 8 vols. (Nancy: Presses Universitaires de Nancy, 1990), 1:561; Danchin, *Restoration*, 2:814–15.

11. Danchin, *Eighteenth* 1:85; Danchin, *Restoration*, 2:803–4.

12. Danchin, *Restoration*, 3:230, 488.

13. Danchin, *Eighteenth*, 1:167. The play, Pix's *The Different Widows* (1703), is discussed in chapter 1.

14. William Wycherley, *The Country Wife*, ed. James Ogden (London: A and C Black, 1991), 102.

15. Ibid., 3:230–31.

16. Women authored eleven and men authored eighty, plus there are twenty-five anonymous paratexts that, given this ratio, would likely add greatly to the male total. See appendix, part 5.

17. Following Larry Carver and Danchin, I am citing from the broadside rather than the 1685 quarto version of the first prologue because the former is likely a more accurate record of performance. See Larry Carver, "Rochester's *Valentinian*," *Restoration and Eighteenth-Century Theatre Research* 4, no. 1 (1989). Richard Morton observes that this may be a "unique example of a prologue and epilogue being bowdlerized between the broadsheet and quarto printings." See Richard Morton, "Textual Problems in Restoration Broadsheet Prologues and Epilogues," *Library* 12, no. 3 (1957): 201.

18. Harold Love, "Was Lucina Betrayed at Whitehall?," in *That Second Bottle: Essays on John Wilmot, Earl of Rochester*, ed. Nicholas Fisher (Manchester: Manchester University Press, 2000), 187.

19. The trope of a male lover teaching a woman the craft of acting recurs in Restoration and eighteenth-century theater lore. For a challenge to the Rochester–Barry story, see Bush-Bailey, *Treading the Bawds*, 46. Bush-Bailey calls this "at best the result of male boasting and at worst yet another example of the appropriation of women's work to male control." The addition of the Cooke story adds weight to her argument.

20. *Memoirs of the Life of Count de Grammont: Containing the Amorous Intrigues of the Court of England in the Reign of King Charles II*, trans. Anthony Hamilton (London: Thomas Payne, 1760), 215. Although *Memoirs* is considered semifictional, Highfill et al. think that it renders the events fairly accurately. See Philip H. Highfill, Kalman A. Burnim, and Edward A. Langhans, *A Biographical Dictionary of Actors, Actresses, Musicians, Dancers, Managers and Other Stage Personnel in London 1660–1800*, 16 vols. (Carbondale: Southern Illinois University Press, 1973).

21. Qtd. in Bush-Bailey, *Treading the Bawds*, 59. After her death, Etherege wrote: "Sarah Cooke was always fitter for a player than for a Mrs., and it is properer her lungs should be wasted on the stage than that she should die of a disease too gallant for her" (Highfill, *A Biographical Dictionary*, 3:475).

22. Oxford English Dictionary, 2nd ed. 1991, s.v. "savin."

23. Cooke delivered a different prologue (author unknown) on the show's second day, featuring standard raillery at the critics. Elizabeth Barry's epilogue (written by a "Person of Quality") connects with women in a different way, by romanticizing Valentinian's rape; according to the epilogue, each woman has "her Valentinan in her heart." A third cloaked prologue, again intended for Barry, was also published with the 1685 quarto; it attacks the Whigs. See Danchin, *Restoration*, 2:514–16.

24. In 1684 the prologue first circulated in broadside form.

25. Danchin, *Restoration*, 2:510, 512.

26. New-style calendar dating.

27. Danchin, *Restoration*, 2:513. The final couplet exists in a folio half-sheet printed by Charles Tebroc but is missing from the 1685 quarto; see Morton, "Textual Problems," 201–2. Danchin prints the Tebroc version.

28. Cheri Davis Langdell, "Aphra Behn and Sexual Politics: A Dramatist's Discourse with Her Audience," in *Drama, Sex, and Politics*, ed. James Redmond (Cambridge: Cambridge University Press, 1985), 115.

29. There is a similarity here between Cooke's prologue about Rochester and Charles Hart referring to his past lover, Nell Gwyn, in the epilogue to *The Conquest of Granada Part 1*. In both cases the body onstage is experienced with the person being described. The motivations, however, are different; the prologue reads as sexually stimulating, while the epilogue tries to divert blame for a delayed play away from the author and toward Gwyn (and perhaps other actresses). Hart in this sense is a scold, not an admirer.

30. Janet Todd, *The Works of Aphra Behn*, 7 vols. (Columbus: Ohio State University Press, 1992), 1:161–63.

31. This prologue and the epilogue discussed later appeared in print independently of the play, in Dryden's 1684 *Miscellany Poems*. The play itself was not published until 1689, and then with a different prologue and epilogue. See Todd, *Behn*, 1:161–63.

32. Robert D. Hume, "The Satiric Design of Nat. Lee's *The Princess of Cleve*," *Journal of English and Germanic Philology* 75 (1976): 133.

33. Michael Cordner, *Four Restoration Marriage Plays* (Oxford: Oxford World's Classics, 1995), xxviii.

34. Ibid.

35. Tara L. Collington and Philip D. Collington, "Adulteration or Adaptation? Nathaniel Lee's 'Princess of Cleve' and Its Sources," *Modern Philology* 100, no. 2 (2002): 197.

36. Danchin, *Restoration*, 2:442.

37. Ibid.

38. "[Jupiter] laughs at the perjuries of lovers." From Tibullus, *Elegies*, III. vi. 49–50.

39. Danchin, *Restoration*, 2:442.

40. Ibid., 1:321.

41. For a discussion of the "drunken" prologue, see chapter 1.

42. Danchin, *Restoration*, 2:442.

43. Ibid., 2:443.

44. Ibid., 2:269.

45. Ibid., 3:39.

46. Joanne Gilbert, *Performing Marginality: Humor, Gender, and Cultural Critique* (Detroit: Wayne State University Press, 2004), 11.

47. Ruth Shade, "Take My Mother-in-Law: 'Old Bags,' Comedy and the Sociocultural Construction of the Older Woman," *Comedy Studies* 1, no. 1 (2010): 80.

48. Robert Markley, "'Be Impudent, Be Saucy, Forward, Bold, Touzing, and Leud': The Politics of Masculine Sexuality and Feminine Desire in Behn's Tory Comedies,"

in *Cultural Readings of Restoration and Eighteenth-Century English Theater*, ed. J. Douglas Canfield and Deborah C. Payne (Athens: University of Georgia Press, 1995), 131; Susan Owen, "Behn's Dramatic Response to Restoration Politics," in *The Cambridge Companion to Aphra Behn*, ed. Derek Hughes and Janet Todd (Cambridge: Cambridge University Press, 2004), 76.

49. Derek Hughes, *The Theatre of Aphra Behn* (Houndmills, Basingstoke, Hampshire: Palgrave, 2001), 149.

50. Robert Markley, "Aphra Behn's *The City Heiress*: Feminism and the Dynamics of Popular Success on the Late Seventeenth-Century Stage," *Comparative Drama* 41, no. 2 (2007): 151.

51. Danchin, *Restoration*, 2:403.

52. Ibid., 3:251.

53. Ibid., 2:403–4.

54. Ibid., 2:405.

55. In a different vein, Deborah Payne reads the epilogue as stressing the economic advantage of liaisons for actresses. See Deborah Payne, "Reified Object or Emergent Professional? Retheorizing the Restoration Actress," in *Cultural Readings of Restoration and Eighteenth Century English Theater*, ed. J. Douglas Canfield and Deborah C. Payne (Athens: University of Georgia Press, 1995).

56. The model for Issachar in Dryden's *Absalom and Achitophel*, Thomas Thynne (1649–1682) lost his life not by his allegiance to the Duke of Monmouth but by his marriage to the fourteen-year-old heiress Elizabeth, Lady Ogle. When she fled the country before the marriage was consummated, he sued for her return and to retain her estates; there is also some evidence of legal action from her side to annul the marriage. An unsuccessful suitor of hers arranged for his murder on 12 February 1682. *The City-Heiress* premiered in April of that year.

57. Danchin, *Restoration*, 1:410.

58. Ibid., 3:111–12.

59. Ibid., 2:92.

60. Ibid., 2:341–42.

61. Ibid., 2:740–41; 2:265; Danchin, *Eighteenth*, 1:19.

62. Eve Kosofsky Sedgwick, *Between Men: English Literature and Male Homosocial Desire*, Gender and Culture (New York: Columbia University Press, 1992), 49.

63. Wycherley, *The Country Wife*.

64. Rene Girard and Yvonne Freccero, *Deceit, Desire, and the Novel; Self and Other in Literary Structure* (Baltimore: Johns Hopkins Press, 1965), 12.

65. Sedgwick, *Between*, 49. Robert A. Erickson has shown that it is also possible to consider Margery Pinchwife a character with more agency than Sedgwick's homosocial triangle permits her. Learning to write letters teaches her "to live independently in a dangerous world" and gives her a sense of personal identity: "I write, therefore I am." Robert A. Erickson, "Lady Fullbank and the Poet's Dream in Behn's Lucky Chance," in *Broken Boundaries: Women and Feminism in Restoration Drama*, ed. Katherine M. Quinsey (Lexington: University Press of Kentucky, 1996), 95–96. Penny Gay makes a related point when discussing Kitty Clive's epilogues: that those epilogues

represent Clive's opportunity "to have the last, indecorous word." See Penny Gay, "'So Persuasive an Eloquence'? Roles for Women on the Eighteenth-Century Stage," in The Public's Open to Us All: Essays on Women and Performance in Eighteenth-Century England, ed. Laura Engel (Newcastle, UK: Cambridge Scholars, 2009), 26.

66. Wycherley, Country Wife, 152.

67. J. L. Styan argues that rather than delicacy or modesty, actresses introduced cynicism, apparent in their characterizations. To me, this quality is particularly apparent in the economy of prologues and epilogues, which employ women's bodies for company profit. See J. L. Styan, Restoration Comedy in Performance (Cambridge: Cambridge University Press, 1986), 49.

68. Peter Holland, The Ornament of Action: Text and Performance in Restoration Comedy (Cambridge: Cambridge University Press, 1979), 182.

69. Richard Ollard, Pepys: A Biography (London: Hodder and Stoughton, 1974), 3.

70. Less well chronicled but also publicly known was Knep's affair with Haines; acting together in the King's Company, the two joined other players going to act in Edinburgh under Thomas Sydserf, and became lovers. Knep died in 1681 while giving birth to Haines's daughter, who also died; and later in "A Rhymeing Supplication to Nell Gwyn," Haines mourns "that delicate Compound of Spiritt & Rump." See Highfill, Burnim, and Langhans, Biographical Dictionary, 9:58; Robert Latham and William Matthews, The Diary of Samuel Pepys, 11 vols., vol. 7 (London: G. Bell and Sons, 1976), "2 January 1666."

71. Wycherley, Country Wife, xvii.

72. Anthony Kaufman, "The Smiler with the Knife: Covert Aggression in Some Restoration Epilogues," Studies in the Literary Imagination 17, no. 1 (1984): 69.

73. Wycherley, Country Wife, 152.

74. Danchin, Restoration, 2:639-40.

75. The Constant Nymph, or, The Rambling Shepherd, a Pastoral (London: Langley Curtis, 1678), 23.

76. Ibid., A2v.

77. Danchin, Restoration, 2:61.

78. Ibid.

79. Ibid.

80. Ibid.

81. Ibid.

82. Gilbert, Marginality, xvii.

PART II

THE IMPACT
OF PARATEXTS

CHAPTER FOUR

~

Vestal Interests:
Anne Bracegirdle's Paratexts

The same actress who punned on death and orgasm in an epilogue was remembered as the "*Diana* of the Stage."[1] To Colley Cibber, Anne Bracegirdle's chaste reputation made her a star: "Never any Woman was in such general Favour of her Spectators, which, to the last Scene of her Dramatic Life, she maintain'd by not being unguarded in her private character. This discretion contributed not a little to make her the *Cara*, the Darling of the Theatre."[2] But onstage, Bracegirdle acted and discussed subjects typical of Restoration theater, such as sex, rape, prostitution, and adultery. Given her proximity to such material, the general taint of theater work, and moralists' attacks on the theater during the heart of her career, how did Bracegirdle establish and maintain her image of virginity?

This chapter offers a case study of how prologues and epilogues helped shape an actress's career. In her nineteen years onstage, Anne Bracegirdle specialized in two types of roles: the tragic victim of sexual violence, and the witty comic heroine who tests her fiancé's fitness for marriage. Her reputation for virginity, sustained despite many allegations to the contrary, gave these roles a credibility that interrupted the apparent clash between the innocence of virginal heroines and the cultural linkage between acting and prostitution. Concurrently, however, she performed several licentious roles wherein her character engaged in extramarital sex yet reassimilated into polite society; similarly, she delivered flirtatious prologues and epilogues that hint at off-stage sexual liaisons. Emphasizing the first half of her career to demonstrate its development, I argue that her sexually experienced characters and bawdy paratexts ironically reinforced Bracegirdle's virginal persona. Whereas what I have been calling "retroactive metalepsis" appeared in many female epilogues where the sexualized actress mocked the naïve heroine—see, for example, my reading of Charlotte Butler's "critiques of love and marriage" epilogue to Behn's *The City-Heiress* in chapter 3—Bracegirdle's paratexts feature a double irony: Since her virgin persona countered the stereotype of the wanton actress, her nonvirginal roles and her sexualized prologues and epilogues accordingly contradicted her virgin persona, creating comic incongruities. Enabled by the virtuous heroine's apparent similitude to the actress, the rakish roles and paratexts ironically reinforced her virginal reputation and carved out an experimental and accommodating theatrical environment. Implicitly poking fun at her virginity, these roles resulted in sexually comic sophistication. Through both virginal and sexually experienced roles, prologues, and epilogues, Anne Bracegirdle sustained a virginal persona.

This chapter balances an empirical approach to Bracegirdle's oeuvre with a study of celebrity formation, itself not necessarily a linear growth. Just as the development of a contemporary celebrity's "It effect"—Joseph Roach's term for stars' "personality-driven mass attraction"—derives from assorted and unsystematically accessed sources, so the development of Bracegirdle's persona emanates from roles, paratexts, other media such as letters and satires, and unrecoverable gossip.[3] But while the development of her persona is roughly chronological, there is no conclusively identifiable causal relationship. Without excluding contradictory evidence, in this chapter I have selected the roles I think most formative to Bracegirdle's persona. While most roles were customized for her, inherited roles also contribute when they were revived frequently, such as her performance of Statira in Nathaniel Lee's *The Rival Queens*.

Recent revisionist histories have called for a questioning of how the stories of Restoration and eighteenth-century actresses have been told—a way that emphasized sexuality over skill—yet I argue that since sexuality is part of performance and since female roles emphasize it, to divide is to distort. Elizabeth Howe first framed this problem within Restoration studies, with her thesis that actresses faced sexual exploitation yet received some acknowledgment as professionals; subsequent texts by such critics as Cynthia Lowenthal, Katherine Eisaman Maus, Kirsten Pullen, Laura Rosenthal, Kristina Straub, Cheryl Wanko, and most recently Gilli Bush-Bailey and Felicity Nussbaum have advanced the call to treat actresses the same way we do actors, studying their craft and their financial success and eschewing undue emphasis on their sexuality, whether that means contextualizing the actress-whore association (Pullen), treating her as more than just a spectacle (Straub), or studying her construction of on- and offstage identities (Bush-Bailey, Nussbaum).[4] Bush-Bailey draws a useful distinction: we need to see an actress's body as the setting for her "craft," without obscuring her body through objectification.[5] While these approaches provide essential information, there is no point in hermetically sealing actresses in a sexless world. As this book demonstrates, sexuality formed the bedrock of actresses' public intimacy. "Sex sells" was as true then as it is now, and theater personnel knew to exploit it. My taxonomy of prologues and epilogues reflects this condition. Cloaked paratexts are impersonal by definition, and while male exposed paratexts can make comedy from additional sources (such as alcohol or donkeys, as chapter 1 demonstrates), this possibility more frequently eluded actresses and to a great extent still eludes female stand-up comedians. In writing about how prologues and epilogues helped fashion Anne Bracegirdle's career, therefore, I emphasize how they promoted her sexuality in a way that ironically buttressed her reputation as virgin. Nussbaum has argued persuasively that Anne Oldfield first transcended the taint of the theater world to mix in genteel society, but Bracegirdle somehow emerged with the credibility of a virgin from that same exploitative theater world.[6] It is the irony of this situation that is fascinating: that Bracegirdle, raised within this world, derived virginity from its sexualized atmosphere.

Credibility of the Virgin Actress: Satires on Bracegirdle

A skilled actress of tragedy and comedy, Anne Bracegirdle enjoyed a lengthy career (1688–1707) and a devoted fan base. Reared by the preeminent theatrical couple Thomas and Mary Saunderson Betterton, Bracegirdle may have debuted at about age eight as the page in Thomas Otway's 1680 tragedy, *The Orphan*; her first confirmed performance was in Thomas D'Urfey's 1685 comedy, *A Commonwealth of Women*, when she was approximately thirteen years old, playing the character of Clita and the epilogue.[7] Joining the United Theatre Company in 1688, Bracegirdle quickly developed a reputation for versatility by playing comic and tragic heroines and delivering witty prologues and epilogues. She inspired and staged all of William Congreve's greatest female roles, and she shared with him a twenty-year friendship that many have speculated was a love affair. D'Urfey, Thomas Southerne, John Vanbrugh, and Nicholas Rowe also wrote many of their most significant female roles for her. She formed a partnership with the great actress Elizabeth Barry: the two played fifty-six roles together in plays such as Southerne's *The Wives Excuse* (1691) and Vanbrugh's *The Provok'd Wife* (1697), where typically the younger, virginal Bracegirdle character questions marriage because Barry's older character has married badly. Among many other career highlights, in 1695 she, Barry, and Thomas Betterton broke away from the United Company and its oppressive manager, and founded their own company at Lincoln's Inn Fields.

Not everybody was convinced of Bracegirdle's virginity, though, and several extant satires asserted the opposite. I suggest, however, that their focus remained persistent because her virginal image was pervasive. That is, the fact that satires on Bracegirdle—those unrelated to her comanagement of Lincoln's Inn Fields—focused on the virginity question throughout her career meant that no one conclusively disproved her status. Lucyle Hook suggests this process when she writes that "it was Mrs. Bracegirdle's unimpeachable private life which gave a new fillip to play-going. First, there was speculation, then incredulity, controversy, and finally admiration and gradual acceptance of the miracle of virtue in an actress."[8]

Satires demonstrate the speculation, incredulity, and controversy surrounding her image, and contrasting the extant satires on other actresses with those on Bracegirdle clarifies a difference: satirists challenge Bracegirdle's virginity but refrain from the accusations of promiscuity they lob at other actresses. As many have argued, satires have often been excerpted and applied to specific actresses in ways that emphasize their sexuality over their professional achievements.[9] And satirists' motivations rarely get discussed; as Bush-Bailey points out, the author of one of the most cited examples, Robert Gould, writes from the perspective of a lifelong playwright rejected by the United Company, whose work remained unperformed but for one production in 1696.[10] As opposed to attacking the promiscuity of other actresses (and, in Gould's case, actors), satires on Bracegirdle focus on the question of her virginity: on the incident, but not the range, of her sexual engagement.

Attacks on other actresses follow one of two patterns: some malign their general promiscuity, while others link them to specific lovers. Gould's "Satyr on the Players" (1685; reprinted 1689, 1709) writes that all actresses try to dupe gullible men into financially supporting them at present and in their wills:

> This is the train that sooths her swift to Vice,
> So she be fine, she cares not at what price;
> Though her lewd Body rot, and her good name
> Be all one blot of Infamy and shame;
> For with good rigging, though they have no skill,
> They'l find out *Keepers*, be they ne'r so ill.[11]

Satires on individual women similarly assert actresses' pollution of their bodies through selling sex. A 1678 lampoon calls Rebecca Marshall a "Proud Curtizan" and suggests that her wayward ways produced a bastard, while Gould's "Satyr on the Players" writes of Charlotte Butler that "mony is the Syren's chiefest Aym," of Susannah Percival (later Verbruggen) that her father "Be Pimp himself, that she may play ye Whore," and of Sarah Cooke that her body is "fuck't & fuck't and as debauch'd as Hell."[12] A satire that goes on to impugn Mrs. Cox and Elizabeth Barry calls Betty Boutell "chestnut-maned Boutell, whom all the Town fucks."[13] Other satires link actresses with specific, sometimes high-profile lovers. The 1683 "Satire on Whigs and Tories" connects Marshall with Sir George Hewitt and claims that Butler gave her lover the clap, which he subsequently passed on to his wife.[14] Both approaches suggest that actresses had a range of lovers and criticize their promiscuity.

Most satires on Bracegirdle assert her lack of virginity, yet they ironically bestow on her an aura of unavailability.[15] One satire mocks Lord Clifford for failing to advance his courtship of her.[16] Tom Brown's "From Worthy Mrs. Behn the Poetess, to the famous Virgin Actress" (1703) exploits Bracegirdle's innocence as an excuse for Behn to instruct her in how to carry on multiple simultaneous love affairs.[17] While the satirist doubts Bracegirdle's virginal reputation, the fact that he questions it only four years before her retirement speaks to its impenetrability. Two satires romantically linking her to costar William Mountfort also suggest that she remains out of reach. Tom Brown's "Elegy on Mounfort [sic]" (1693), written in the wake of Mountfort's murder, is the earliest extant satire involving Bracegirdle and perpetuates the allegation that Mountfort and Bracegirdle were lovers. Yet like many of the other satires, it conveys a sense of male failure to win Bracegirdle; while the couplet "Let not ev'ry vain Spark think that he can ingage / The Heart of a Female, like One on the Stage" sarcastically elevates Bracegirdle's status, it also taunts male audience members about their apparent inadequacy.[18] The anonymous novel *The Players Tragedy* (1693) also describes Bracegirdle as a tough sell; although written to capitalize on the scandalous murder of Mountfort and, by association, his supposed affair with Bracegirdle, the novel otherwise portrays her as unattainable to the admiring narrator, "Montano," who attends her plays and develops a crush.[19] As opposed to "Elegy on Mounfort," this portrayal, far from being sarcastic, drives Montano to great lengths to attain her, and he is ultimately duped by a woman impersonating the actress. Surely the novel, which by its publication record appears to have failed, would have capitalized on more juicy details if any were to be had. Even after his death, Mountfort remained a subject of satire; Brown writes of an imagined encounter between two gentlemen and the actor:

> "Oh, gentlemen," says he, "I am glad to see you; but I am troubled with such a weakness in my back, that it makes me bend like a Superannuated Fornicator." "Some strain," said I, "got in the other world with Overheaving yourself." "What matter how t'was got," said he, "can you tell any thing that's good

for't?" "Yes," said I, "get a good warm Girdle and tie round you, 'tis an excellent Coroboratick to strengthen the loins." "Pox on you," says he, "for a bantering dog, how can a single girdle do me good, when a Brace was my destruction?"[20]

Again, while the satire questions Bracegirdle's reputation for chastity, its main target is her lover.

The many satires insinuating a relationship between Bracegirdle and Congreve also either leave open the possibility that she remains a virgin or suggest that she has tricked him into marrying her, thus making her unavailable to others. Like many of the other satires, they direct their accusations at him rather than her. "Animadversions on Mr. Congreve's Late Answer to Mr. Collier" insinuates Bracegirdle's unchasteness but directs the satire against Congreve: "he need not covet to go to Heaven at all, but to stay and Ogle his Dear Bracilla, with sneaking looks under his Ha[t], in the little side Box."[21] Yet another Tom Brown satire best captures the comic incongruity of Bracegirdle maintaining her virginal reputation, despite proximity to sex. Describing her relationship with Congreve in 1702, he writes:

> he Dines with her almost ev'ry day, yet She's a Maid, he rides out with her, and visits her in Publick and Private, yet She's a Maid; if I had not a particular respect for her, I should go near to say he lies with her, yet She's a Maid. Now I Leave the World to Judge whether it be His or Her fault that She has So long Kept her Maidenhead.[22]

Like the satire mocking Lord Clifford, Brown keeps alive the prospect of her virginity even as he implies that it is a fiction, and Congreve's sexuality is also impugned. A 1707 poem suggests that she and Congreve have married, implying that Congreve acceded to her wishes: "But at length the poor Nymph did for Justice implore, / H'as married her now, tho he'd—her before."[23] Well into Bracegirdle's career, the scale and perpetuation of this vein of satire attest to the continued perception that she is unavailable—due to either virginity or a relationship with Congreve—and accordingly reveal her public's fascination with the actress.

Bracegirdle's Self-Constructed Virginity

For Bracegirdle to become the celebrated virgin actress, she had to both convince the public of her sexual status and mitigate virginity's threatening association with female independence and self-governance. Virginity's implications of bodily inviolability and self-control resonated with Restoration fears of cuckoldry. Its indeterminacy sparked male fears of marrying another man's mistress, prompting early modern scientists to attempt verification. Despite admonition from Andreas Vesalius that the hymen is not the telltale sign of virginity (he famously said that the presence of the hymen is only confirmable at the moment of its destruction), anatomists tried to determine virginity by associating outwardly observable conditions and diseases—such as womb-fury, hysteria, and chlorosis or greensickness—with the virgin body.[24] Portraits of Elizabeth I represented the chastity of the "Virgin Queen" artistically by symbolizing it as a sieve, jewel, or ermine.[25] Bracegirdle asserted hers performatively. Peter Holland argues that the Restoration actor's appropriateness for a role gives to the play an air of "truth," but he restricts this claim to comedy because it better approximates everyday modes of speech.[26] In fact, he specifically argues against this association in tragedy: "This sort of imaginative consideration of the similarity of a comic situation with a possible real event is completely alien to tragedy in the period and hence the tragic style of acting cannot involve this sort of identification."[27] Holland's thesis, however, need not be limited by generic and linguistic verisimilitude. Bracegirdle's performances of virginity derived from and strengthened her own spotless reputation. Her tragic heroines radiated virginity, and their losses became dramatic centerpieces. By modulating performances of virginity according to sociological concerns, Bracegirdle developed a credible persona.

Her face served as synecdoche; its brightness and youth signified the intact hymen. Descriptions of customized characters reference her attributes. A character in *King Edward III* describes her as "A glorious Woman: how her eyes sparkle, and how the bloud juts in and out upon her cheecks, as if it hop'd some good were coming toward her. . . . Her lips are made of Velvet, smooth, soft, and plyable."[28] The same speaker later calls her "my blossome of a Colly-flower, my cherry-colour'd-bean with a black eye."[29] Blushes connote a first flush of love; when saying, in *The Rover*, that she wishes to experience love before she is banished to life as a nun, Hellena suggests that blushes are also a side effect of love.[30] Black eyes have a special association; many Restoration plays and fictional heroines feature black-eyed virginal heroines, even though few of the audience members could verify this trait. And such descriptions are echoed in eyewitness accounts of the actress. Tony Aston describes her as follows:

> She was of a lovely Height, with dark-brown Hair and Eye-brows, black sparkling Eyes, and a fresh blushy Complexion; and, whenever she exerted herself, had an involuntary Flushing in her Breast, Neck and Face, having continually a chearful Aspect, and a fine Set of even white Teeth; never making an exit but that she left the audience in an imitation of her pleasant countenance.[31]

The "involuntary" aspect of Bracegirdle's blushes connotes a sincerity of emotional expression that appears to verify the sexual innocence Aston refers to when he compares her to the Roman goddess of chastity.[32]

Raped Heroines: The Virtuous Nonvirgins

As the pivotal actress in the development of she-tragedy, Bracegirdle effected a new dramatic treatment of rape, where the raped characters are divested of blame. It was the actress herself, and her virginal celebrity, that drove this subgenre. Female characters in Restoration dramas who have even nonconsensual sex are normally held accountable, often by their own internalized mores. The blame, Jean Marsden says, extends to a character that resists rape or enjoys sex under false pretenses (such as with a man impersonating her husband, as Monimia does in Otway's *The Orphan*).[33] Since the actresses who played raped characters prior to Bracegirdle—Elizabeth Barry, Mary Saunderson Betterton, Elizabeth Boutell, Mary Lee, and Rebecca Marshall—practiced marital or extramarital sex, their performances did not signify a lasting metatheatrical sense of injustice and violation.[34]

Whereas earlier in the Restoration, rape had been but one element of a play, in Bracegirdle's she-tragedies, rape was now the central feature and emphasized the significance of the crime through ennobling the victim. The attacks on Bracegirdle's characters showcase absolute male force and female passivity, and therefore cast blame only on the perpetrator. Antecedents to Richardson's *Clarissa*, William Mountfort's *The Injur'd Lovers* (February 1688) and Elkanah Settle's *The Distres'd Innocence* (October 1690) feature Bracegirdle's characters being drugged beforehand, so that consent or resistance is impossible. Similarly, her heroines in Powell's *Alphonso King of Naples* and Nicholas Brady's *The Rape* (February 1692) appear tied to a tree, the former by her hair. After the attack they appear physically and emotionally disheveled, confirming that the sexual encounter was not of their doing.[35] The result, as Cynthia Lowenthal points out, is "an explosive, if short-lived, discursive subjectivity for the victim, trauma that leads her to exteriorize her pain and attempt to perform her wounded interiority."[36] The later heroines also emphasize the value of their virginity when they desire revenge upon rather than marriage to the rapist—the latter being the English judiciate's usual compensation for proven rapes. Raped characters are often offered recompense, such as class elevation or immortality. These plays are hardly protofeminist—the raped woman must die—but in contrast with the extremely low conviction rate of rapists in Restoration society, every onstage villain is punished.[37] Bracegirdle's characters' rapes therefore divide the Restoration synonyms "virginity" and "virtue"; they have lost the former but retain the latter.[38]

There has been some dispute over what inspired the production of so many rape plays during the Restoration, but one overlooked factor is the cultural intervention, by later-Restoration plays, into the treatment of rapists—work best accomplished by an apparently virgin actress. Whereas Elizabeth Howe and Jean Marsden have argued that the rise of rape plays was a direct result of the rise of the actress, Derek Hughes has countered that rape was a trope responsive to early Restoration cultural issues of sex and power, and the late Restoration periods of frenetic political activity.[39] Hughes distinguishes rape and attempted rape plays from those containing unfortunate but unforced sexual activity, such as *The Orphan*, where Monimia willingly engages in sex, although under false pretenses.[40] In the process, however, he argues against both the association of rape plays with star actresses and the increased prominence that later Restoration plays allot to rape. In the earlier years, Mary Betterton played many of the rape roles, such as Lucrece in *Lucius Junius Brutus* and Florinda in *The Rover*, but these were secondary.[41] The two major rape roles during this period come from Renaissance plays adapted in the Restoration: Ravenscroft's adaptation of Shakespeare's *Titus Andronicus* and Rochester's adaptation of Fletcher's *Valentinian*. Marsden documents the rise of she-tragedy, with rape normally its centerpiece, as occurring in the late 1680s, coinciding with the birth of Bracegirdle's career.[42] Hughes inexplicably neglects the eight rape plays he names as occurring between 1688 and 1695 but calls the nine rape plays that premiered between 1696 and 1700 "an explosion."[43] In fact, he overlooks four additional plays featuring rape or attempted rape from those earlier years: Shadwell's *The Amorous Bigotte* (1690), Dryden's *King Arthur* (1691), Motteux's *The Rape of Europa*, and D'Urfey's *Don Quixote Part II* (both 1694). Just as the incidence of prologues and epilogues more than doubled once the actress arrived on the public stage, so the number of she-tragedies and the amount of space they devote to rape owes something to the genre's star.

While Hughes and James Peck cite many examples of late Restoration stagings of rape as political analogues, what needs to be considered is how staged rape responds to cultural and juridical responses to rape as a crime. Peck argues convincingly that several plays dramatize a Whiggish ideology of rape as property crime and Tory tyranny, and he concurs with Marsden that the rape portrayals eroticize the victim rather than authentically represent her suffering.[44] Coexistent with the political narrative, however, is a link to a real crime. That is, the rapes and rape attempts that Bracegirdle dramatized correspond to many of the qualifications for rapes to be prosecuted in English society. These qualities include the credibility of the virgin character-actress, the distinction between calling the event rape rather than ravishment, and the steps taken to show that the heroine could not resist the attack. Garthine Walker, discussing in *Crime, Gender and Social Order in Early Modern England* the low prosecution and even lower conviction rate of rapists, cites techniques women used to build evidence against the men they accused of rape. The primary goal was to distinguish rape from consensual sex. Women did this by claiming to have been drugged or unconscious, or by construing rape as a property crime; so do Bracegirdle's heroines. In addition, the fact that no dramatic rape victim survives means that she would never reveal the pregnancy that would confirm her complicity; since conception was thought to take place only if both man and woman orgasmed, pregnancy would give the lie to claims of violence.[45] Finally, the fact that every one of Bracegirdle's rapists is punished must have been a satisfying conclusion for female and male audiences who themselves directly or proximately suffered due to rape.

This last point marks one of the two biggest differences between earlier staged rapes and those in Bracegirdle's plays: with few exceptions, the later plays showcase rather than marginalize rape, and they punish the aggressor. Before Bracegirdle came to the stage, there were three plays with rape as their main event, two of which are adaptations of Renaissance plays. The third, *The Orphan*, construes its rape as instead a tragic case of mistaken identity, thus making it hard to recognize as rape to Restoration and some modern-day audiences.[46] During her first eleven years on the stage, in contrast, Bracegirdle acted in triple this number of plays that feature attempted or achieved rape as their central action.[47]

As virginity came to define her persona, so its loss took center stage in she-tragedies. Bracegirdle's first major character, Antelina in *The Injur'd Lovers*, ranks virginity above royalty. Antelina and her lover, Rheusanes (played by William Mountfort), are each desired by, respectively, the king and his daughter, Oryala (Barry). The royals trick the lovers; first, they pretend to arrange the wedding of Antelina and Rheusanes, but through masquerade, engineer marriage and consummation between Rheusanes and Oryala. The audience then learns that between the acts, the king has raped Antelina. Act 4 opens with Antelina cursing the king, who admits that he used duplicitous tactics to rape her, a scene that confirms her nonconsent. She emphasizes the significance of virginity when mourning for herself as "a wandring Virgin" and "a Ravish'd Virgin in a stranger World."[48] These appellations reposition her as the play's most consequential character, shifting the focus entirely to grief and revenge. The king subsequently offers to elevate Antelina to queen; when she refuses, the king's sister rhetorically asks him what possible reparations he could make for the loss of her virtue, thereby valuing virginity above the prospect of royalty. (This stands in striking opposition to actual rape aftermaths, where the desired outcome was for the rapist to marry the victim.[49] As such, some audiences may have found Antelina's refusal of the king's offer risible.) Finally, the king begs Antelina to take pity on him, but she wants justice; she poisons them both, and as he dies, he still apologizes.

The implication that a royal rapist is tormented and dies because of his crime suggests that rape has supreme consequences and creates an over-criminalization of rape in the play compared to contemporaneous cultural views. Here is a challenge to cultural discourse about rape victims and their compensation. The rape victim has to have been a virtuous virgin, but nevertheless a shift is happening, and it can happen via Bracegirdle because of her reputation. At the same time, these moments may create interesting effects for women in the audience. Borrowing from Mulvey, Marsden cites the female spectator's dilemma: to side with the victim is masochistic, but to side with the rapist creates a "masquerade," which is also masochistic.[50] But there are also the pleasures of imagining a rape and of seeing a rapist punished.[51] And the histrionics of this final scene affirm Antelina as agent; she executes her own and her lover's deaths. By the end, therefore, she has gained a god-like agency, and she dies a virtuous nonvirgin.

The linguistic representations of virginity in George Powell's *Alphonso King of Naples* (1691) are even more prevalent. The warring lovers are Cesario (Mountfort), whom Urania loves, and Ferdinand, to whom she has been contracted. Fearing that his rival will return from war a military hero, Ferdinand arranges for the king to shun Cesario's homecoming and deny his marital hopes. Cesario and Urania escape to the woods, but when Cesario is drawn into a brawl, two bandits tie Urania to a tree by her hair and attempt to rape her. After Cesario intervenes and Urania reassures him that "I am yet spotless," he describes her character as inherently virtuous:

> I believe thee,
> For thou'rt all Truth, the Innocence on that Face
> Says thou art chaste, the guilty cannot speak
> So heavenly as thou dost.[52]

These lines represent Bracegirdle's face and voice as proof of virginity. Whereas the theme of deceptive appearances permeates many Restoration plays, her face undoes this logic, suggesting that her virginity is outwardly affirmable. Although the attack itself is minor, Urania's reaffirmations of her virginity reverberate throughout the text. At the end, Powell describes her suicide as self-rape: she has stabbed herself and enters "bleeding, her hair hanging loose, led by two Women." In an example of what Christopher J. Wheatley identifies as Restoration tragedy's combination of sex and death through "morbid wit," she has burst her synecdochic virginity, ruining the white purity of her face.[53] Witnessing Ferdinand and Cesario mortally wound each other in a duel over her, Urania again feels compelled to confirm her maidenhood; first she tells Cesario:

> in that
> Cold Bridal Bed, I shall not be deny'd
> To lie a sleeping Virgin by thy side

and then informs the crowd, "Free from Loves grosser and impurer Charms, / I die a Virgin in my Husband's Arms."[54] This couplet creates the paradox of the "virgin wife" and demonstrates that, like the "virgin actress," she can exist. The audience, therefore, witnesses Urania/Bracegirdle affirm her virginity and then, by extension, destroy it.

Even in plays where they were sexually experienced at the start, Bracegirdle's characters are recast as virgins, adding credence to the actress's own public persona. In Elkanah Settle's play, *The Distres'd Innocence*, Bracegirdle's character, Cleomira, has a ten-month-old son. Her husband, Hormidas (Mountfort), returns home a war hero, but the evil Otrantes, angry because Hormidas publicly shamed him for cheating soldiers out of their pay, sets a Christian temple on fire and lays the blame on Hormidas. To punish the supposed culprit, the king and his daughter, Orundana (Barry), give his son to barbarians and Cleomira to Otrantes, who drugs and rapes her. The removal of her baby allows her to be seen in a different light because evidence of her past sexuality is no longer present, and the use of a drug renders her blameless for the rape. Afterward, images of lost virginity surround her. Her husband elevates her by calling her "thou bleeding *Lucrece*," "Oh mourning Philomel," and "a Bleeding Martyr."[55] The rape symbolism continues when another man wants to rape her but stabs her instead. As she dies, Cleomira speaks quasi-religiously of going to her "new Bridal."[56] Paganism's challenge to Christianity, an allegory for religious war, is embodied in the suffering heroine.[57] By removing signs of her marital state, drugging her, alluding to rapes of other virgins, and suggesting that she is still fit to marry, *The Distres'd Innocence* thus remakes Cleomira as a virgin so that her rape is more consequential, a plot move that bolsters Bracegirdle's persona.

Although her character in the wildly successful 1690 revival of Nathaniel Lee's *The Rival Queens* does not experience rape, Bracegirdle demonstrates and personalizes the power of virginity. The 1677 creation of the virgin heroine, Statira, won Elizabeth Boutell praise, but during the twenty-plus revivals, Bracegirdle made the role more plausible. In an unusual form of infidelity, the intended second wife of Alexander the Great, Statira, must endure his philandering with his first wife, Roxalana, after he promised to refrain. Discovering his unfaithfulness, Statira first resolves to never see him again, then tempers this vow into never again engaging in sexual behavior with Alexander. In maintaining this resolve, she possesses the ability of the virgin to order her world, which in this case nullifies the king's rule. Here, virginity has the potential to threaten men by insinuating a chosen world without them. While the play itself was travestied, Bracegirdle's performance remained admired. Colley Cibber, author of one such burlesque, nevertheless commented, "If any thing could excuse that desperate Extravagance of Love, that almost frantick Passion of *Lee's Alexander the Great*, it must have been when Mrs. *Bracegirdle* was his *Statira*."[58] The parallels between Bracegirdle's heroine and her public persona seem especially strong when, in the play, Mountfort's Alexander exclaims that she is "*Diana's* Soul, cast in the flesh of *Venus!*"[59]

Rape Roles with Prologues or Epilogues

The process of retroactive metalepsis, where the epilogue speaker comments, often satirically, on the play, may appear especially jarring when that play contains a rape. If a female character has been raped in the play, meaning that she has died as a direct or indirect result, what material is left to comically critique? In *The Rape, The Amorous Bigotte, King Arthur,* and *The Ambitious Step-Mother*, Bracegirdle's character suffers a rape or rape attempt, then returns in the epilogue to comment on it or offer a counter-characterization.[60] This creates an unusual process whereby she presents a sympathetic character in line with her growing stack of credible virginal heroines, and then steps out of that series through commentary. In the epilogue to *The Rape*, Bracegirdle performs as if oblivious to her character's rape and death. In the other three plays, she ironically reinforces her virginal persona through the sexually suggestive epilogue.

In the play that Marsden calls the period's "archetypical representation" of the crime, Brady's *The Rape* (1692) depicts the simultaneous valuation and exploitation of its heroine. Like many others, the play features the rape taking place between acts 2 and 3, with much buildup beforehand and an attenuated denouement during the remaining three acts. In the play, the king's advisor, Genselaric, desires the former king's daughter, Eurione

(Bracegirdle), and rapes her to prevent her marriage to the king's "son" (who later turns out to be a woman). Anticipating the rape, he fantasizes about how he will "rifle all the Treasures of her Beauty":

> Methinks I see already
> Her dying Looks, her seeming faint Resistance,
> And feel the mighty Transports of hot Love![61]

These lines show that Genselaric does not distinguish between rape and consensual sex, markedly contrasting with the violent aftermath. After the rape takes place, other characters emphasize its brutality and affirm Eurione's innocence. In a stage direction that belies Genselaric's fantasy of "seeming faint resistance," following the rape she is found "gagg'd and bound to a Tree, her hair dishevel'd as newly Ravish'd, a Dagger lying by her."[62] One of his cohorts protests the violence: "methinks 'tis strange / That Pleasure forc'd shou'd give such vast delight." Genselaric responds imperviously: "she strugled so / I could not get the Gag into her Mouth / So soon as I design'd it."[63] The scene juxtaposes the sexualized spectacle of Eurione/Bracegirdle with the barbarity of her rapist, thereby removing any reasons for blaming her (such as her resistance), and implying that for the actress, as for the character, no less than rape would part her from her virginity. The rape prompts a manhunt sanctioned by the king, a full confession, followed by the murder of Genselaric, and finally Eurione stabbing herself from shame. Jacqueline Pearson points out that the raped woman is sexually contradictory: she is "innocent but 'polluted.'"[64] The action reinforces this contradiction—Eurione still must kill herself, despite the gravity with which others treat the crime.

In a different but certainly not whorish mode, Bracegirdle then delivers a cloaked, political epilogue. Written by Shadwell, the epilogue features Bracegirdle taunting the beaux who are present at the theater and not away at war. In one sense, this impersonal epilogue reflects the difficulty of the cloaked category; given how Bracegirdle's reputation had grown, most of the audience would have recognized her despite her lack of self-reference, and perhaps interpreted the epilogue's impersonal lines as somehow reflecting a personal attribute of the speaker. On the other hand, it speaks to Bracegirdle's stature, even at that early point in her career, that she could deliver a cloaked epilogue criticizing, by name, three prominent courtiers for refusing to serve in the Nine Years' War.[65]

Despite the fact that rape was used for laughs in Restoration comedies, her appearance as victim in two such roles nevertheless continued to build her virginal reputation. Shadwell's comedy, *The Amorous Bigotte* (1690), reflects the trend throughout Restoration drama of featuring rape in comedies. In this play, attempted rape is given slapstick treatment. Bracegirdle plays a minor role, the Spanish Rosania, who twice has to fend off the Irish friar Tegue O'Divelly, played by comedian Anthony Leigh. Friar Tegue is the latest in a long line of "foolish old men" characters that includes Sir Feeble Fainwou'd in Behn's *The Luckey Chance*. Scenes between the veteran Leigh and the approximately eighteen-year-old Bracegirdle are thus prime for risibility; add Friar Tegue's thick brogue and the result could have been uproarious. (Lucyle Hook suspects that Bracegirdle's success as Rosania may have led to her taking over of the role of Hellena in *The Rover*.[66]) Nevertheless, the overt sexualization of Bracegirdle, combined with her bawdy epilogue, furthered the development of her persona.

In the first of two attempted rape scenes, Friar Tegue sexualizes Rosania by having her recount sexual dreams during Confession, then forces himself on her. His additions to her narrative build the comic tension until he takes the part of her imaginary lover:

Rosania: I dreamt last night that a fine young Gentleman came and took me by the hand.

Tegue: Very vell, and I warrant dee he did shtroake dy Ame to dy Elbow, dush dush.

Ros. Yes indeed I dreamt so.

Teg. And he did squeesh dy shweet hand, and kish it hard dush? dush, dush Joy.

Ros. Hold, hold, Father, what d' ye mean?

Teg. I do only maake demonstraation phaat dis young man did unto deetrot, By my shoul she has maude great inflamaation upon me, and if she vil not agree and beat under me, I vill maake a raape upon her Body. [*Aside.*] But predee spaake didst dou not dream shomphat further?

Ros. Yes, Heaven forgive me, I did dream that he took me hard about the waste, and did kiss me.

Teg. Vell gra, an dou vert not angry vid him Joy?

Ros. No, no, I was too well pleas'd Heaven help me.

Teg. Phaat he did taake de about middle and did kish de, dush, dush, dush, dush, dush.

Ros. Hold, hold, hold.

Teg. Peash de kish of de Priesht vil absolve de prophaane kish of de Lay Maan, vell and he did trow dee downe upon de plaash, I vill show de how.

Ros. No, no, I dreamt not so far.

Teg. He did, dou dousht not spaak right, and I vil show de how by my Shoul; I vill maake a Raape upon her.

[He lays hold on her.

Ros. Help, help, help, help, ah, ah.[67]

Here Tegue, a ridiculous audience surrogate, potentially induces laughter while advancing the sexualization of Bracegirdle. Rosania resists this—Tegue has coaxed her into revealing her dream, and he, not she, delights in the details. He talks through his stroking of her arms, squeezing of her hands, and the like, so the audience recognizes her as a desirable being but does not implicate her in the sexual activity. The Catholic friar instead becomes the object of sexual decadence and impurity, taking the taint away from the young girl. In the name of exorcising a demon from her body, Tegue tries again in act 4, using her resistance as proof that the demon exists. The articulated fondling of Rosania combines with her resistance to maintain simultaneous sexualization and innocence.

In the epilogue, Bracegirdle creates betweenness by maintaining her Spanish character yet praising English customs. The "tendentious" and "solidarity" epilogue turns on the theme, increasingly popular in the 1690s, of the treatment of women in England versus in Spain. Speaking as Rosania still, she claims that the Spanish custom of women remaining locked up at home can have sexual advantages: lovers will not grow tired of their faces, and since they are only rarely released from home, they never defer pleasure. But while Spanish women are wiser as a result, their English counterparts are happier because they can run off with a gallant and not have to fear for their lives; their kinsmen will just "hunt on and drink."[68] Bracegirdle thus recalls the violence her character nearly suffered in the play and combines it with the pose of offering advice to women on how to cheat, a pose made comic when contrasted with her persona. The epilogue establishes her as an English Protestant woman, reinforcing the treatment of the Catholic friar as ridiculous, yet also satirizing her own countrymen for not paying enough attention to their women and teasing them with the prospect of cuckolding. That she has a virginal reputation adds to the comedy, since she gives advice that she will never follow.

In plays where her character withstands a serious rape attempt, the language also intimates the supreme value of virginity and complements the actress's persona. In Dryden's semi-opera, *King Arthur*, Bracegirdle plays the role of Emmeline, the young blind daughter of Arthur's military second-in-command. The play contains lines about Emmeline that exploit the actress's physique while affirming the character's innocence. When learning about the function of sight, Emmeline paradoxically invites audience voyeurism while dissuading Betterton's King Arthur from such a reaction:

> If you can see so far, and yet not touch,
> I fear you see my Naked Legs and Feet
> Quite through my Cloaths; pray do not see so well.[69]

King Arthur reassures her that his gaze aims higher:

> Fear not, sweet Innocence;
> I view the lovely Features of your Face;
> Your Lips Carnation, your dark shaded Eye-brows,
> Black Eyes, And Snow-white Forehead; all the Colours
> That make your Beauty, and produce my Love.[70]

In these two passages, Dryden provides a seductive view that invites the audience to search for her nudity, yet counters it with a chaste, above-the-neck description of the heroine. The play also considers her virginity just as important as the security of the future kingdom.[71] Because the enemy, Oswald, holds her prisoner for most of the play, her goodness and virginity shine by comparison. These passages resemble a dramatic version of amatory fiction, the term Rosalind Ballaster defines as the narrative dehistoricization of political events into romances that empower the heroine.[72] When Oswald takes Emmeline prisoner, he promises Arthur not to rape her, but the mere mention of rape provokes the king's consternation. When a second evil character makes for her a prison within Oswald's prison, we think the rape is about to happen. Emmeline ultimately owes her safety to Arthur's war victory, and her regained vision to a magical potion the male spirit, Philidel, pours into her eyes at the king's instigation. This scene depicts a more innocent way for a man to treat a woman's body: By administering magic into the openings, Philidel gives to rather than takes from her. The actions of three men, themselves representing companies at war, make Emmeline's virginity and the prospect of rape consequential.

The moment where Philidel pours the potion into her eyes is also the first of many where a maneuver with sexual overtones reverses course and testifies to Bracegirdle's virginity. Here we have a man putting a liquid with special properties into a woman's open orifice, with results that alter her body—but within the play context, and reinforced by Bracegirdle's persona, it reads as a generous and innocent gesture, a kind of virtuous violation. Granted, Philidel is a cross-dressed role and was played by Charlotte Butler. But he merely carries out Merlin's orders; Merlin produces the potion and Arthur, disappointed that he cannot dispense it himself, orders it administered immediately. All three male characters thus transgress the bounds of her body, and yet the move only confirms Emmeline's and by extension Bracegirdle's virginity. An offstage example, where the presence of Bracegirdle also overrides sexual overtones, comes from an anecdote recorded by Aston:

> Her virtue had its reward, both in applause and specie; for it happen'd, that as the Dukes of Dorset and Devonshire, Lord Hallifax, and other Nobles, over a bottle, were all extolling Mrs. Bracegirdle's virtuous behavior, "Come," says Lord Hallifax—"you all commend her virtue, &c. but why do we not present this incomparable woman with something worthy her acceptance?"—his Lordship deposited 200 guineas, which the rest made up 800, and sent to her, with encomiums on her virtue.[73]

Aston describes an unconventional version of virtue rewarded, in which a group of men discuss an "incomparable woman" over drinks and give her a sizeable sum not to buy sexual favors but to celebrate her virtue. Driven by onstage scenes where normally sexual maneuvers demand virtuous rereadings, Bracegirdle ekes out a virgin image that anecdotes like Aston's confirm.

While the exposed, sexually self-referential epilogue Bracegirdle delivers at the end of King Arthur does not exhibit betweenness—Bracegirdle's persona appears, abandoning Emmeline—it personalizes the role of virginity. Knapp has called this quick shift from character to actor an "inarticulate metamorphosis." The premise of the epilogue, that Bracegirdle will select her favorite among the many men courting her, inaugurates what became a popular epilogue conceit, where the actress possesses sexual agency. (We next see this conceit in Miss Allison's virgin epilogue to John Dennis's 1697 comedy, A Plot and No Plot, after which it becomes a mainstay of the eighteenth century.) The props, "a Dozen Billet-Doux," convey Bracegirdle's control over her sexuality; she threatens to expose the identities of the writers, among them courtiers or lawyers, and says she will desist only if they stop writing. In one sense, she facetiously inverts Emmeline's first meeting with King Arthur, since Bracegirdle possesses the power to reveal her lovers' secrets. Ultimately, she manipulates the audience into expressing appreciation of the play, saying "he that likes the Musick and the Play / Shall be my Favourite Gallant to Day." [74] Political and cultural resonances abound;

the would-be lovers suggest meetings with Bracegirdle at specific locations around London.[75] But regarding the development of her virgin image, this epilogue establishes a key device: it places Bracegirdle in charge and portrays her rejecting every lover, actively reinforcing her virginity. Several surviving anecdotes seem like permutations on this theme; Horace Walpole perpetuated the story that Lord Burlington "sent her a present of some fine old china. She told the servant he had made a mistake; that it was true the letter was for her, but the china for his lady, to whom he must carry it. Lord! the Countess was so full of gratitude when her husband came home to dinner!"[76] The enduring persona of Bracegirdle resisting and rerouting lovers owes its birth to the epilogue to *King Arthur*.

As late as 1701, Bracegirdle created roles where her character's blameless rape takes center stage. Ostensibly, Nicholas Rowe's tragedy *The Ambitious Step-Mother* focuses on its titular character, but as the play progresses, the rape of Bracegirdle's virginal character, Amestris, grows in importance. The play concerns two half-brothers' war over their dying father's throne: Artaxerxes, the estranged elder son, challenges Artaban, son by the eponymous stepmother. Artaxerxes and Amestris have yet to consummate their recent marriage when the queen's henchman, Mirza, takes captive the couple and Amestris's father, Memnon. But at this halfway point, Mirza falls for his pretty prisoner, and in three asides describes her beauty and his lust, until the fourth aside, when he rationalizes raping her as a means of restoring his youth. After Amestris is taken from her husband and father, Artaxerxes imagines sex with her, while Memnon raises the specter of her rape. Mirza and Amestris then engage in a violent scene, lasting over nine pages, where Mirza describes her sexual assets and attempts to rape her until she stabs him and he reciprocates. Artaxerxes and Memnon discover her as she dies, awash in symbolic blood and mourning, "Are these the Joys of Brides?" prompting Artaxerxes to commit suicide.[77] The prospect of rape thus dominates the second half of the play and results in three deaths.

Throughout the lengthy attempted rape scene, words and deeds reinforce Amestris's virtue. She is a "married virgin"—she and Artaxerxes have not had a chance to consummate their marriage—and therefore she speaks of her virginity as augmenting the crime Mirza would commit if he rapes her, while his language reflects the fact that this would clearly be a rape, not consensual sex. In a plotting aside, he says, "Force is a sure resort," and calls her his "prey," while she calls herself "Chaste Diana" and begs him to "spare my virgin honour."[78] And the ending may be the most satisfying of all within this genre, as Amestris gets to play a rapist of a sort when she stabs Mirza. The play thus follows in the tradition of establishing the virginity and virtue of

Bracegirdle's character through words and deeds, and then portraying others exacting revenge on the rapist.

The tendentious epilogue echoes the tropes that by 1701 had publicly established Bracegirdle as virgin. It is not a revived epilogue, as Bracegirdle critiques her character rather than reanimating her. Immediately evoking the death-orgasm pun, Bracegirdle poses as being disgusted with her role and claims the play drove Amestris to her death. The epilogue then turns on the "King Arthur" conceit, as she seeks the most enthusiastic male patron to be her "Monarch" and her "Phoenix."[79] Further mocking the audience, she says she cannot find such a lover because men have defected to the other playhouse and its inferior offerings: "Must Shakespeare, Fletcher, and laborious Ben / Be left for Scaramouch and Harlequin?"[80] Both the play, with its stress on her character's virginity, and the epilogue, where Bracegirdle asserts sexual agency, thus further the development of her celebrity persona.

Nonvirgin Roles

Her virgin persona enabled Bracegirdle to perform sexually experienced characters without their qualities adhering to her reputation. Like her virgins, these characters are redeemed: they are either restored to the upper echelons of society or removed from it for noble, shame-free reasons. Critics have often reported the "shock value" of Bracegirdle performing parts unaligned with her persona; what requires further examination, however, is the accommodation of her rakes.[81] Despite their overt affairs, these characters are not reviled within the play, and at least two of them enable their plays' success. Of the five appearances of this character type in Bracegirdle's early career, two comedies, Thomas Shadwell's The Squire of Alsatia (1688) and D'Urfey's The Marriage-Hater Match'd (1692), and one tragedy, John Bancroft's Henry II, with the Death of Rosamond (1692), feature characters who are seduced but not condemned. The comic characters turn out much better off than earlier seduced figures in comedies, such as Bellinda in Etherege's The Man of Mode (1676), who ends up friendless and alone. And Rosamond is more consequential and treated more respectfully than previous seduced characters in tragedies, such as Eugenia in Henry Neville Payne's The Fatal Jealousy (1672), who suffers rape in addition to seduction. These roles fit Derek Hughes's observation that "[o]n the few occasions on which the stereotypically virtuous Anne Bracegirdle is cast in an unchaste role, the casting helps to defamiliarize and reassess the character of the transgressor."[82] The fourth play, Southerne's comedy The Maid's Last Prayer (1693), showcases blatant rakishness, because Bracegirdle's character directs her own sexuality.

A few years later, in D'Urfey's *The Intrigues at Versailles* (1697), her adulterous character emerges more advantageously than the other philanderers in the play. As early as the first few years of her career, the virgin actress expanded the theatrical sphere to admit these sexual yet redeemable figures.

In Shadwell's extremely popular play, *The Squire of Alsatia*, seduction does not necessitate abandonment. Bracegirdle plays Lucia, an attorney's daughter who is seduced by Belfond Junior (Mountfort). Belfond Junior also behaves cruelly to a former mistress, and when he meets his future wife, his promise to reform is as unconvincing as any of Aphra Behn's rovers. Experience with the genre leads us to anticipate Belfond Junior abandoning Lucia, and the play seems headed in that direction when he makes empty promises to visit her often. Although he does not repair Lucia's broken heart, by lying about her sexual status Belfond Junior does enable her social reassimilation. At the end of the play, he declares publicly that she is a virgin, which (in a fictional precursor to the Aston story about the gentlemen taking up a collection to honor her virtue) prompts his astonishingly kind-hearted uncle to pay her £1500 as reparation for her formerly debased reputation. With good name intact and coffers full, she may then reenter the marriage market. Biographer Lucyle Hook calls the play "revolutionary" in its sympathy for Bracegirdle's "seduced but innocent" character and locates in it early elements of sentimental comedy.[83] Bracegirdle's first role in a successful play thus helps establish a new character type: that of a woman who engages in sex yet remains socially acceptable.

D'Urfey's popular comedy, *The Marriage-Hater Match'd*, similarly engineers a place for the seduced female that is not just compensatory but actually desirable.[84] When the play begins, we learn that Sir Philip, the marriage-hater (Mountfort), has seduced Bracegirdle's character, Phoebe. To attain his lawful inheritance from his friend's widow, Lady Subtle, Sir Philip has the lovelorn Phoebe masquerade as a young man, Lovewell. Instead of social banishment, then, the seduced woman enjoys male agency, and the actress thus becomes a more prominent spectacle. The play then revolves around the love triangle of Sir Philip, Lady Subtle, and Phoebe/Lovewell; at various points, all three possible pairs exchange kisses. At the end, Phoebe wins both the jewels and the man: in a combination of trickery and good fortune, she joins Sir Philip in a wedding that he thinks is a sham, but is in fact legitimate. While Shadwell's Lucia successfully remarketed herself, Phoebe/Lovewell does even better by marrying the man she loves (putting Sir Philip in the embarrassing position of having married his mistress) *and* gaining a fortune. Her character thus avoids stigma, moves freely in society, and ascends to the most desirable social position.

The breeches prologue by Mountfort and Bracegirdle anticipates this surprising rehabilitation of the fallen woman and maintains the façade begun in *King Arthur* of Bracegirdle simultaneously pointing out and disavowing her exposed body. As Emmeline, she identified her body while bidding Arthur withhold his sight, and in the epilogue she established her sexual desirability while purporting to send men along their merry way. In this prologue, Mountfort's bid for the breeches-clad Bracegirdle to come onstage and deliver the prologue attests to her popularity as a paratextual performer:

> Nay madam, there's no turning back alone;
> Now you are Enter'd, faith you must go on;
> And speak the *Prologue*, you for those are Fam'd,
> And th'Play's beginning.[85]

Calling her breeches costume "Nauseous," Bracegirdle then conveys her reluctance to speak: "Spite of myself, I must appear a Man; / Pray let me beg ye not to like me less / Than when you see me in my Maiden Dress."[86] Bracegirdle is thus able to maintain her virginal persona in serious and comic plays, virginal and seduced roles, prologues and epilogues; her betweenness melds genres, builds credence, and fosters public intimacy.

Even John Bancroft's tragedy, *Henry II, King of England with the Death of Rosamond*, reveals a more sympathetic way of viewing the seduced heroine. The premise resembles that of *The Rival Queens*: alienated from his queen, the king becomes infatuated with the virginal Rosamond (Bracegirdle) and seduces her. Naturally, the queen views Rosamond as a threat and tries to kill her in an attempt to win back the king. But her plan backfires; Rosamond's death necessitates the queen's banishment from England. If Rosamond were played by another actress, her death might reflect condemnation for female sexuality because she is seduced rather than raped, but here she dies nobly and is duly mourned. Unlike the figure of the sympathetic whore, Rosamond is not punished for acting on her sexuality; rather, the queen recognizes her as better suited to the king and tries to kill her out of jealousy. Defined initially by their lost virginity, Lucia, Phoebe, and Rosamond represent the rejection of the extreme binary of virgin and whore, carving out new characters in the theatrical sphere.

The revived epilogue to *Henry II* converts the death of Rosamond into a comedy that corresponds with Bracegirdle's public persona. In act 5, to avoid being stabbed by the queen, Rosamond drinks poison. The epilogue's last couplet, however, reinterprets poison in a comically sexual way and as a supposed threat to Bracegirdle's public persona. In this couplet, the actress maintains poison's deadly connotation but treats it as the death of Anne

Bracegirdle, Virgin. When she concludes, "But I was drench'd to day for lov-ing well, / And fear the Poyson that would make me swell," she reinvents the poison as sperm that would invalidate her public image through pregnancy.[87] In this case, however, poisoning of either kind ironically reinforces her care-fully crafted virginal persona.

Perhaps the character most out of alignment with Bracegirdle's public im-age is Lady Trickitt in Southerne's *The Maid's Last Prayer*. She and Elizabeth Barry's Lady Malepert are married yet prostitute themselves. Lady Malepert defeats herself; she thinks she has sex with "Sir Ruff," but the man she loves has actually masqueraded as this blunderbuss and he now hates her for pros-tituting herself. The play ends, therefore, with her downfall. Lady Trickitt, on the other hand, has sex with two lovers yet laughingly jilts both of them. Her statement, "I'll light upon a Man that has sense enough to value his own pleasure, without invading mine," indicates her steely agency throughout the play.[88] The distance between Bracegirdle's persona and her character is wide; as Peter Holland notes, this discrepancy flags the play as social satire.[89] Al-though it seems not to have succeeded—Robert Hume says the play's "hard comedy" was too much for the times—*The Maid's Last Prayer* increased the range of Bracegirdle's comedy and its social accommodation.[90] Its epilogue furthers the comic incongruity between Bracegirdle's character and persona. Using her character's frustration with her husband, in this female solidarity epilogue Bracegirdle advises her female audience not to hold out for their dream man, because "there's no urging / These Sparks, to take an Antiquated Virgin."[91] The comedy comes from her ironically not promoting virginity. Her conclusion, "every Woman's Business is a Man," continues the comic betweenness of her depraved character and virginal persona, since she herself is so clearly an exception to such mixed messages.

Like Lady Trickitt, Bracegirdle's part in D'Urfey's *The Intrigues at Versailles* is a sexual agent who cuckolds her husband yet gains the other characters' sympathy and respect. The pairing again with Barry makes the adultery of Bracegirdle's Lady Sancerre minor; whereas she has one affair, Barry's char-acter prostitutes herself with four different characters, rejoices in cheating on one with another, and celebrates her self-pimping, at one point singing, "Money, Money, Money, Money, Money, Money."[92] Lady Sancerre's hus-band also receives a limited portrayal—all he cares about is catching her in the act of infidelity—making his character appear sinister, and prompting an older Count who trusts his own wife (mistakenly, it turns out) to humiliate him. This wife's lover also conspires against her and then feels guilty for do-ing so, and when at the end of the play she tricks her husband into believ-ing her faithful, the tone combines relief for her escape with admiration of her craftiness.[93] Together, these five nonvirgin characters find redemption through their actress. When played by Bracegirdle, such characters can be married, mourned, and socially accommodated.

The Height of Fame: Bracegirdle's Prologue to Congreve's *Love For Love*

Bracegirdle and William Congreve ultimately cemented each other's fame. Her role as Araminta in *The Old Bachelor* (1693) greatly contributed to the play's fourteen-performance premiere, and during her career she performed the role at least twenty-five times. *The Double Dealer* (1694) ran for eight nights, the she-tragedy *The Mourning Bride* (1697) for another thirteen, and *The Way of the World* (1700) for five. Although modern audiences favor the last play, Restoration players and audiences alike preferred *Love for Love* (1695). Performed at the opening of the new Lincoln's Inn Fields theater, a heralded event that restored to London a second theater company after thirteen years of a dramatic monopoly, *Love for Love* became a smash hit, playing for fifteen straight performances and for a minimum of twenty-three performances over the course of Bracegirdle's career. It was an actors' favorite as well; in a touching theatrical moment, Thomas Betterton chose it for his final benefit performance (with Bracegirdle and Barry coming out of retirement for this sole show), and played the hero, Valentine, supported on either side by Barry and Bracegirdle.

A study of Bracegirdle's breeches and solidarity prologue to *Love for Love* reveals the rakish comedy generated from the contrast of flamboyant lines with her virgin persona. While the prologue's history suggests that it was never performed—it was "sent from an unknown hand"; the four extant broadsides say it was "spoken by Mrs. Bracegirdle," but they circulated in advance of the premiere; and quartos instead say it was "propos'd to be spoken by Mrs. Bracegirdle"—its wide circulation and the play's vast success indicate its relevance to her career. It was also reprinted on a broadside at the time of the farewell benefit performance for Betterton.

The sexual prologue jokingly denies that the "three Bs" negotiated to obtain the new theater company. In this way it confirms Elizabeth Howe's thesis that portrayals of women's sexuality accompanied their professional achievements; this prologue in fact conflates the two elements, suggesting Bracegirdle traded sexual favors for the new theater company.[94] What interests me in this case, however, is the continuous portrayal of Bracegirdle's persona—the comic contradiction between the apparent public knowledge of her chastity, and the prologue's insinuation that Bracegirdle used sex to obtain the new company.

Bracegirdle's prologue to *Love for Love* demonstrates that two opposing forces—self-objectification and rebuff of male sexual control—can comically coexist. The prologue breaks with the tradition of welcoming patrons to the new theater in a cloaked, Bettertonian fashion. Because the actress presents herself this way—and in *Love for Love*'s prologue, Bracegirdle wears breeches and refers to earning money for sexual favors—she also controls what gets objectified and mocked. As I argued in the introduction, it is why what is commonly known as self-deprecating comedy should instead be considered the recognition and celebration of one's own body as a comic source, which the speaker then strategically presents for material benefit and personal satisfaction. As Joanne Gilbert has argued, self-deprecatory humor can transmit as social critique, and its sources do not necessarily accord with the personae they project, as is the case for Bracegirdle.[95] The woman who appears onstage alone to deliver a prologue or epilogue to a feisty audience already exhibits strength; that she understands her body as a comic tool and turns the fact of objectification into her own comedy means that she directs what can be objectified and in so doing, unobjectifies herself.

Bracegirdle's comic persona is signaled immediately because the prologue's anonymous author envisions her wearing breeches. The choice to have Bracegirdle wear the breeches costume is apparently justified in the prologue's early lines, "But Women, you will say, are ill at Speeches, / 'Tis true, and therefore I appear in Breeches."[96] While it was common for actresses to deliver breeches prologues and epilogues, it might be thought that this would signal a series of masquerades during the play. But Bracegirdle's character, Angelica, does not cross-dress; she only "disguises" her feelings for Valentine. So what emerges in the prologue is a betweenness, a skewed version of Bracegirdle's persona and an adjunct to her customary display of virtue. In addition to being a play paratext, the prologue, therefore, is a genre in its own right. This is a moment when comedy does not foreshadow themes in the play, but rather builds on the audience's supposed knowledge of Bracegirdle, so that they may appreciate her beauty and recognize a comic incongruity between the actress they presume to know and the woman who inspired the prologue.

To begin, Bracegirdle plays on male fears of female infidelity. Commenting on men's desire to marry money, in the lines "Was it for gain the Husband first consented? / O yes, their Gains are mightily augmented," she suggests that husbands' only marital gain is cuckold status.[97] The 1695 text and all subsequent editions that include this prologue record the joke with a stage direction for Bracegirdle "Making Horns with her Hands over her Head." While cuckoldry generally makes fools of men in comedies, and revengers in tragedies, to introduce it independently of a plot and suggest members of the audience may themselves suffer from it insinuates that it is a quotidian, widespread condition. Whether or not Bracegirdle ever made the sign of the cuckold onstage, the action as recorded in print represents a daring joke. While the joke arguably stands on its own, the stage direction augments it, possibly indicating a reason for the prologue's later excision.[98]

Bracegirdle continues to mix her virginal persona with risqué allusions for comic effect when she coyly implies that she obtained the new theater through sex:

> But you perhaps, wou'd have me here confess
> How we obtain'd the Favour;—Can't you guess?
> Why then I'll tell you, (for I hate a Lye)
> By Brib'ry, errant Brib'ry, let me dye:
> I was their Agent, but by Jove I swear
> No honorable Member had a share
> Tho' young and able Members bid me Fair.[99]

This myth mixes truth-telling and bribery, oaths and opportunistic sex. The prologue creates a virtual back-and-forth exchange between the audience, cast as inquisitors, and Bracegirdle, the teasing woman in charge of her sexuality. She resolves to tell the truth but then promptly undercuts this by swearing to bribery as her method. In the final triplet, she swears a second oath, this time overtly to God, that her method was prostitution. The trade of sex for the stage is made more overt by words like "dye" and "Member," the latter in this case also indicating a Member of Parliament.[100] Citations of bribery and jabs at MPs therefore comically undercut apparent truth-telling. Bracegirdle's lines reflect what Susan Staves has said about oaths: that their usage in the later Restoration theater reflected a general loss of confidence in mere words.[101] These lines take that loss for granted. Bracegirdle seduces her audience through a mix of confession, oath, and comic prevarication.

Next, she delivers an even more direct triplet:

> I chose a wiser way to make you willing,
> Which has not cost the House a single Shilling;
> Now you suspect at least I went a Billing.[102]

According to these lines, sexual exchange is the wise way of achieving fiscal sense. By referring to her "billing," Bracegirdle implies that she delights in the audience imagining her playing this role.[103] This is an actress, or a representation of an actress, controlling and commodifying her sexuality through comedy and creating a titillatingly blurry boundary between her roles and her persona.

Finally, Bracegirdle turns her approach into a mock moral. To conclude the prologue, first she details her technique in playing this offstage "role":

> I Laugh'd, and Sigh'd, and Sung, and Leer'd upon ye;
> With Roguish Loving Looks, and that way won ye:
> The Young Men kiss'd me, and the Old I kiss'd,
> And luringly, I led them as I list.[104]

The lines combine courtship methods in a way befitting their breeches-clad speaker. Sighing, singing (for which she was highly respected), and being kissed by young men are behaviors found in many a comic female role, including several of Congreve's lesser female characters, such as Mrs. Frail, Barry's part in *Love for Love*. Leering, throwing roguish looks, kissing, and laughing are behaviors typical of male characters in the great sex comedies of the mid-1670s; one thinks of the looks Dorimant throws Harriet or the kisses Horner liberally bestows on Mrs. Pinchwife's "brother." Ending the prologue with a couplet discussing the advantages of bribery, "Thus Bribing, or thus Brib'd, fear no Disgraces; / For thus you may take Bribes, and keep your Places," she suggests that the sex-for-theater trade disgraces none of its participants, a critique which complicates her joke. She is known for her chastity, yet in this prologue not only does she joke about engaging in sexual behavior but endorses it as a way to get things done. Her "moral" thus contradicts her reputation for morality.

Love for Love's two prologues and an epilogue each comment differently on the new dramatic circumstances; as we have seen, Bracegirdle's prologue insinuates her sexual help in obtaining the theater. In contrast, Betterton's cloaked prologue first philosophically likens the actors' discontent with the United Company to a farmer attempting to till unyielding ground, and then compares the new theater to Eden and describes the play as "The First-fruit Offering, of a Virgin Play." Finally, he declares that Congreve has written much-needed social satire, which "this Crying Age" has not experienced since Wycherley.[105] Like the prototypical cloaked prologue to *The Way of the World*, discussed in chapter 1, this prologue comes across as being spoken by a voice of reason uninflected by personal self-reference. The different degrees of individual representation in Bracegirdle's and Betterton's prologues typify the difference between cloaked and exposed paratexts.

Congreve wrote a song, set to music by Henry Purcell, which has long been associated with Bracegirdle and which reinforces her persona. The poem seems inspired by a line she performed in Southerne's *Sir Anthony Love* (1690): her young virginal character imagines being able to "perswade [Sir Anthony] to make a Sinner of me, rather than suffer my Father to make me a Saint, so much before my time."[106] Congreve appropriated the theme, offering a male perspective:

> PIOUS Celinda goes to Pray'rs,
> Whene'er I ask the Favour;
> Yet, the tender Fool's in Tears,
> When she believes I'll leave her.
> Wou'd I were free from this Restraint,
> Or else had Power to win her!
> Wou'd she cou'd make of me a Saint,
> Or I of her a Sinner![107]

This song articulates a potentially sinister male desire that encapsulates an ideal response to Bracegirdle's persona. The description of Celinda's piety befits Bracegirdle's tragic heroines, but the male perspective seems one that her savvy public persona activates and exploits. In her work on nineteenth- and twentieth-century American comic female characters, Nancy Walker has defined the *eíron* in a way that needs little modification to accommodate Bracegirdle. "The *eíron* is the figure, who, by pretending to be innocent, points out society's faults through his own naïve questioning of the world around him."[108] Walker's figure is a mix of innocence, which generates the humor and self-awareness that allow a critique of the dramatized inequalities. Bracegirdle's persona unites both.

By creating a virginal persona of the type that Walker describes, Anne Bracegirdle ingeniously directed her reputation. Her combination of charm, agency, and semiotic inventiveness demonstrates that she figured out how to perform comedy, with all its accompanying privileges, and be rewarded for it. The "virgin or whore" stereotype of actresses, therefore, should be deemed only a starting point when considering how audiences felt about a certain actress, and should not translate into a belief that actresses lacked all forms of agency. My case study of Bracegirdle demonstrates how, by performing prologues and epilogues alongside their roles, the first Restoration actresses exercised a circumscribed agency to shape their own personae and reception.

Notes

1. Pierre Danchin, *The Prologues and Epilogues of the Restoration 1660–1700*, 4 vols. (Nancy: Presses Universitaires de Nancy, 1981–1988), 3:62–63; Anthony Aston, *A Brief Supplement to Colley Cibber, Esq. His Lives of the Late Famous Actors and Actresses* (London, 1747), 8.

2. Colley Cibber, *An Apology for the Life of Colley Cibber*, ed. B. R. S. Fone (New York: Dover 1968, reprint, 2000), 97.

3. Joseph R. Roach, *It* (Ann Arbor: University of Michigan Press, 2007), 3.

4. Gilli Bush-Bailey, *Treading the Bawds: Actresses and Playwrights on the late-Stuart Stage* (Manchester: Manchester University Press, 2006); Elizabeth Howe, *The First English Actresses: Women and Drama, 1660–1700* (Cambridge: Cambridge University Press, 1992); Cynthia Lowenthal, *Performing Identities on the Restoration Stage* (Carbondale: Southern Illinois University Press, 2003); Katharine Eisaman Maus, "'Playhouse Flesh and Blood': Sexual ideology and the Restoration Actress," *English Literary History* 46 (1979); Felicity Nussbaum, *Rival Queens: Actresses, Performance and the Eighteenth-Century British Theater* (Philadelphia: University of Pennsylvania Press, 2010); Kirsten Pullen, *Actresses and Whores: On Stage and in Society* (Cambridge: Cambridge University Press, 2005); Laura Rosenthal, "'Counterfeit Scrubbado': Women Actors in the Restoration," *Eighteenth Century* 34, no. 1 (1993); Kristina Straub, *Sexual Suspects: Eighteenth-Century Players and Sexual Ideology* (Princeton, NJ: Princeton University Press, 1992).

5. Bush-Bailey, *Treading the Bawds*, 16.

6. Nussbaum, *Rival Queens*, 101.

7. There is confusion about Bracegirdle's age because when she died in 1748 her tombstone listed her as eighty-five. Her baptism, however, took place in November of 1671. For a discussion of Bracegirdle's birthdate, see Lucyle Hook, "Anne Bracegirdle's First Appearance," *Theatre Notebook* 13 (1959): 133–36.

8. Lucyle Hook, "Mrs. Elizabeth Barry and Mrs. Anne Bracegirdle, Actresses. Their Careers from 1672 to 1695: A Study in Influences," PhD diss., New York University, 1949, 227.

9. Bush-Baily, *Treading the Bawds*, 61. Bush-Bailey provides a valuable rereading of Robert Gould's "A *Satyr* on the players," a much-sampled text when it comes to discussing specific actresses' reputations, but rarely consulted when discussing male actors' reputations, despite its sexual insinuations about them. Rosenthal, "'Counterfeit Scrubbado,'" 4; Cheryl Wanko, *Roles of Authority: Thespian Biography and Celebrity in Eighteenth-Century Britain* (Lubbock: Texas Tech University Press, 2003), 56.

10. Bush-Bailey, *Treading the Bawds*, 55.

11. Robert Gould, "The Play-House. A Satyr," in *Poems, chiefly consisting of satyrs and satyrical epistles* (London: 1689), 181–82.

12. Bush-Bailey, *Treading the Bawds*, 60, 59. For further discussion of this satire's treatment of Sarah Cooke, see my chapter 3.

13. "The Session of Ladies," in John Harold Wilson, ed., *Court Satires of the Restoration* (Columbus: Ohio State University Press, 1976), 206.

14. "Satyr on the Whigs and Tories," in *MS Harleian* (British Library, 1683), 241–42. Butler's lover is named "Whorwood": either an actual person or, more probably, a male lover of whores. In the same stanza, a man named May has "left his wife with Barry to F—k on," implying Barry as a teacher of prostitution.

15. Later satires attest to the significant power she held in the London theater world. After she, Barry, and Betterton formed the new company at Lincoln's Inn

Fields, satires criticized the ruling power of the "Three Bs." See, for example, *The Lunatick*, a 1705 comedy by "Frank Telltroth" (possibly a pseudonym for William Tavernor).

16. William J. Cameron, ed., *Poems on Affairs of State*, vol. 5 (New Haven: Yale University Press, 1971), 370 n. 32.

17. Tom Brown, "From the Worthy Mrs Behn the Poetess to the Famous Virgin Actress," in *A Continuation or Second Part of the Letters from the Dead to the Living* (London, 1703), 270–78.

18. Tom Brown, "Elegy on Mountfort" (Huntington Library, 1693). In subsequent collections of Brown's work the poem was republished as "The Ladies Lamentation for their Adonis."

19. Anon., *The Player's Tragedy. Or, Fatal Love* (London, 1693).

20. Tom Brown, "Bully Dawson to Bully Watson," in *A Continuation or Second Part of the letters from the Dead to the Living* (London, 1703), 128.

21. Anon., *Animadversions on Mr. Congreve's Late Answer to Mr. Collier* (London: John Nutt, 1698), [a4v].

22. Tom Brown, *Amusements Serious and Comical, Calculated for the Meridian of London*, 2nd ed. (London: John Nutt, 1702), 51–52. See also "The Tryal of Skill," reproduced in Howard Erskine-Hill, *William Congreve* (London: Routledge, 1995), 189.

23. Anon., *Poems on Affairs of State*, vol. 4 (London, 1707), 4, 50.

24. Marie H. Loughlin, *Hymeneutics: Interpreting Virginity on the Early Modern Stage* (Lewisburg, PA: Bucknell University Press, 1997), 30, 35.

25. Roy Strong, *The Cult of Elizabeth: Elizabethan Portraiture and Pageantry* (Berkeley: University of California Press, 1977), 47, 149, 153–54.

26. Peter Holland, *The Ornament of Action: Text and Performance in Restoration Comedy* (Cambridge: Cambridge University Press, 1979), 56–60.

27. Ibid., 59.

28. John Bancroft, *King Edward the Third, with the Fall of Mortimer* (London: Hindmarsh, 1691), 32.

29. Ibid.

30. Aphra Behn, "The Rover," in *The Works of Aphra Behn*, electronic edition, ed. Janet Todd (Charlottesville, VA: InteLex Corporation, 2004), 5:455.

31. Aston, *Brief Supplement*, 9–10.

32. Ibid., 8.

33. Marsden demonstrates that literary depictions of rape in this period only spare females who behave passively. See Jean I. Marsden, "Rape, Voyeurism, and the Restoration Stage," in *Broken Boundaries: Women and Feminism in Restoration Drama*, edited by Katherine M. Quinsey (Lexington: University Press of Kentucky, 1996), 187–90.

34. Betterton and Lee were married by the time of their rape performances; Barry, Boutell, and Marshall were lampooned for promiscuity. It should, however, be noted that this list may be incomplete, since cast lists are unavailable for Ravenscroft's *Titus Andronicus* (1678), Settle's *The Female Prelate*, Tate's *The Ingratitude of a Commonwealth* (1681), D'Urfey's *The Injur'd Princess* (1682), and Sedley's *Bellamira*

(1687). Anne Gibbs apparently performed in William Rowley's *All's Lost by Lust* in 1661, probably before she married Thomas Shadwell and before satires of her promiscuity were published.

35. Jacqueline Pearson correctly names female-authored plays as the ones absolving women of guilt. I extend this category, arguing that regardless of the author's gender, Bracegirdle was the catalyst for the rape victim's absolution. See Marsden, "Rape, Voyeurism, and the Restoration Stage," 187–90; and Jacqueline Pearson, *The Prostituted Muse: Images of Women and Women Dramatists, 1642–1737* (New York: St Martin's Press, 1988), 96.

36. Lowenthal, *Performing Identities*, 145.

37. For information on rapists' conviction rates, see Nazife Bashar, "Rape in England between 1550 and 1700," in *The Sexual Dynamics of History*, ed. London Feminist History Group (London: Pluto, 1983), 28–42.

38. Bracegirdle later played raped characters in the anonymous masque "The Rape of Europa" (1694) and Charles Hopkins's *Boadicea Queen of Britain* (1697). Her characters endure rape attempts in D'Urfey's *Don Quixote Part II* (1694), Peter Motteux's *Beauty in Distress* (1698), and Mary Pix's *Queen Catherine* (1698).

39. Howe, *First English Actresses*, 43; Marsden, "Rape, Voyeurism, and the Restoration Stage," 185; Derek Hughes, "Rape on the Restoration Stage," *Eighteenth Century* 46, no. 3 (2005): 228, 232. James Peck strengthens the link between Bracegirdle's virginity and the political situation surrounding the Glorious Revolution; see James Peck, "Albion's 'Chaste Lucrese': Chastity, Resistance, and the Glorious Revolution in the Career of Anne Bracegirdle," *Theatre Survey* 25, no. 1 (2004).

40. Hughes, "Rape on the Restoration Stage," 227.

41. For discussions of rape in *The Rover*, in addition to Marsden and Hughes, see Adam R. Beach, "Carnival Politics, Generous Satire, and Nationalist Spectacle in Behn's *The Rover*," *Eighteenth-Century Life* 28, no. 3 (2004); Anita Pacheco, "Rape and the Female Subject in Aphra Behn's *The Rover*," *English Literary History* 65, no. 2 (1998).

42. Jean I. Marsden, *Fatal Desire: Women, Sexuality, and the English Stage, 1660–1720* (Ithaca, NY: Cornell University Press, 2006), 65.

43. Hughes, "Rape on the Restoration Stage," 232.

44. Peck, "Albion's 'Chaste Lucrese,'" 99; Marsden, "Rape, Voyeurism, and the Restoration Stage," 186.

45. Garthine Walker, *Crime, Gender and Social Order in Early Modern England* (Cambridge: Cambridge University Press, 2003), 55–60.

46. Hughes reads the scene in question as not "forcible rape" but "intercourse achieved under false pretenses," a condition that, he correctly observes, Restoration courts did not consider rape. The problem with this argument is that Restoration courts had a narrow definition that excluded spousal rape and many other forms of what plays like *The Orphan* portray as crimes and that today we would consider rape. See Hughes, "Rape on the Restoration Stage," 227. Thanks to Nico Dicecco for this observation.

47. These plays are: *The Injur'd Lovers, Alphonzo King of Naples, King Arthur, The Distres'd Innocence, The Rape, Henry the Second, Beauty in Distress, Queen Catherine,* and *The Ambitious Stepmother.*

48. William Mountfort, *The Injur'd Lovers,* 1st ed. (London: Sam Manship, 1678).

49. Bashar, "Rape in England between 1550 and 1700."

50. Marsden, "Rape, Voyeurism, and the Restoration Stage," 196.

51. Written by a "Gentlewoman of York" and spoken by Mrs. Pearson, the second epilogue to William Hunt's *The Fall of Tarquin* (1713) suggests women attend rape trials to imagine themselves as the victims and to enjoy hearing "a smutty word." See Pierre Danchin, *The Prologues and Epilogues of the Eighteenth Century,* 8 vols. (Nancy: Presses Universitaires de Nancy, 1990), 1:520.

52. George Powell, *Alphonso King of Naples,* 1st ed. (London: Abel Roper and Thomas Bever, 1691), 22.

53. Christopher J. Wheatley, "Tragedy," in *The Cambridge Companion to English Restoration Theatre,* ed. Deborah Payne Fisk (Cambridge: Cambridge University Press, 2000), 71.

54. Powell, *Alphonso,* 46.

55. Elkanah Settle, *The Distres'd Innocence: or, the Princess of Persia,* 1st ed. (London: E. J. for Abel Roper, 1691), 46, 44.

56. Ibid., 60.

57. Bridget Orr identifies the play as representing both the Turks' threat to Christianity following the Austro–Turkish War and the domestic challenges to the Protestant church. See Bridget Orr, *Empire on the English Stage 1660–1714* (Cambridge: Cambridge University Press, 2001), 43.

58. Cibber, *Apology,* 98.

59. Nathaniel Lee, *The Rival Queens, or The Death of Alexander the Great,* ed. Chadwyck-Healey (London: James Magres and Richard Bertley, 1677), 39.

60. This phenomenon also occurs in Motteux's *Beauty in Distress* (1698).

61. Nicholas Brady, *The Rape: or, the Innocent Impostors,* 1st ed. (London: R. Bentley, 1692), 21.

62. Ibid., 25. There is theatrical precedent for this manner of rape in Thomas Rawlins, *Rebellion* (1640), and in John Dryden, *Amboyna* (1673). For a discussion of the former, see Dale B. J. Randall, *Winter Fruit: English Drama 1642–1660* (Lexington: University Press of Kentucky, 1995), 34. Jean Marsden reproduces the latter's frontispiece, an illustration of a woman tied to a tree by her hair, in Marsden, *Fatal Desire,* 77.

63. Brady, *The Rape,* 27.

64. Pearson, *The Prostituted Muse,* 98.

65. The three men were Charles Talbot, the Earl and Duke of Shrewsbury; Henry Sidney, Earl of Romsey; and Aubrey de Vere, Earl of Oxford. Shadwell criticizes them for not volunteering to fight France's increased aggressiveness in the Nine Years' War. The criticism seems unfair, since all three had previous battle experience. See Danchin, *Restoration,* 3:55–58.

66. Hook, "Mrs. Elizabeth Barry," 244.

67. Thomas Shadwell, *The Amorous Bigotte*, 1st ed. (London: James Knapton, 1690), 22.

68. Danchin, *Restoration*, 2:804.

69. John Dryden, *King Arthur: or, The British Worthy*, 1st ed. (London: Jacob Tonson, 1691), 4.

70. Ibid., 4–5.

71. The struggle over the kingdom reflects the beginning of the Jacobites. Originally, the play was written in 1684 to honor Charles II. When Dryden collaborated with Purcell on the 1691 version, he was the subject of ongoing attacks regarding his conversion to Catholicism. James Winn points out that *King Arthur* is remarkably politic, because the play can be interpreted as supporting either the Jacobite or the Williamite factions. See James Anderson Winn, *John Dryden and His World* (New Haven, CT: Yale University Press, 1987), 448–49.

72. Rosalind Ballaster, *Seductive Forms: Women's Amatory Fiction from 1684–1740* (Oxford: Oxford University Press, 1992), 34–35.

73. Aston, *Brief Supplement*, 10.

74. Danchin, *Restoration*, 3:21; Peter Motteux recycles the billet-doux in his epilogue for Bracegirdle in *Beauty in Distress* (1698).

75. Editor Vinton Dearing has traced these locations; see Vinton A. Dearing, ed., *The Works of John Dryden*, vol. 16 (Berkeley: University of California Press, 1996), 342.

76. W. S. Lewis, Warren Hunting Smith, and George L. Lam, eds., *Horace Walpole's Correspondence with Sir Horace Mann and Sir Horace Mann the Younger*, 48 vols. (New Haven, CT: Yale University Press, 1971), 25:74.

77. Nicholas Rowe, *The Ambitious Step-Mother* (London: 1701), 75.

78. Ibid., 68, 70.

79. Ibid., "The Ambitious Step-Mother," in *The Works of Nicholas Rowe* (London: 1728), 2: ix.

80. Ibid.

81. Pearson, *The Prostituted Muse*, 26.

82. Derek Hughes, *English Drama 1660–1700* (Oxford: Clarendon, 1996), 5–6.

83. Hook, "Mrs. Elizabeth Barry," 220.

84. Thomas D'Urfey, *The Marriage-Hater Match'd* (London: Richard Bentley, 1692).

85. Danchin, *Restoration*, 3:48.

86. Ibid., 49.

87. John Bancroft, *Henry the Second, King of England, with the Death of Rosamond* (London: Jacob Tonson, 1693), A4r.

88. Thomas Southerne, *The Works of Thomas Southerne*, ed. Robert Jordan and Harold Love, 2 vols. (Oxford: Clarendon, 1988), 1:424.

89. Holland, *Ornament of Action*, 155.

90. Hume, *The Development of English Drama in the Late Seventeenth Century* (Oxford: Clarendon, 1976), 388.

91. Danchin, *Restoration*, 3:92. Interestingly, Danchin editorializes in response to these lines: "Apparently, Mrs. Bracegirdle's 'chastity' was not above open sexual

suggestion!" This may recapture a typical response among those incredulous about her reputation.

92. Thomas D'Urfey, *The Intrigues at Versailles* (London: Saunders, Buck, and Parker, 1697), 38.

93. My reading of the ending differs from that of Derek Hughes. Hughes sees Barry's character as exposing Bracegirdle's Lady Sancerre and values the Duke of Sancerre's censoring of his wife. In my reading it is Bracegirdle's character that outs Barry's, and the Duke of Sancerre is ridiculed throughout. See Hughes, *English Drama*, 404.

94. Howe, *First English Actresses*, xi.

95. Joanne Gilbert, *Performing Marginality: Humor, Gender, and Cultural Critique* (Detroit: Wayne State University Press, 2004), 140.

96. Danchin, *Restoration*, 3:180.

97. Ibid.

98. The play went through four authorized editions (two in 1695, one in 1697, and one in 1704), all of which contained the Bracegirdle prologue, until Congreve's collaboration with Jacob Tonson on the *Works* of 1710 excised it. Other publishers eventually followed suit, and the last eighteenth-century edition to contain it was published in 1731. The prologue reappeared in the 1920s in a Romanian printing of the play and then began appearing more frequently beginning in the 1960s. To this day, it continues to be published inconsistently with editions of the play. In *The Works of William Congreve*, D. F. McKenzie republishes it not alongside the other prologue, but in the endnotes.

99. Danchin, *Restoration*, 3:180–81.

100. Malcom Kelsall observes this in William Congreve, *Love for Love*, ed. M. M. Kelsall, 2nd ed. (London: Ernest Benn, 1999), 30.

101. Susan Staves, *Players' Scepters: Fictions of Authority in the Restoration* (Lincoln: University of Nebraska Press, 1979).

102. Danchin, *Restoration*, 3:181.

103. Oxford English Dictionary, 1991, vol. 2, 193, 195, s.v. "bill": *v.* 2.2. To stroke bill with bill (as doves). 3. *transf.* To caress, make show of affection; usually (of reciprocal action) *to bill and coo.* billing, *ppl. a.* That bills or caresses like a pair of doves.

104. Danchin, *Restoration*, 3:181.

105. Ibid., 182–83.

106. Thomas Southerne, *Sir Anthony Love* (London: Joseph Fox and Abel Roper, 1691), 23.

107. Hook, "Mrs. Elizabeth Barry," 246. The song was first published in Henry Purcell, *Orpheus Britannicus* (London: J. Heptinstall for Henry Playford, 1698), 63.

108. Nancy Walker, "Agelaste or Eiron: American Women Writers and the Sense of Humor," *Studies in American Humor* 4, no. 1/2 (1985): 105.

~

CHAPTER FIVE

Bawdy Language: The Reception History of Addison's Epilogue to *The Distrest Mother*

The Business of an *Epilogue*, they say,
Is, to destroy the Moral of the Play:
To wipe the Tears of Vertue from your Eyes;
And make you Merry,—lest you should grow Wise.

—Ambrose Philips, epilogue to *Humfrey, Duke of Gloucester* (1723),
spoken by Anne Oldfield

Whereas chapter 4 examined the significance of many prologues and epilogues in one player's life, chapter 5 traces the lifespan of one epilogue. First performed by Anne Oldfield, the epilogue to Ambrose Philips's tragedy, *The Distrest Mother* (1712), became a showpiece for twenty-seven different actresses, including Peg Woffington, Hannah Pritchard, and Sarah Siddons. Addressing women and critiquing marriage, this exposed epilogue features bawdy talk about female sexuality and masturbation. Such material coincided with the height of the publication of anti-onanism tracts. For these and related reasons, the epilogue occasioned a lot of press. A *Spectator* debate about this particular epilogue and the general seemliness of comic epilogues following tragedies prompted the authors to conclude that epilogues are *not* parts of plays, a contention challenged by the entirety of this book. As revivals of Philips's popular tragedy broke custom by featuring the original epilogue, Samuel Richardson incorporated it into *Pamela* as an example of theater at its worst, while Samuel Johnson advanced inconsistent views of its merits. While it generated more discussion than most, the epilogue is one of a number of Restoration and eighteenth-century paratexts that occasioned important discussions of dramatic theory and practice. For all of these reasons, the epilogue to *The Distrest Mother* demonstrates how prologues and epilogues influence the consumption of many other texts, some far outside the theatrical sphere.

The Bawdy Epilogue: Why All the Fuss?

Always delivered by actresses, what distinguishes what I am calling the bawdy epilogue is its sexually comic reinterpretation of the tragic play. In such an epilogue, the actress playing a primary character who had exhibited morally upstanding behavior now disrupts that characterization with flippant comedy. This formerly genteel, now salacious character disrupts the play's alternate universe. The epilogue's new urban temporality creates an incongruous comedy and returns the audience to a familiar, mocking world—at the expense of the play's themes and structural consistency. Tragic catharsis is abbreviated; the primary character's grief and death, the audience's purgation of its flaws, and the restoration of an ordered society all precede the bawdy epilogue, whose speaker reintroduces disorder by interrupting the audience's prior conception of the heroine. The enduring presence of the bawdy epilogue (of which the revived epilogue is a subset) indicates that London authors, theater managers, and publishers frequently brushed aside the integrity of role and genre to accommodate some spectators' desire for female sex comedy.[1]

In the process of taxonomizing prologues and epilogues, this book has tended to focus on their appreciative audiences. Part of my fascination with these paratexts is their licensing of actresses to deliver ribald comedy and receive applause in return. Yet many writers protested their proliferation. Upper-class Restoration women were supposed to find their "indecent" vocabulary unintelligible.[2] Others objected to the upset of genre and morality ironically celebrated in this chapter's epigraph. Bawdy epilogues certainly disordered the dramatic location and time of their tragedies. To maintain the tragic frame, characters need to remain in the play's normally rural fantasy world, but the epilogues swiftly relocated them to London.

Published in a late eighteenth-century collection of prologues and epilogues, "A prologue upon epilogues" points out its disordering of tragedy:

> The epilogue, which always deck'd with smiles,
> In female accent, tragic care beguiles:
> That when exalted thoughts, the mind impress,

> A trivial jest must make the pleasure less.
> Ludicrous custom, which compels to show,
> The cap of folly, in the rear of woe;
> Portrays a smile, emerging from a sigh,
> And pleasure starting from affliction's eye;
> Makes joy's bright beam in sorrow's face appear,
> And Quibble dry the sentimental tear.[3]

In its call to arms, the prologue then points out the perversity of ending a comedy with "a doleful ditty."[4] This prologue confirms that female comic epilogues remained so influential as to stand in for *all* epilogues. It also indicates why some would find bawdy epilogues to tragedies unsettling. Such epilogues occurred despite Restoration theories that spectators derived pleasure from tragedy's moral structure and affect. Earlier theories of tragedy, which emphasized either design or emotional response as the genre's foundation, combine in the work of René Rapin, the Restoration-era interpreter of Aristotle.[5] An influence on Dryden and Addison, Rapin advocates both internal unity and emotional reactions. The rules of unity, he says, will prevent playwrights from "joining things naturally incompatible, *mixing Tygers with Lambs, Birds with Serpents, to make one body of different species.*"[6] Rapin could have added tragedies with bawdy epilogues to the list.

Regarding bawdy epilogues, theater commentators were often contradictory. One of the few to maintain a consistent opinion, Jeremy Collier complains that actresses' performances of *all* prologues and epilogues are problematic:

> the *Actors* quit the *Stage*, and remove from Fiction into Life. Here they converse with the *Boxes*, and *Pit*, and address directly to the Audience. . . . And to make it the more agreeable, Women are Commonly pick'd out for this Service. . . . If a Man would study to outrage *Quality* and Vertue, he could not do it more Effectually.[7]

Fielding also decried bawdy epilogues yet composed some himself, including the epilogue to Charles Bodens's *The Modish Couple.*[8] In this epilogue, Clarissa/Susannah Cibber warns men that they have a greater chance of being cuckolded because wives, from seeing fine Greek and Roman heroes perform onstage, now have higher sexual standards: "Her Fancy fir'd with *Hector* or with *Caesar*; / What can a *Haberdasher* do to please her?"[9] Colley Cibber wrote a couple for Oldfield, but in the epilogue to Fielding's *The Miser* he calls them "Ragouts of Smut and Ribaldry."[10] Garrick's were cleaner but sexually allusive; although (as Knapp points out) they lacked innuendo, they often referenced famous risqué moments, such as the china scene in *The Country Wife*.[11] And while Johnson loved the epilogue to *The Distrest Mother*, he registered a touch of disapproval for the genre at large: In *Idler* no. 40 he calls it an "inconvenience" that "the salutary sorrow of tragick scenes is too soon effaced by the merriment of the epilogue."[12] For authors and managers purporting to reform the stage, the bawdy epilogue remained an inconclusive site.

Addison's Paratextual Contribution to Philips's *The Distrest Mother*

The epilogue to *The Distrest Mother* transformed discussions of theatrical decorum.[13] First performed by Anne Oldfield on 17 March 1712, the epilogue converts the suffering heroine into a figure of lustful cunning. Enraptured audiences demanded that revivals of the play include the original epilogue, an exception to theatrical custom.[14] Although attributed at the time to his cousin Eustace Budgell, the epilogue was likely authored by none other than that eighteenth-century arbiter of taste, Joseph Addison. And in *Spectator* no. 341, Addison and Budgell justify such an epilogue concluding a tragedy.[15] To make their case, they determine that *all* epilogues are thematically and structurally divorced from their plays, a problematic formulation which my book seeks once and for all to rectify. By altering dramatic characters and genres to accommodate the epilogue, no. 341 contradicts one of the primary purposes of the *Spectator* as stated in Addison's Horatian chiasmus: "to enliven Morality with Wit, and to temper Wit with Morality."[16] As a result, despite increasing theatrical censorship, *The Distrest Mother*'s original epilogue continued to be performed and published throughout the century. This pattern suggests, therefore, that regarding dramatic prologues and epilogues, the history of censorship throughout eighteenth-century theater should also be considered a history of inclusion.[17] Tracts, licensing acts, authors, and audiences not only bowdlerized but also sanctioned certain forms of indecency.

Prologues and epilogues punctuated the career of star actress Anne Oldfield. One testament to her fame is the myth of her ascent: as the story goes, in 1707 she and Anne Bracegirdle played the same part, the amorous widow, in Betterton's eponymous play; although Bracegirdle was well received, Oldfield brought the house down. Although dates do not align with this anecdote, it reflects the acclaim for both actresses, Bracegirdle for representing the standing pinnacle of achievement and Oldfield for launching stardom. By the time she acted as Andromache in *The Distrest Mother*, she had already inspired several great characters, including Cibber's Lady Betty Modish in *The Careless Husband* and Farquhar's Mrs. Sullen in *The Beaux' Stratagem*.

Prologues and especially epilogues represented an important part of her reputation; many people, including her lover, Arthur Maynwaring, contributed
paratexts for her to perform, and as Felicity Nussbaum notes, the fact that
a 1741 biography lists all of her epilogues stresses their importance to her
career.[18] She was buried in Westminster Abbey, and posthumous evidence,
such as a prologue to a 1756 performance of Congreve's *The Mourning Bride*,
indicates her enduring influence.[19]

Oldfield excelled at playing Andromache and performing the epilogue
to *The Distrest Mother*, which she accomplished at least fifty-one times. One
of the twelve most popular tragedies of the era, Philips's play was staged numerous times through to the end of the century (the *London Stage* lists 197
known performances, and the play also traveled). Usually mounted early in
the theater season, when playhouses were likely to take in more revenue, the
play was frequently chosen by actors for their benefit nights for the same reason. And writers often attributed the play's success to Oldfield's performance
of its epilogue. At the first three performances, she accommodated audience
demand for encores.[20] One of Oldfield's earliest biographers, Edmund Curll,
credited Oldfield's "manner of speaking the very humorous EPILOGUE" as
having "greatly contributed to the Run of the last Play; and which whenever
revived, the Audience always have insisted on."[21] Following Oldfield's death
in 1730, many actresses played Andromache as a signature piece, and at least
eleven, including Susannah Cibber and George Anne Bellamy, performed the
original epilogue. In 1781 Samuel Johnson proclaimed it "the most successful
Epilogue that was ever yet spoken on the English theatre," and observed that
"whenever [The Distrest Mother] is recalled to the stage . . . the Epilogue is
still expected, and is still spoken."[22] No fan of the epilogue herself, Hester
Thrale Piozzi wonders at its popularity: "What I cannot comprehend at all is
that since my time—nay since Mrs. Siddon's [sic] time—the Gallery always
will call for this Epilogue, which is now unreservedly given to Addison; but
how the Gallery people came to know its value so well I guess not."[23] By the
mid-nineteenth century, the play had gone through nearly sixty editions and
issues, most of which included the epilogue. More so than most, therefore, this
epilogue remained integral to the play in both performance and publication.

Judging by its performance and publication histories, *The Distrest Mother*
was one of the most beloved tragedies of the eighteenth century.[24] On a first
reading, the play might seem unlikely to spawn debate. *The Distrest Mother*
is Philips's adaptation of Racine's *Andromache* (1667), itself an adaptation of
Euripides's same-named tragedy.[25] Imagining the Trojan War's effects upon
individual love relationships, the play portrays Andromache as the loyal Trojan widowed mother, torn between remaining faithful to the memory of her

dead husband, Hector, and saving their son by marrying the Greek leader, Pyrrhus. Resolving to marry Pyrrhus but kill herself immediately afterward, Andromache unintentionally provokes his murder by an enraged mob, the resulting suicide of Pyrrhus's lover, Hermione, and finally, the madness of Hermione's lover, Orestes. Andromache successfully saves her son's (and her own) life, but at great human cost.

Although one contemporary spectator faults Philips for being *too* faithful to Racine, Philips in fact prefers Racine to Euripides because the French play better accords with his own strict morality.[26] Instead of having Andromache grieve over the impending murder of the son she bore to her second husband, Racine recentered the myth around her initial son, Astyanax, by her first husband, Hector. In the preface, Philips says that he adopts this shift because "Considered in this Light, no doubt, she moves our Compassion much more effectually, than she could be imagined to do in any Distress for a Son by a Second Husband."[27] The last two words indicate Philips's sense of propriety; to lose a son provokes less sympathy if the mother conceived him with her *second* sexual partner.

Contrasting with Philips's moralizing preface, the lighthearted epilogue reduces plot and character, Aristotle's two most important aspects of tragedy, to their sexual elements. The epilogue reimagines Andromache as a sexual opportunist who now speculates on the night of sex she might have had with Pyrrhus, and who attributes her love for Hector to his sexual skill. In the wake of other characters' murder, suicide, and insanity, Andromache abruptly transitions from grieving for Pyrrhus during the last scene of the play, to gloating over her successful plan to save her son. At the beginning of the epilogue she signals the betweenness of character and actress by saying, "I Hope you'll own that with becoming Art / I've play'd my Game, and topp'd the Widow's Part."[28] When one thinks of the "I" as originating from Andromache, then these lines generate a suspicion of her character. Implying that she faked suffering, Andromache suggests that the situation actually worked out well for her because of her craftiness in both saving her son and remaining loyal to Hector. Instead of a play within a play, here we have a role within a role, played by a single entity. Whereas during the play, Andromache came across as a faithful heroine, these lines suggest that her earlier loyalty is suspect.[29] They make Andromache sound cunning: she has rescued her son without having to consummate her marriage to Pyrrhus. Because Pyrrhus was murdered just before their wedding night, Andromache's assertion of freedom also makes her suspect. At once, Andromache is both moral and devious. Her double entendre further complicates this characterization and places her within the witty world of London sexual comedy. "Topp'd" implies many situations: her attaining chief position in her family, her having cheated and won at a dice game, or her having "tupped" (copulated) with Pyrrhus.[30]

The couplet gains additional resonance when applied to Oldfield. In 1712, many in the audience would have known that Oldfield was living with Arthur Maynwaring, secretary to the Duchess of Marlborough. A great theater patron, Maynwaring wrote several prologues and epilogues for Oldfield. Due to poor health, he had been out of the public eye for the past two years, so references to mortality might evoke Oldfield's impending "widowhood." More significant, though, was the part's reassignment from its original actress, Jane Rogers. When she first came to the stage in 1692, Rogers followed the example of Anne Bracegirdle in promoting her virtue. But she could not resist her handsome costar and subsequent theater manager, Robert Wilks, and during their short-lived relationship Wilks apparently fathered the child she bore in 1700. Rogers initially received the role of Andromache, only to endure Philips and Wilks reassigning it to Oldfield. Her supporters disrupted the opening night, and then Rogers penned a protest about her lost role in "The Memorial of Jane Rogers: Humbly Submitted to the Town."[31] "Topp'd the Widow's Part" may therefore have reminded some of Oldfield's triumph.

The same salacious content dominates the rest of the epilogue. In revisiting her brief marriage to Pyrrhus, Andromache recasts herself as motivated by sex. In the epilogue's third stanza, she reconsiders her decision to kill herself rather than remain married to Pyrrhus:

> 'Twas a strange Scape! had *Pyrrhus* liv'd till now
> I had been finely hamper'd in my Vow.
> To dye by ones own Hand, and fly the Charms
> Of Love and Life in a young Monarch's Arms!
> 'Twere an hard Fate—ere I had undergone it
> I might have took one Night—to think upon it.[32]

Whereas during the play Andromache finds Pyrrhus odious, here she emphasizes his attractiveness. The last line makes light of her vow to kill herself rather than be unfaithful to her dead first husband. In *Players' Scepters*, Susan Staves names the protagonists of *Venice Preserv'd* and *Lucius Junius Brutus* as oathbreakers; their breaches ensure tragedy but compel audience sympathy.[33] In Philips's play, Orestes vows numerous times to stay away from Hermione and complains that she caused his perjury; his resulting madness signals tragedy and potentially provokes sympathy. We might think, therefore, that Andromache would also castigate herself at the thought of breaking her original marriage vow, and approve of her subsequent resolve to kill herself rather than go to bed with Pyrrhus. The last line, however, implies a sexual hint, since the "one night" Andromache refers to would be hers and Pyrrhus's wedding night. The dash and the metrical weight of the word "think" suggest that in performance it was emphasized; this would heighten the joke that if Andromache had indeed taken a night to think about her marriage to Pyrrhus, she would have been doing more than just thinking.

Context and date also support my interpretation of the phrase "To dye by ones own Hand" as indicating both suicide and masturbation—the latter considered a disturbing practice particularly associated with women. Referring to suicide, the line represents a literal death by a metonymic means; referring to masturbation, it signifies a metaphoric orgasm by a literal device. Given the prevalent death/orgasm association, the line both connotes and connects suicide and masturbation.[34] In *Solitary Sex: A Cultural History of Masturbation*, Thomas Laqueur describes how anti-onanism tracts reflected cultural anxieties about the masturbating—hence sexually self-sufficient—woman through metaphors of suicide. Laqueur also dates the anti-onanism movement as beginning "in or around 1712," when John Marten's popular *Onania; or, The Heinous Sin of Self Pollution, and all its Frightful Consequences, in both SEXES Considered* was first published.[35] Marten's campaign had begun a few years earlier, when his pamphlet on venereal disease—a suicide of the bloodline—listed masturbation as a source of infection.[36] According to Laqueur, Kant considered masturbation to be worse than suicide; while the latter destroys the life of one person, the former scorns the survival of the species.[37] Given its cultural context, "To dye by ones own Hand, and fly the charms / Of Love and Life in a young Monarch's Arms!" suggests that Andromache dreamed up a third way of saving her son: to survive, ironically, by masturbating.

This option comically interferes with tragic characters who approach their problems fatalistically rather than strategically; and it contests Aristotle's description of tragedy as serious and complete in itself. Like the burgeoning anti-onanism tracts, Andromache's survival technique alludes to male fears about female self-control, but then she tempers it with the comment, "'Twere an hard Fate." The passage provides another example of the ribald discourse that survived theatrical censors.

The fourth stanza continues the sexual innuendo:

> But why you'll say was all this Grief exprest
> For a first Husband, laid long since at Rest?
> Why so much Coldness to my kind Protector?
> —Ah Ladies! had you known the good Man *Hector!*[38]

These lines unite the faithful character of Andromache with the gossip about Oldfield. Andromache/Oldfield's appeal to only the ladies in the audience, and the pun on the word "known" as indicating sexual intimacy, implies that Hector would trump any other lover Andromache (or Oldfield) could experience. In the body of the play, Andromache's fidelity elevates her practically to warrior status; because of her loyalties to the Trojan side's supreme combatant, Andromache faces an Antigone-like decision: to survive with the victors or honor the dead. Presented in the play as a sign of her merit, Andromache's devotion becomes an object of ridicule in the epilogue. The joke—that Andromache remains committed to a now-dead man because of his adeptness in bed—is augmented by the feminine rhyme "Protector/Hector." It may also refer to the dying Maynwaring; the line implies that Oldfield's loyalty to him will also be short-lived. (Maynwaring died on 13 November, less than eight months after the premiere of *The Distrest Mother*.)[39] This sequence comically reimagines the play's thematic consideration of what constitutes "good" behavior. Whereas during the play Andromache qualifies as good because she struggles with the ethical conflict of choosing between husband and son, here the idea that her fidelity stems from memories of good intercourse deflates her earlier high-mindedness and further subsumes her sensibility within the epilogue's betweenness.

The final stanza comically revises the play's pitiful conclusion to solicit the audience's approval:

> At length howe'er I laid my Weeds aside,
> And sunk the Widow in the well-dress'd Bride.
> In you it still remains to grace the Play,
> And bless with Joy my Coronation Day:
> Take then, ye Circles of the Brave and Fair,
> The Fatherless and Widow to your Care.[40]

To re-fill seats at future performances, epilogues often beg the audience to return or promote the play's worth. These lines, however, contain two stances—Andromache/Oldfield asks the audience to sympathize with her as widow *and* celebrate her as queen—thus maintaining the comic recasting of the play's ending. The brashest statement in this stanza refers to her "Coronation Day," since her new title comes at the expense of Pyrrhus's death. And the final couplet exploits the many meanings of the word "Care." From an economic standpoint, it reflects the hope that audience members will circle back to the theater and express their care for the play through future ticket purchases. Coming from Andromache, the couplet also suggests that the audience should maintain sympathy for her both abstractly, as helpless widow, and actively, as sexual agent. This second meaning, a come-on, also extends to the soon-to-be-partnerless Oldfield, who may be lining up post-Maynwaring lovers.

Her delivery of this epilogue both changed the pattern of epilogues' associations with plays and led to more such performances for Oldfield. Whereas most revived plays featured a new prologue and epilogue, revivals of *The Distrest Mother* not only retained the original epilogue but also used it as a source of advertisement. While it remains uncertain whether epilogues and prologues were performed during the first performance only, during the first three performances, or throughout the play's entire first run, scholars agree that revivals generally did not feature performances of the original paratexts. But the *London Stage* lists twenty-eight performances of *The Distrest Mother* between 1712 and 1800 that specify "With the original epilogue." The actual number of performances that included it was higher, especially because only five of Oldfield's thirty-three known performances are so designated. An advertisement for a 13 March 1727 performance, which specifies "And the usual Epilogue by Mrs. Oldfield," indicates that inclusion of the epilogue was standard.[41] Sybil Rosenfeld also mentions performances at Bath, Bristol, Canterbury, and York, some of which may have included the original epilogue.[42]

How to Watch Epilogues: *The Spectator* Weighs In

The first recorded response to the epilogue came, rather disingenuously, from its author and his collaborator: Addison and Steele. They treat it as a case study in order to discuss the relationship between plays and epilogues. Their finding, that all epilogues are structurally divorced from plays, does not account for two of the issues I have raised in this book: the "both-and" relationship that Genette describes as existing between main text and paratext, wherein each can function singly or in tandem according to audience desire; and the "betweenness" that combines elements of a main play's character with the persona of its performer.

Before launching into this discussion, it is necessary to clarify the authorship of the epilogue, since that is not a straightforward matter. Although in the playtext Eustace Budgell receives credit, several sources confirm the real author to be Joseph Addison. Johnson notes that Addison's family and friends confirmed him as the author; and according to Boswell, Somerset Draper said he and copublishers Jacob and Richard Tonson also knew that the epilogue was Addison's.[43] Most stage histories also question the attribution to Budgell; those who claim outright Addison's authorship include John Genest and, more recently, Richard Bevis and Charles Knight.[44] Most sources consider Budgell a mediocre author and a hanger-on to his cousin, who helped him with his writing.

My analysis of the bawdy epilogue seems at odds with Addison, the arbiter of decorum. It is not my aim to dwell on any apparent hypocrisy, as a text can of course produce meanings unintended by the author. In this case, it may be safest to say that bawdiness is in the eye of the beholder. The above interpretation is contextual; although at least one near-contemporary of Addison's found the epilogue shockingly bawdy (described below), these points are circumstantial, not speculation on Addison's intentions.

While established writers frequently contributed prologues and epilogues to plays by their less-experienced colleagues, on this occasion Addison and Steele were more enthusiastic than most. The title of an anonymous play critique, *A Modest Survey Of that Celebrated Tragedy The Distrest Mother, So often and so highly Applauded by the Ingenious Spectator*, reflects the extremity of their support.[45] They heavily promoted Philips's endeavor, contributing both prologue and epilogue, attending multiple performances, and lauding the play in no fewer than six *Spectator* papers. In the first of these, no. 290, Steele praises the play for elements that conflict with its epilogue.[46] Six weeks before opening night, Steele heaps praise on *The Distrest Mother*'s portrayal of innocents. Whereas most tragic characters suffer the consequences of their own sins, says Steele, Philips's excel because they are free from vice, suffering instead from their unfortunate proximity to the evils of war. To see the play is thus a moral endeavor: "The Town has an Opportunity of doing it self Justice in supporting the Representation of Passion, Sorrow, Indignation, even Despair it self, within the Rules of Decency, Honour and good Breeding."[47] Steele's approval accords with the *Spectator*'s mission of stressing these qualities in everyday life. In fact, a reader of no. 290 might have easily identified the author of these prologue lines:

> Our Author . . . makes Propriety his Care.
> Your Treat with study'd Decency he serves;
> Not only Rules of Time and Place preserves,
> But strives to keep his Characters intire,
> With *French* Correctness and with *British* Fire.[48]

Steele touts decorum here with elegant and witty phrases. His praise of Philips's neoclassical symmetries is consistent with his advocacy of steady moral behavior, both points of view that he ostensibly shares with Addison.

In *Spectator* no. 335, where he narrates Sir Roger de Coverley's trip to see Philips's play, Addison avoids mentioning the epilogue. Distributed on March 25 after *The Distrest Mother*'s first five performances, no. 335 concentrates less on describing the play itself than on recording Sir Roger's scene-by-scene emotional responses. These range from properly timed admiration of Andromache's heroic struggle to solemnity during the play's climax and denouement. Although he claims that Sir Roger viewed every part of the performance, Addison neglects to mention the epilogue: "As we were the first that came into the House, so we were the last that went out of it."[49] While readers know how Sir Roger felt during every turn of the play, we do not learn his reaction to the epilogue.

When Addison, Budgell, and Steele ultimately discuss the epilogue, they stage a mock debate about epilogues, morality, and theatrical decorum. In no. 338, the correspondent, "Physibulus," advocates audience agency when he writes of his desire that tragedy be left intact:

> it is always my Custom, when I have been well entertained at a new Tragedy, to make my Retreat before the facetious Epilogue enters; not but that those Pieces are often very well writ, but having paid down my Half Crown, and made a fair Purchase of as much of the pleasing Melancholy as the Poet's Art can afford me, or my own Nature admit of, I am willing to carry some of it home with me, and can't endure to be at once trick'd out of all, tho' by the wittiest Dexterity in the World. However, I kept my Seat t'other Night, in hopes of finding my own Sentiments of this Matter favour'd by your Friends; when, to my great Surprize, I found the Knight entering with equal Pleasure into both Parts, and as much satisfied with Mrs. *Oldfield*'s Gaiety, as he had been before with *Andromache*'s Greatness. Whether this were no other than an Effect of the Knight's peculiar Humanity, pleas'd to find at last, that after all the Tragical Doings, every thing was safe and well, I don't know. But for my own part, I must confess, I was so dissatisfied, that I was sorry the Poet had sav'd *Andromache*, and could heartily have wish'd that he had left her stone-dead upon the Stage.[50]

Like the epilogue itself, this passage is both an in-joke among Addison, Budgell, Philips, and Steele, and a set-up for no. 341's endorsement of the bawdy epilogue. Physibulus apparently attends the theater to participate in the discussion of "this Matter favour'd by your Friends." He rejects both the bawdy epilogue itself and the enthusiasm for it that Sir Roger ("the Knight") displays. In this passage, Physibulus finds himself at odds with Sir Roger, whose easy transition from low to high spirits contradicts *Spectator* no. 335's endorsement of his emotional involvement.

To set everything right—that is, to make moments of bawdy humor (and cronyism) acceptable while still demonstrating good deportment—*Spectator* no. 341 accommodates the bawdy epilogue within polite society. This can only occur through a detachment that threatens the play's neoclassicism:

> I can by no means allow your melancholy Correspondent, that the new Epilogue is unnatural, because it is gay. If I had a mind to be learned I could tell him, that the Prologue and Epilogue were real Parts of the ancient Tragedy; but every one knows that on the *British* Stage they are distinct Performances by themselves, Pieces intirely detached from the Play, and no way essential to it.
>
> The Moment the Play ends, Mrs. *Oldfield* is no more *Andromache*, but Mrs. *Oldfield*; and tho' the Poet had left *Andromache stone-dead upon the Stage*, as your ingenious Correspondent phrases it, Mrs. *Oldfield* might still have spoke a merry Epilogue.[51]

His wish, that Andromache be left "stone-dead," recasts Physibulus as a fuddy-duddy and accommodates the bawdy epilogue. Despite citing an era that recognized the prologue and epilogue as part of the play, no. 341 makes room for future bawdy epilogues by glossing over their sexual content and claiming that since they are disconnected from their plays, they interrupt nothing. In the second paragraph, their description of Andromache's death indicates that Addison and Budgell view the actor as an empty vessel that the playwright fills with words. No collaboration between writer and actor takes place. The division of Oldfield and Andromache similarly supports the concept of the epilogue as a tacked-on afterthought. This reasoning does not leave open the possibility I am exploring here: that the epilogue's betweenness of the actress's character and public persona influences interpretations of the play. To the authors, Andromache ceases to exist in act 5, and Oldfield presents herself in the epilogue; any correlation between the two has ended. Their justification of the bawdy epilogue thus relies on a conception of a divided theater where characters, actors, playwrights, and authors of epilogues offer mutually exclusive contributions—in short, the opposite of my book's argument for a wide possibility of collaborations and interpretations.

Pamela as Theater Critic

Samuel Richardson recognizes the epilogue's layers of innuendo, however, and disapproves. The appearance of *The Distrest Mother*'s epilogue in Richardson's *Pamela* further illuminates its impact, and more generally, the power of bawdy epilogues. In *Licensing Entertainment: The Elevation of Novel Reading in Britain, 1684–1750,* William Warner argues that we should view the rise of the novel as a series of attempts made by Daniel Defoe, Richardson, and Henry Fielding to reform reading practices by deriding yet co-opting and sanitizing earlier novels of amorous intrigue by Aphra Behn, Delarivier Manley, and Eliza Haywood. In particular, he claims, the male novelists imitate their female contemporaries by writing a great deal of lurid sex into their books but surrounding it with moral commentary.[52] In *Pamela,* however, Richardson derides yet co-opts the epilogue to *The Distrest Mother* in the same manner as he treats the novel of amorous intrigue.[53] By extension, the epilogue's appearance within his first attempts to teach virtuous behavior and advance generic integrity suggests that Richardson may also have considered the tragedy with a bawdy epilogue as a device requiring reform. Through Pamela's disparagement, he reconceives the epilogue as more disturbing than its initial reception would demonstrate.[54] And his treatment of the epilogue demonstrates gender implications: Its orator rouses different responses from male and female audience members. These responses attest to the agency wielded by the actress as performer and the female audience member as theater critic. My reading demonstrates, through Pamela's negative reaction, the power of tragedies with bawdy epilogues.

After spending the first part of the novel exemplifying how a virtuous servant girl may secure her employer as a husband, Pamela turns theater critic in letters to her sister-in-law, commenting on the tragedy, and then on a comedy, an opera, and a masquerade. In Book IV, letter 11, Pamela writes to Lady Davers about her experience of attending a performance of *The Distrest Mother.* She gives a plot summary, discusses what she likes and doesn't like about the play, and singles out the epilogue for unequivocal condemnation. Her assessment of the epilogue is worth quoting in its entirety:

> But judge, my dear Lady, what, after the Play was over, I must think of the Epilogue, and indeed of that Part of the Audience, which called out for it.
>
> An Epilogue spoken by Mrs. Oldfield in the Character of *Andromache,* that was more shocking to me, than the most terrible Parts of the Play; as by lewd, and even senseless *Double Entendre,* it could be calculated only to efface all the tender, all the virtuous Sentiments, which the Tragedy was design'd to raise.
>
> The Pleasure this was receiv'd with by the Men, was equally barbarous and insulting; every one turning himself to the Boxes, Pit, and Galleries, where Ladies were, to see how they look'd, and how they stood an emphatical and too well pronounc'd Ridicule, not only upon the Play in general, but upon the Part of *Andromache* in particular, which had been so well sustain'd by an excellent Actress; and I was extremely mortify'd to see my favourite (and the only perfect) Character, debas'd and despoil'd, and the Widow of *Hector,* Prince of

Troy, talking Nastiness to an Audience, and setting it out with all the wicked Graces of Action, and affected Archness of Look, Attitude, and Emphasis.

I stood up—Dear Sir!—Dear Miss!—said I.

What's the Matter, my Love? said Mr. B. smiling, who expected, as he told me afterwards, to see me mov'd by this vile Epilogue—for it is always call'd for, it seems.

Why have I wept the Distresses of the injur'd *Hermione*? whisper'd I: Why have I been mov'd by the Murder of the brave *Pyrrhus*, and shock'd by the Madness of *Orestes*? Is it for this? See you not *Hector's* Widow, the noble *Andromache*, inverting the Design of the whole Play, satirizing her own Sex, but indeed most of all ridiculing and shaming, in my Mind, that Part of the Audience, who have call'd for this vile Epilogue, and those who can be delighted with it, after such Scenes of Horror and Distress?

He was pleas'd to say, smiling, I expected, my Dear, that your Delicacy, and Miss's too, would be shock'd on this preposterous Occasion. I never saw this Play, Rake as I was, but the Impropriety of the Epilogue sent me away dissatisfy'd with it, and with human Nature too: And you only see, by this one Instance, what a Character that of an Actor or Actress is, and how capable they are to personate any thing for a sorry Subsistence.

Well, but, Sir, said I, are there not, think you, extravagant Scenes and Characters enough in most Plays, to justify the Censures of the Virtuous upon them, that the wicked Friend of the Author must crown the Work in an Epilogue, for fear the Audience should go away improv'd by the Representation? It is not, I see, always Narrowness of Spirit, as I have heard some say, that opens the Mouths of good People against these Diversions.[55]

Pamela first objects to the idea of betweenness. Her preceding nineteen-page analysis of the play demonstrates that she prioritizes character over plot. This predilection contradicts Aristotle's ordering of tragic events. Pamela reverses Aristotle's hierarchy in three ways: the number of lines (154) she cites from the play (as a good "writer," she includes quotations to examine their language, not to retell the plot); her analyses of these lines with respect to character, with plot mentioned secondarily; and the disordered sequence of the quotations. The fact that she quotes scenes out of order indicates that fidelity to plot sequence is not Pamela's first motive. Her reflection over the Andromache–Hermione exchange instead exemplifies her priorities: "Why should [Philips] chuse to make Andromache's Part thus nobly moving at the Expence of the other Character, in a Point, where Justice, Generosity, and Humanity, were so much concern'd?"[56] Such comments typify her endorsement of character as a vehicle for promoting virtue, and my interest in the way that character becomes hybridized and disrupts the tragedy in the epilogue.

Her attribution of the play's inversion to Andromache indicates Pamela's anxiety over character inconsistency, an anxiety that influences the shape of fiction. The contrast Pamela draws between "my favorite (and the only perfect) Character" and her "debas'd and despoil'd" state in the epilogue demonstrates her high level of investment in Andromache's virtue. This point mirrors the novelistic shift Warner points out, where heroines in earlier novels of romantic intrigue engage in self-pleasure and thus provide readers with nonvirtuous entertainment. Richardson then co-opts plot and character types from these novels while simultaneously criticizing their spheres of immorality. Readers of Richardson therefore become absorbed with the protagonist's quest for virtue while being titillated by the lurid details preserved from the earlier novels. Pamela at the theater represents this invested reader; Andromache's swing away from the path of virtue toward a flippant character-actress amalgam derails Pamela's impassioned "reading." As Toni Bowers points out, this change in Andromache's character also cleaves Pamela from her identification with the heroine as exemplifying noble motherhood.[57] During the play, Pamela suffers pleasurably along with the anguished Andromache; during the epilogue, however, she suffers because Andromache's character no longer suffers.

Pamela's method of describing the epilogue also emphasizes the importance of considering this play as a performance. Her dual roles as eyewitness and correspondent to Lady Davers allow her to both discuss the responses of "her" audience and react as an emotional member of a group. Through the lens of scornful distaste for the epilogue, she manages to give important performance details, including the description of Oldfield's physical mannerisms and the apparent call-and-response interaction between Oldfield and a section of the audience. Interestingly, by stubbornly calling the epilogue's speaker "Andromache," despite the popular fervor for Oldfield, Pamela shows herself in sympathy with the contributor to Spectator no. 338. In this manner, Pamela describes how the saucy epilogue elicits her own emotionalism, which she blames on the epilogue's lack of virtue but which also suits the passionate theater environment she has just described. Considering the epilogue in performance, therefore, shows us how it spawns additional audience "performances." I call these performances rather than reactions because they differ from the customary reactions of tears to tragedy, laughter to comedy. Rather, as Pamela demonstrates, they involve leaving one's chair and turning oneself into a more visible spectacle.

Pamela also experiences an anxiety related to the disruption of genre. She seems psychologically invested in the idea of tragedy, particularly its closing catharsis. As such, Pamela is a naive viewer. Especially given its sexual content, the comic epilogue disabuses such members, demanding that they adjust their conception of the tragic theater. Since the epilogue was so famous, audiences of all but the premiere performance would have anticipated viewing it, a collective anticipation that must have intervened with the reception of the tragic ending. In adhering to an association between genre and morality, Pamela tries to protect this function of tragedy. The audience members, on the other hand, seem like spectators who favor a perverse source of appended pleasure that threatens the intactness of an established whole. The one "moment" of comedy threatens to upset the genre of tragedy in a way that troubles Pamela and delights a theatergoing audience with a taste for something besides tragedy or sentimental comedy. The generic disruption therefore provokes an amoral appreciation of comedy in the majority of the audience, but a moral response from Pamela.

Mirroring the instability created by the epilogue's generic disruption of the play, Pamela arrives at an inconsistency regarding the epilogue function that is akin to the state reached by the *Spectator* exchange. When deemphasizing plot in relation to character, Pamela claims that the epilogue disrupts plot but cannot make up her mind as to the outcome. Therefore she claims both that Andromache is "inverting the Design of the whole Play" and that the epilogue itself is an "unnatural and unexpected Piece of Ridicule, tack'd to so serious a Play, and coming after such a Moral."[58] These lines suggest the ways that the epilogue troubles the tragedy. For an epilogue to invert a tragedy's design might mean to reverse it in comedic fashion; to be tacked to it suggests a way of concluding tragedy in a trite yet connected way that upsets plot and character. Pamela cannot decide and is outvoted by the populace in her objections to the generic upset. This last point indicates the favored status of such epilogues and the cultural accommodation (at least) or embrace (more likely) of the tragedy with a bawdy epilogue.

Pamela's protectiveness of her sympathy for Andromache's plight reflects on theories of audience pleasure attained from tragedy. Eric Rothstein identifies two forms of tragedy theory that influenced the Restoration: the fabulist, which he associates with Hobbes's conception of pleasure as originating in the contrast between the safe audience member and the imperiled characters; and the affective, which he connects to Dryden's interpretation of Aristotle associating pleasure with pity for another.[59] Pamela's reaction to the epilogue illuminates both forms. Suddenly, Andromache/Oldfield's sexuality becomes a joke, a means of connecting with members of the audience, most of whom are able to transition from tragedy to comedy. For Pamela, whose preservation of her virginity has enabled her to make a virtuous marriage, Andromache's comic disruption of this ideal not only occasions her critical scorn but also physically upsets her because, in the Aristotelian sense, it dislodges her identification with or pity for the tragic heroine, or, in the Hobbesian sense, it disrupts her sense of safety. In being forced to recognize Andromache/ Oldfield's inconsistency, Pamela's own consistency of character is violated. The comic epilogue is thus a provocative factor in the development of works like *Pamela*, where authors strive to involve the reader empathically with the virtuous struggles of their protagonists.

Her discontent demonstrates how the tragedy with a comic epilogue has particular implications for the female viewer. In *Interpreting Ladies: Women, Wit and Morality in the Restoration Comedy of Manners*, Pat Gill discusses how the comedies of Etherege, Wycherley, and Congreve reestablished the idea of a consistent selfhood, in part by advancing the idea that dramatic obscenity rests in the eye of the beholder.[60] Congreve in particular uses this idea to rebuff female critics of *The Double Dealer*, telling them that they themselves are generating any smut they may perceive. This line of reasoning genders sexual innuendo as male and carries anxieties for women who recognize it; they therefore recognize the disruption of their virtuous simplicity. It is no wonder that, just as Pamela refuses to recognize sexual innuendo, she rejects it in the epilogue to *The Distrest Mother*. That Andromache/Oldfield delivers it disrupts this amalgamated character's virtuous simplicity; that Pamela recognizes it (which she definitely does) threatens her own.

Interrogating the men's response as itself part of the "barbarous" theater taking place, Pamela describes their reaction as if they themselves become part of the spectacle, and only women remain audience members. Laughing and turning to face the women in the audience, the men bodily align themselves with Andromache. The epilogue thus cleaves the audience by gender and gives each a distinct agency: the men physically support the orator, while the women sit (or in Pamela's case, stand) in judgment. This dynamic is then seen again in miniature, with Mr. B. waiting cunningly for Pamela to weigh in on the scene and then agreeing with her, one suspects, to preserve marital harmony.

Their qualified endorsement of bawdy epilogues demonstrates that Addison and Steele's goal of advocating the delightful integration of ideas at times licensed ribald immorality. Nos. 338 and 341 justify this example at the expense of their purpose for *The Spectator*. Elsewhere the authors promote simplicity, genteel manners, and consistency, but here they create a loophole for dissymmetry. They claim to wrest wit from its indecorous Restoration usage, but the epilogue to *The Distrest Mother* would have fit right in with the period's most lascivious plays. As we have seen, Addison pointedly condemns the tragicomedy and the double-plotted tragedy because they distract from the tragic plot. But his authorship of the epilogue and subsequent analysis in the *Spectator* contradict Addison and Steele's larger project. Addison's *Cato*, produced the following year, includes an epilogue by Dr. Samuel Garth that claims women who swear oaths of virginity, even in convents, are masochists. The scope of dramatists who offer inconsistent opinions about the bawdy epilogue, moreover, provides important information about how much eighteenth-century theater instigated reform. That actresses performed bawdy epilogues throughout the rest of the century suggests that we need to rethink the nature and success of the efforts to censor London Theater. By challenging character, genre, and moral boundaries within his performance as "the Spectator," Addison, it seems, created a betweenness for himself.

Beginning with Nell Gwyn's performance in Dryden's *Tyrannick Love*, the bawdy epilogue sacrificed strict integrity of role and genre to create a comic betweenness of character and actress. Through its continued performance and publication, the eighteenth century's most celebrated example, the epilogue to *The Distrest Mother*, inspired an ongoing dialogue among the literati concerning epilogues' relation to their plays, and more generally, to standards of morality and decorum. Above all, we cannot underestimate the importance of paratexts to the period's drama; for, in a statement that likewise holds true for epilogues, the prologue speaker to Jane Wiseman's *Antiochus the Great* tells the audience, "'Tis a hard Tax upon the Stage we know, / That without Prologue, you'll no Play allow."[61]

Notes

1. Besides the revived epilogues, other bawdy epilogues cited in this book include Bracegirdle's epilogues to Dryden's *King Arthur* and Rowe's *The Ambitious Step-Mother*.

2. "Indecent" is Mary Knapp's rather judgmental term. See Mary Etta Knapp, *Prologues and Epilogues of the Eighteenth Century* (New Haven, CT: Yale University Press, 1961), 103.

3. *The Spouter's Companion* (London: J. Cook, ca.1770), 9.

4. Ibid.

5. Eric Rothstein, *Restoration Tragedy: Form and the Process of Change* (Westport, CT: Greenwood Press, 1978), 3–14.

6. Rene Rapin, *Reflections on Aristotle's Treatise of Poesie. Containing the necessary, rational, and universal rules for Epick, dramatick, and the other sorts of poetry* (London: T. N. for H. Herringman, 1674), 14–15. On the other hand, as Judith Fisher points out, the proximity to the action for audience members seated onstage could make for comic interferences to tragedy. See Judith W. Fisher, "Audience Participation in the Eighteenth-Century London Theatre," in *Audience Participation: Essays on Inclusion in Performance*, ed. Susan Kattwinkel (Westport, CT: Praeger, 2003), 63.

188   ~   Chapter Five

7. Jeremy Collier, *A Short View of the Immorality, and Profaneness of the English Stage*, 1st ed. (London, S. Keble, 1698; reprint, 1996), 13–14.

8. For a discussion of Fielding's plentiful criticism of prologues and epilogues—criticism often occurring in the paratexts to his own plays—see Knapp, *Prologues*, 25–29.

9. Charles Bodens, *The Modish Couple* (London: J. Watts, 1732), [75]. Fielding's *The Covent-Garden Tragedy*, a 1732 burlesque of *The Distrest Mother*, also features an epilogue where the betweenness of character Isabel and actress Kitty Raftor (later Clive) is prominent. For a discussion of the burlesque, see Peter Lewis, "Fielding's *The Covent-Garden Tragedy* and Philips's *The Distrest Mother*," *Durham University Journal* 37 (1976): 33–46.

10. Pierre Danchin, *The Prologues and Epilogues of the Eighteenth Century*, 8 vols. (Nancy: Presses Universitaires de Nancy, 1990), 2:552.

11. Knapp, *Prologues*, 298.

12. W. J. Bate, John M. Bullitt, and L. F. Powell, eds., *The Yale Edition of the Works of Samuel Johnson*, vol. 2 (New Haven, CT: Yale University Press, 1963), 2:126.

13. Autrey Nell Wiley and Mary Knapp have identified the textual responses to this epilogue; see Autrey Nell Wiley, "Female Prologues and Epilogues in English Plays," *Publications of the Modern Language Association (PMLA)* 48 (1933): 1078–79; Knapp, *Prologues*, 12, 22–23, 295–97, 299–300. Danchin incorporates these passages into his analysis. See Danchin, *Eighteenth*, 1:502–3.

14. Between 1712 and 1800, the *London Stage* lists twenty-eight performances of *The Distrest Mother* that specify "With the original epilogue." The actual number of performances that included it was higher, especially because only five of Oldfield's thirty-three known performances were so designated.

15. Editor Donald F. Bond claims that although no. 341 bears Budgell's signature, his "contributions are clearly written by way of assistance to Addison, or even perhaps with his collaboration" (li). For a discussion of author identification, see Donald Frederic Bond, *The Spectator*, 5 vols. (Oxford: Clarendon, 1965), 1:xliii–lix.

16. Ibid., 1:44.

17. Matthew Kinservik makes a related claim about the 1737 Licensing Act "disciplining" rather than censuring satire. See Matthew Kinservik, *Discipling Satire* (Lewisburg, PA: Bucknell University Press, 2002), 11.

18. Felicity Nussbaum, *Rival Queens: Actresses, Performance, and the Eighteenth-Century British Theater* (Philadelphia: University of Pennsylvania Press, 2010), 106. For a discussion of the paratexts Maynwaring wrote for her, see Henry L. Snyder, "The Prologues and Epilogues of Arthur Maynwaring," *Philological Quarterly* 50 (1971): 610–29.

19. Danchin, *Eighteenth*, 3:567.

20. *Spectator* no. 341 says that Oldfield performed the epilogue nine times during the first three performances; Johnson says she performed it six times. Bond, *The Spectator*, 3:265–69; Samuel Johnson, "Ambrose Philips," in *The Lives of the Most Eminent English Poets* (London: C. Bathhurst et al., 1781), 4:297.

21. Edmund Curll, *Memoirs of the Life of Mrs. Oldfield* (London, 1731), 35. The *London Stage* lists thirty-one performance announcements specifying that "the Original epilogue" would be performed.

22. Johnson, "Ambrose Philips," 4:297–98. Knapp points out that Johnson recognized the epilogue's similarity to that of Edmund Smith's *Phaedra and Hippolitus* (1707); see Knapp, *Prologues*, 295. Samuel Johnson, "Life of Philips," in *Lives of the English Poets*, ed. George Birkbeck Hill (Oxford: Clarendon, 1905), 3:315 n.4; qtd. in Knapp, *Prologues*, 23.

23. As Knapp notes, Johnson's editor George Birkbeck Hill claims to have seen Piozzi's marginal note on a copy of *Spectator* no. 341. See Knapp, *Prologues*, 23.

24. Lincoln Faller names it as among the top twelve tragedies performed between 1700 and 1776. See Lincoln B. Faller, *The Population of Addison's Cato and Lillo's The London Merchant* (New York: Garland, 1988), 2. In addition, Henry Fielding parodies Pyrrhus and Andromache in his farce, *The Covent-Garden Tragedy*, a full twenty years after Philips's play premiered.

25. John Crowne also translated Racine's play, which played to an unreceptive audience during the summer season at Dorset Garden in 1674. For analyses of Philips's adaptation of Racine, see Katherine Ernestine Wheatley, *Racine and English Classicism* (Austin: University of Texas Press, 1956); Paul E. Parnell, "The Distrest Mother, Ambrose Philips' Morality Play," *Comparative Literature* 11, no. 2 (1959): 111–23.

26. *A Modest survey of that Celebrated Tragedy The Distrest Mother, so often and so highly applauded by the ingenious Spectator* (London: Redmayne and Morphew, 1712), 23, 29, 52. The author objects to Andromache misleading Pyrrhus about her love for him and to her suicide plan. Ultimately, the author argues that British writers need to clean up "French Importations."

27. Ambrose Philips, *The Distrest Mother*, 1st ed. (London: Sam. Buckley, 1712), A5r.

28. Ibid., 58:1–2.

29. Her delivery of this epilogue both changed the pattern of epilogues' associations with plays and led to more such performances for Oldfield. Despite his criticism of the form, Cibber seized on the idea and wrote for Oldfield bawdy epilogues to two tragedies: his own adaptation of *Le Cid*, entitled *The Heroick Daughter* (28 November 1712), and Charles Johnson's *The Victim* (5 January 1714).

30. "Tupped" is an alternate spelling of "topped." *Oxford English Dictionary*, 1991, s.v. "topped."

31. Judith Milhous and Robert Hume reprint the unique copy of "Memorial" and discuss this affair in Judith Milhous and Robert D. Hume, "Theatrical Politics at Drury Lane: New Light on Letitia Cross, Jane Rogers, and Anne Oldfield," *Bulletin of Research in the Humanities* 85, no. 4 (1982): 412–29.

32. Philips, *Distrest Mother*, 58:11–16.

33. Susan Staves, *Players' Sceptors: Fictions of Authority in the Restoration* (Lincoln: University of Nebraska Press, 1979), 234.

34. Oxford English Dictionary, 1991.

35. Thomas Laqueur, *Solitary Sex: A Cultural History of Masturbation* (New York: Zone Books, 2003), 13.

36. Ibid., 29, 424 n. 10.

37. Ibid., 58–60.

38. Philips, *Distrest Mother*, 58:17–20.

39. Oldfield's biographer, Joanne Lafler, chronicles Maynwaring's illness and death on 13 November 1712. See Joanne Lafler, *The Celebrated Mrs. Oldfield* (Carbondale: Southern Illinois University Press, 1989), 99–102.

40. Philip, *Distrest Mother*, 59:28–33.

41. Emmett Avery, *The London Stage, 1660–1800*, vol. 2, 1700–1729 (Carbondale: Southern Illinois University Press, 1960), 912.

42. Sybil Rosenfeld, *Strolling Players and Drama in the Provinces, 1660–1765* (Cambridge: Cambridge University Press, 1939), 138, 180, 232.

43. See Johnson, "Ambrose Philips," 6. James Boswell, *Life of Johnson*, ed. R. W. Chapman (Oxford: Oxford University Press, 1990), 749. Oldfield's 1730 and 1731 biographers attribute it to Budgell, but Lafler questions their credibility.

44. John Genest, *Some Account of the English Stage, from the Restoration in 1660 to 1830*, 10 vols. (London: H. E. Carrington, 1832), 2:496. Richard Bevis, *English Drama: Restoration and Eighteenth Century, 1660–1789* (New York: Longman, 1988); Charles A. Knight, *Joseph Addison and Richard Steele: A Reference Guide, 1730–1991* (New York: Simon and Schuster, 1994).

45. *A Modest survey.*

46. These are nos. 290, 335, 338, 341, 541, and 555.

47. Bond, *Spectator*, 3:33.

48. Philips, *Distrest Mother*, A5v:17–24.

49. Bond, *Spectator*, 3:242.

50. Ibid., 252.

51. Ibid., 266. Wiley's term "merry epilogues" for epilogues following tragedies comes from this passage.

52. William B. Warner, *Licensing Entertainment: The Elevation of Novel Reading in Britain, 1684–1750* (Berkeley: University of California Press, 1998), xiii–xv.

53. Knapp cites the passage as appearing in the third edition of *Pamela* (1742). The passage also appears in the first and sixth editions, which would indicate that it may have helped augment and sustain what Warner terms the "Pamela Media Event." See Knapp, *Prologues*, 297; Warner, *Licensing*, 176–230.

54. Warner defines a media event as centered on the advent of one medium that occasions other media, in the form of commentary, imitations, and spinoffs. My naming of *The Distrest Mother*'s epilogue a media event in one sense ironizes Warner's treatment of *Pamela*, since Warner says *Pamela* causes a media event. Here I read it as a response to an earlier media event occasioned by Oldfield's epilogue.

55. Samuel Richardson, *Pamela, or, Virtue Rewarded*, 6 ed., vol. 4 (London, 1772), 85–87.

56. Ibid., 79.

57. Toni Bowers, *The Politics of Motherhood: British Writing and Culture, 1680–1760* (Cambridge: Cambridge University Press, 1996), 183.

58. Richardson, *Pamela*, 4:87.

59. Rothstein, *Restoration Tragedy*, 3–14.

60. Pat Gill, *Interpreting Ladies: Women, Wit, and Morality in the Restoration Comedy of Manners* (Athens: University of Georgia Press, 1994), 5.

61. Jane Wiseman, *Antiochus the Great; or, the Fatal Relapse*, 1st ed. (London: William Turner and Richard Bassett, 1702), A3r: 1–2.

~

Conclusion

The number of Restoration prologues and epilogues is vast, and so is the variety of related subjects. To bring order to the archive, this book proposes a taxonomy and then offers one case study delineating an actress's oeuvre and a second tracing the performance and publication path of one epilogue. But there are many subsequent directions that theater scholars can pursue. Ironically, one direction is renewed attention to male-authored examples; whereas the recovery work on female playwrights has been more likely to analyze their prologues and epilogues, with few exceptions the same attention has not been brought to those of male playwrights. Gardiner's collection of Dryden's prologues and epilogues is sitting there, waiting for a critical analysis—meaning 103 texts by the greatest Restoration writer have been virtually untouched. The editors of *The Works of John Dryden* have provided excellent annotations, but the nature of their work has been to unite the author's total body of work, not to single out subgenres for further consideration. Out of the most frequent speakers of prologues and epilogues, I have only had space to consider Anne Bracegirdle's collectively; Elizabeth Barry, Thomas Betterton, Joseph Haines, Anne Oldfield, Mary Porter, and others deserve the same treatment. While chapter 3 singles out actresses' addresses to female audiences, future scholarship should consider those that female playwrights wrote for actresses, of which there are thirty-seven. As genres, prologues and epilogues deserve temporal consideration, given that those from the 1660s differ markedly from those from the 1710s. Where possible, I have heeded Danchin's guidance that work on prologues and epilogues needs to account for their evolution, but much more work is needed here to characterize paratexts temporally. And many paratexts tell stories, both individually and collectively; to name two examples, Nell Gwyn's "hat and belt" prologue encapsulates a rivalry between the two theater companies, and many prologues and epilogues meditate on their own genres. These are just a few of the subjects that lie waiting for critical analysis.

~

Appendix: Actresses' Prologues and Epilogues by Type

This appendix is meant to be a first step for anyone conducting further scholarship on actresses' prologues and epilogues. Categorizing prologues and epilogues is not a science and is of necessity somewhat messy. Prologues and epilogues often address many subjects very quickly and therefore may appear in more than one category, and some categories, such as "breeches," include many topics within their conceit. Breeches, revived, and virgin paratexts are simple to pick out, but the other three main categories have required judgments on my part where the reader might disagree. To supplement chapter 5, there is a category listing bawdy epilogues to tragedies. I have also created a category of "other exposed": paratexts that are definitely exposed but do not neatly fit into one of the six subcategories; almost all of these examples feature an actress in character and are thus the most similar to male exposed paratexts. The paratexts discussed at length in the book appear in *italics*.

Date of Performance	Play Title	Author of Play	Author of Prologue or Epilogue	Actress	Prologue or Epilogue
1. Cloaked					
4 Feb 1668	Horace	Katherine Philips	Philips	Anne Scott, Duchess of Monmouth	P
c.June 1672	Prologue for the Women	n/a	John Dryden	n/a	P
July 1674	Epilogue to University of Oxford	n/a	Dryden	Betty Boutell	E
Aug 1674	Andromache	John Crowne	Crowne	a woman	E
c.1675–1676	Beauties Triumph	Thomas Duffett	n/a	a young lady	E
Sept 1679	*The Young King*	*Aphra Behn*	*Behn*	*Elizabeth Barry "as nymph"*	*E*
Jan 1680	The Loving Enemies	Lewis Maidwell	Thomas Shadwell	Barry	E
c.1680–1681	Sophonisba	Nathaniel Lee	Lee	"Sophonisba" (Cox) or "Rosalinda" (Boutell)	E
Jan 1681	Second Part of the Rover	Behn	Behn	Barry	E
Jan–Mar 1681	Henry VI, with the Murder of Humphrey Duke of Gloucester	Crowne	Crowne	a woman	E
Oct 1681	Mr Turbulent	n/a	n/a	Mary Lee, Lady Slingsby	P
Oct 1681	The London Cuckolds	Edward Ravenscroft	"a friend"	Barry	P1
Apr 1682	*The City-Heiress*	*Behn*	*Thomas Otway*	*Barry*	*P*
10 Aug 1682	Romulus and Hersilia; or, The Sabine War	Behn	Behn	Charlotte Butler	P
12 Nov 1683	Constantine	Lee	Dryden	Sarah Cooke	E
Feb 1684	*Valentinian*	*Rochester*	*Behn*	*Barry*	*P3*
1685–1686 or 1686–1687	Titus A.., or, The Rape of Lavinia	Ravenscroft	n/a	a woman?	E1
Mar 1687	The Emperour of the Moon	Behn	Behn	Cooke	E

Date	Title			a woman	
4 Dec 1689	Don Sebastian, King of Portugal	Dryden	Dryden	a woman	P[1]
late Mar 1690	The Amorous Bigotte	Shadwell	Shadwell	Butler	P[2]
Nov 1690	King Edward III	n/a	n/a	Anne Bracegirdle	E
Early to mid-1690s	Aristomenes	Anne Finch	Finch	Finch	P
Early to mid-1690s	Aristomenes	Finch	Finch	Finch	E
Feb 1692	*The Rape; or, The Innocent Imposters*	*Nicholas Brady*	*Shadwell*	*Bracegirdle*	*E*
c.Jan 1694	Prologue upon her Majesty's coming to see the Old Bachelor	William Congreve	n/a	Barry	P
Feb 1694	The Fatal Marriage	Thomas Southerne	Southerne	Bracegirdle	P
Apr 1696	Pausanias	Richard Norton	Anto. Henley	Susannah Verbruggen	E
Apr 1696	The Country Wake	Thomas Doggett	Doggett	Barry	P
June 1696	The Husband his own Cuckold	John Dryden Jr	John Dryden Sr	Bracegirdle	E[1] & E[2]
14 Nov 1696	The Anatomist, or, The Sham-Doctor	Ravenscroft	Peter Motteux	Barry	P[1]
c.Spring 1699	Prologue to the Princess	n/a	Congreve?	Bracegirdle	P
Apr 1699	Princess of Parma	Henry Smith	Motteux	Bracegirdle	E
Mar 1701	The Double Distress	Mary Pix	Pix	Mary Porter (not in cast)	E
Dec 1701	Tamerlane	Nicholas Rowe	Rowe	Bracegirdle	E
Jan 1703	The Governor of Cyprus	John Oldmixon	Oldmixon	Porter (not in cast)	E
Mar 1703	The Fair Penitent	Rowe	Rowe	Bracegirdle	E[3]
Apr 1703	The Fickle Shepherdess	anon	n/a	Porter	P
c.Nov 1703	*The Different Widows*	*Pix*	*Pix*	*Porter*	*E*
Sept 1704	The Metamorphosis	John Corye	Corye	Bradshaw	P[2]
25 Nov 1704	The Biter	Rowe	Rowe	Bracegirdle	E

(continued)

Date	Play Title	Author of Play	Author of Prologue or Epilogue	Actress	Prologue or Epilogue
16 Feb 1705	Gibraltar; or, The Spanish Adventures	John Dennis	a Friend	"Leonora, a young Spanish Lady"	E
7 Mar 1706	The Temple of Love	Motteux	Motteux	Lucretia Bradshaw (not in cast)	E
30 Mar 1706	Camilla	Bononcini/Owen Swiney	Richard Estcourt	Oldfield	E
22 Mar 1707	Sganarell, or, the Cuckold in Conceit	John Vanbrugh	Vanbrugh	probably a woman	E
9 Feb 1708	Irene; or, The Fair Greek	Charles Goring	Goring	Porter	E[4]
14 Dec 1708	The Fine Lady's Airs	Thomas Baker	Baker	Bradshaw	E
7 Apr 1709	Love for Love	Congreve	n/a	Barry	E
3 May 1709	The Modern Prophets	Thomas D'Urfey	D'Urfey	Bradshaw	P
20–25 Mar 1710	Epilogue	n/a	n/a	Francis Mary Knight	E
19 Jan 1712	The Perplex'd Lovers	Susannah Centlivre	Centlivre	Oldfield	E

2. Revived Epilogues

Date	Play Title	Author of Play	Author of Prologue or Epilogue	Actress	Prologue or Epilogue
24 June 1669	Tyrannick Love	Dryden	Dryden	Nell Gwyn	E
Aug 1673	Herod and Mariamne	Samuel Pordage	Pordage	"Mariamne"	E
1675	private perf. at Belvoir Castle	Thomas Shipman	Shipman	"P.L."	P[5]
Aug 1675	Piso's Conspiracy	anon	anon	"Poppea"	E[6]
Sept 1675	Alcibiades	Otway	Otway	Mary Lee	E
Oct 1679	The History and Fall of Caius Marius	Otway	Otway	"Mrs Barry, who acted Lavinia"	E
10 Aug 1682	Romulus and Hersilia	Behn	Behn	Lady Slingsby	E
Feb 1684	Valentinian	Rochester	a person of quality	Barry	E
late Apr 1688	Darius King of Persia	Crowne	Crowne	"Barzana"	E[7]

Date	Title	Author	Adapter/Source	Actress	Code
Dec 1689	Dido and Aeneas	Nahum Tate and Henry Purcell	Tate and Purcell	Lady Dorothy Burk	E
1690	The Maid's Tragedy Alter'd	Edmund Waller	Waller	"Aspasia bleeding"	E[8]
mid-Apr 1692	Cleomenes	Dryden	Dryden	Bracegirdle	E
8 Nov 1692	Henry II, King of England	John Bancroft or William Mountfort	Dryden	Bracegirdle	E1 & E2
mid-Apr 1700	The Fate of Capua	Southerne	Colonel Codrington	Barry	E
Dec 1700	*The Ambitious Step-Mother*	*Nicholas Rowe*	*Rowe*	*Bracegirdle*	*E*
Nov 1701	Antiochus the Great	Jane Wiseman	a Friend	Barry	E
28 Jan 1710	Valentinian	Rochester	n/a	Hester Santlow	E
5 Jan 1714	The Victim	Charles Johnson	Colley Cibber	Anne Oldfield	E
3. Breeches					
Feb 1663	The Slighted Maid	Sir Robert Stapylton	Stapylton	Gibbs	E
7 Nov 1667	The Tempest	Davenant and Dryden	Dryden	Long	P[9]
Dec 1670	The Conquest of Granada I	Dryden	Dryden	Gwyn	P[10]
June 1671	The Generous Enemies	Corye	Corye	actress in breeches	E
c.June 1672	The Parson's Wedding (all female)	Thomas Killigrew	Killigrew	Marshall	P
c.June 1672	The Parson's Wedding	Killigrew	Killigrew?	Rebecca Marshall	E
June/July 1672	Secret-Love	Dryden	Dryden	Boutell	P
June/July 1672	Secret-Love	Dryden	Dryden	Ann Reeves	E
Nov 1674	Love and Revenge	Elkanah Settle	Settle	"Nigrello"	E
15 Feb 1675	Calisto	Crowne	Crowne	Intended for Lady Henrietta Maria Wentworth	E[11]

(continued)

Date	Play Title	Author of Play	Author of Prologue or Epilogue	Actress	Prologue or Epilogue
May 1675	The Conquest of China by the Tartars	Settle	Settle	Lee	E
July 1677	The Constant Nymph	"a person of Quality"	"a person of Quality"	Lee	P
28 May 1678	The Counterfeits	John Leanerd?	Leanerd?	Barry	E
Sept 1679	The Woman Captain	Shadwell	Shadwell	Barry, "the Woman-Captain"	E
Jan 1680	The Loving Enemies	Lewis Maidwell	Shadwell	Barry	E[12]
11 Mar 1682	The Heir of Morocco	Settle	Settle	"Spoken by Mrs. Coysh's girl, as Cupid"	E
10 Aug 1682	*Romulus and Hersilia*	*Behn*	*Behn*	*Lady Slingsby*	*E*
4 Dec 1689	Don Sebastian, King of Portugal	Dryden	Dryden	S. Mountfort	P2
Jan 1690	The Treacherous Brothers	George Powell	Mountfort	Butler	E
mid-Dec 1690	The Mistakes; or, The False Report	Joseph Harris (& maybe Mountfort)	Tate	Butler	E
Mar 1691	Bussy D'Ambois	D'Urfey	D'Urfey	n/a	E
mid-Apr 1691	Greenwich Park	Mountfort	Mountfort	a woman and Mrs Knight	E
10 July 1691	A Long Prologue to a Short Play	n/a	n/a	a woman "Drest like a Sea Officer"	P
Jan 1692	The Marriage-Hater Match'd	D'Urfey	D'Urfey	Mountfort & Bracegirdle	P
21 Mar 1694	The Ambitious Slave	Settle	Settle	Jane Rogers as "Mirvan, a Persian Eunuch"	E
30 Apr 1695	*Love for Love*	*Congreve*	*Congreve*	*Bracegirdle*	*P*

Date	Title	Author	P/E Author	Speaker	Type
Sept 1695	She Ventures and He Wins		Ariadne	Elizabeth Bowman	P
Dec 1695	Agnes de Castro	Catharine Trotter	Trotter	Verbruggen	E
Dec 1695	The Lover's Luck	Thomas Dilke	Dilke	Howard	E
late Dec 1695	The She-Gallants	Lord Lansdowne	Lansdowne	Bracegirdle	E
5 May 1697	A Plot and No Plot	John Dennis	Dennis	Betty Allison	E
late June 1697	The World in the Moon; an Opera	Settle	Settle	Miss Denny Chock	E
May 1703 (unacted)	Hypermnestra; or, Love in Tears	Robert Owen	Owen	intended for Porter	P[13]
3 July 1703	The Pilgrim	Vanbrugh	Vanbrugh	Bickerstaff	E
28 Jan 1710	Valentinian	Rochester	n/a	Santlow	E
4 Feb 1710	*Don Quixote II*	*D'Urfey*	*n/a*	*Santlow*	*E*
7 Feb 1710	The Gamester	Centlivre	n/a	Santlow	E
c.Early spring 1710	Epilogue	Aaron Hill	Hill	a woman	E
20 Jan 1711	The Generous Husband	Charles Johnson	Johnson	Bradshaw	E
29 Jan 1713	The Humours of the Army	Charles Shadwell	Shadwell	S. Mountfort II	E[14]

4. Virgin

Date	Title	Author	P/E Author	Speaker	Type
6 Apr 1670	The Faithful Shepherdess	Beaumont and Fletcher	n/a	Lady Mary Mordaunt	E[15]
c.1674–1675	The Indian Emperour	Dryden	Dryden	a girl	E
8 June 1676	Don Carlos	Otway	Otway	a girle	E
1676	Abdelazer; or, The Moor's Revenge	Behn	a friend	"Spoken by little Mrs. Ariell"	E
c.1680s	Prologue at a Boarding School	n/a	n/a	a girl	P
c.1680s	Another prologue at a Boarding School	n/a	n/a	a girl	P
c.1680s	Epilogue spoken by a little girl	n/a	n/a	a girl	E
late Feb 1680	The Orphan	Otway	Otway	Butler	E
c.Sept 1680	Fatal Love, or, the Forc'd Inconstancy	Settle	Settle	a woman	E

(continued)

Date	Play Title	Author of Play	Author of Prologue or Epilogue	Actress	Prologue or Epilogue
Oct or Nov 1681	Sir Barnaby Whigg	D'Urfey	D'Urfey	a new actress	E
11 Mar 1682	The Heir of Morocco	Settle	Settle	"Spoken by Mrs. Coysh's girl, as Cupid"	E
c.1683–1684	The Indian Empress	16 year old writer	same	"some young Ladyes at Green-wich"	2P+E
Aug 1685	A Commonwealth of Women	D'Urfey	D'Urfey	probably Bracegirdle	E
Dec 1689	Dido and Aeneas	Nahum Tate and Henry Purcell	Tate and Purcell	Lady Dorothy Burk	E
1690	The Prophetess	Thomas Betterton (adaptation)	Dryden?	a woman	E
Sept 1695	Bonduca, or, The British Heroine	Powell?	Powell?	Chock	E
Sept 1695	The Mock-Marriage	Thomas Scott	Scott	Letitia Cross	P
Nov 1695	Don Quixote III	D'Urfey	D'Urfey	Mr Horden and Cross	P
Dec 1695	Philaster, or, Love Lies a Bleeding	Beaumont & Fletcher, revised by Settle	Settle	a girl	E
Dec 1695	The Lover's Luck	Dilke	Dilke	Howard	E
mid-Dec 1695	Cyrus the Great	John Banks	Banks	the boy and girl	E[16]
1696	Don Carlos	Otway	Finch	young ladies	P
Jan 1696	Love's Last Shift	Cibber	Cibber	Cross	E
Mar 1696	The Lost Lover	Delarivier Manley	Manley	Cross	E
Apr 1696	The Royal Mischief	Manley	Manley	Bradshaw (not in cast)	E
late May 1696	Ibrahim, The 13th Emperour of the Turks	Pix	Pix	Cross	P

Date	Title				
late Spring 1696	Ibrahim: a new prologue	Pix	n/a	Cross	P
June or July 1696	The Cornish Comedy	n/a	Haines	Chock	E
Nov 1696	Roman Bride's Revenge	Charles Gildon	Gildon	Allison	E
21 Nov 1696	*The Relapse*	*Vanbrugh*	*Vanbrugh*	Cross	*P*
Dec 1696	The City Lady	Dilke	Dilke	Howard (not in cast)	E
Jan 1697	Woman's Wit	Cibber	Cibber	Cross	E
5 May 1697	A Plot and No Plot	Dennis	Dennis	Allison	E
late June 1697	The World in the Moon; an Opera	Settle	Settle	a new girl	P
late June 1697	The World in the Moon	Settle	Settle	Chock	E
Nov/Dec 1697	The Deceiver Deceived	Pix	Pix	Bradshaw (not in cast)	E
Feb/Mar 1698	Caligula	Crowne	Crowne	spoken by a girl	E
late Mar/early Apr 1698	Phaeton	Gildon	Gildon	Cross and Mr Powell	P
June 1698	The Revengeful Queen	William Philips	Philips	Chock	E
mid-late June 1698	Victorious Love	William Walker	Walker	Cross	E
late June 1698	Queen Catharine	Pix	Pix	Porter	E
18–20 Oct 1698	The Wheel of Fortune	Thomas Neale	Neale	"Fortune"	E1
18–20 Oct 1698	The Wheel of Fortune	Neale	Neale	"Fortuna and Astraea" (Porter and Chock)	E2 & E3
c.1698–1699	epilogue for Mrs Lucas	(in D'Urfey's *Wit and Mirth*)	n/a	Lucas	E
May 1699	The Rise and Fall of Massaniello Part 2	D'Urfey	D'Urfey	Mary Ann Campian	E
Feb 1700	The Generous Choice	Francis Manning	Manning	Porter	E
31 Dec 1702	The Stolen Heiress	Centlivre	Centlivre	Prince	P
3 July 1703	The Pilgrim	Vanbrugh	Vanbrugh	Bickerstaff	E
24 June 1704	The Wit of a Woman	Thomas Walker	Walker	Bradshaw	P2
Summer 1705–1706	Timon of Athens	Shakespeare	John Froud	J. Power	E

(continued)

Date	Play Title	Author of Play	Author of Prologue or Epilogue	Actress	Prologue or Epilogue
5 Apr 1706	The Wonders in the Sun	D'Urfey	D'Urfey	Porter with "the little girl"	E
June 1706	The Adventures in Madrid	Pix	Pix	"the little girl"	E
Aug 1706	Love at a Venture	Mrs Carrol (Centlivre)	Centlivre	J. Power	E
24 Oct 1706	The Recruiting Officer	George Farquhar	n/a	Babb	P
3 Jan 1710	Elfrid; or, The Fair Inconstant	Aaron Hill	Hill	Santlow	E

5. Tendentious

Date	Play Title	Author of Play	Author of Prologue or Epilogue	Actress	Prologue or Epilogue
On/after Mar 1662	Selindra	Killigrew	Killigrew	a woman	E[17]
Feb 1663	The Slighted Maid	Sir Robert Stapylton	Stapylton	Gibbs	E
c.Spring 1663	The Four Hours Adventure	n/a	n/a	a woman	E
20 Sept 1670	The Forc'd Marriage	Behn	Behn	a woman	E
June 1672	Philaster	Beaumont & Fletcher	n/a	Marshall	P
c.Spring 1672	Prologue to the Lady-Actors	n/a	Waller	a woman	P
Mar 1673	The Spanish Rogue	Thomas Duffett	Duffett	Boutell	P
Mar 1673	The Spanish Rogue	Duffett	Duffett	Knep	E
c.Late spring 1674	The Mock Tempest	Duffett	Duffett	Mr Haines and Mackarel	P
c.1675–1700	The Lovers Stratagem	n/a	n/a	"Macquerella"	P
29 Jan 1676	Gloriana; or, The Court of Augustus Caesar	Lee	Lee	Mrs. Rochester	P
Mar 1677	The Country Innocence	Thomas Leanerd	Leanerd	Knep	E
Mar or Apr 77	The French Conjurer	Thomas Porter	Porter	a woman	P

Date	Title		Author	Actor	Code
5 Apr 1678	Friendship in Fashion	Otway	Otway	Barry	E
Nov 1678, or earlier	The Destruction of Troy	Banks	Banks	Anne Quin	E
Mar 1679	The Feign'd Curtizans; or, A Night's Intrigue	Behn	Behn	Betty Currer	P
8 Apr 1679	misc. pro. found in Bodleian ms.	unknown	unknown	a woman	P
Sept or Oct 1679	The Merry Milkmaid of Islington	n/a	n/a	a woman	E[18]
Sept or Oct 1679	Love Lost in the Dark	n/a	n/a	a woman	E
Sept or Oct 1679	The Politick Whore	n/a	n/a	"Portia, the Politick Whore"	E
Jan 1680	The Loving Enemies	Maidwell	Shadwell	Barry	E
8 Dec 1680	Lucius Junius Brutus	Lee	Lee	Barry	E
1680–1681	History of King Lear	Tate	Tate	Barry	E
1681	The Lancashire Witches	Shadwell	Shadwell	"Mrs Barry and Tegue."	E
4 Feb 1682	The Loyal Brother, or, The Persian Prince	Southerne	Southerne	Cooke	E
Mar 1682	Like Father, Like Son	Behn	Behn	Butler	P
Apr 1682	*The City-Heiress*	*Behn*	*Behn*	*Butler*	*E*
31 May 1683	Dame Dobson; or, The Cunning Woman	Ravenscroft	Ravenscroft	Currer	P
Feb 1684	Valentinian	Rochester	n/a	Cooke	P2
Feb 1684	Valentinian	Rochester	n/a	Barry	E
mid-Mar 1684	The Northern Lass	Richard Brome	Brome	Butler	E
c.July 1686	An Epilogue. Spoken to University of Oxon	n/a	n/a	Cooke	E
20 Nov 1689	The Widdow Ranter	Behn	Dryden	a woman	P
4 Dec 1689	Don Sebastian, King of Portugal	Dryden	Dryden	a woman	P
c.1690	The Maid's Tragedy Alter'd	Waller	Waller	a woman	E

(continued)

Date	Play Title	Author of Play	Author of Prologue or Epilogue	Actress	Prologue or Epilogue
Jan 1690	The Successful Straingers	Mountfort	Mountfort	Bracegirdle	P
Jan 1690	The Treacherous Brothers	Powell	Mountfort	Knight	P
late Mar 1690	The Amorous Bigotte	Shadwell	Shadwell	Bracegirdle	E
late Sept 1690	Sir Anthony Love, or, The Rambling Lady	Southerne	Southerne	Bracegirdle	P
May or June 1691	King Arthur; or, The British Worthy	Dryden	Dryden	Bracegirdle	E
Apr 1692	Cleomenes	Dryden	Dryden	Bracegirdle	E
8 Nov 1692	Henry II, King of England	Bancroft or Mountfort	Dryden	Bracegirdle	E2
9 Mar 1693	The Old Bachelor	Congreve	Congreve	Bracegirdle	P
9 Mar 1693	The Old Bachelor	Congreve	Congreve	Barry	E
late Mar 1693	The Wary Widow, or, Sir Noisy Parrat	Henry Higden	n/a	Lassells	E
Feb 1694	The Fatal Marriage; or, The Innocent Adultery	Southerne	Southerne	Verbruggen	E
21 Mar 1694	The Ambitious Slave	Settle	Settle	Rogers ("Mirvan, a Persian Eunuch")	E
30 Apr 1695	Love for Love	Congreve	Congreve	Bracegirdle	E1 & E2
Sept 1695	She Ventures and He Wins	Ariadne	Ariadne	Bowman	P
Dec 1695	Agnes de Castro	Trotter	Trotter	Verbruggen	E
mid or late 1690s	Epilogue for Mrs. Verbruggen	n/a	n/a	Verbruggen	E1
Mar 1696	The Lost Lover, or, The Jealous Husband	Manley	Manley	Cross	E
c.Nov 1697	Boadicea Queen of Britain	Charles Hopkins	Hopkins	Bowman	E

Mar 1698	The Pretenders	Dilke	Dilke	Henrietta Moor	E
Feb 1700	The Generous Choice	Francis Manning	Manning	Porter	E
5 Mar 1700	The Way of the World	Congreve	Congreve	Cross	E
Oct 1700	The Perjured Husband	Centlivre	"a Gentleman"	Oldfield	P
23 Nov 1700	Love at a Loss	Trotter	Trotter	"Lesbia"	E
c. Dec 1700	*The Ambitious Step-Mother*	Rowe	Rowe	*Bracegirdle*	*E*
c.1700–1701	St Stephen's Green	William Phillips	Phillips	"Lady Volant"	E
c. Mar 1701	The Czar of Muscovy	Pix	Lee/Burnaby	a woman	E
Feb 1702	The False Friend	Vanbrugh	Vanbrugh	Oldfield	E
Dec 1702	The Twin Rivals	Farquhar	Farquhar	Mary Hook	E
mid-Oct 1703	Marry or do Worse	Walker	Walker	Porter	P
9 Apr 1705	The Loves of Ergasto	Giacomo Greber	Greber	Bracegirdle	E
23 Nov 1705	Ulysses	Rowe	Rowe	Bracegirdle	E
21 Apr 1707	Phaedra and Hippolytus	Edmund Smith	Smith	Oldfield	E
1 Nov 1707	The Double Gallant	Cibber	Cibber	probably a woman	E
1709	Love and Liberty	Johnson	Lee/Burnaby	a woman	E[19]
12 Dec 1709	The Man's Bewitch'd	Centlivre	Cibber	Oldfield	E
20 Apr 1710	The Force of Friendship	Johnson	Johnson	Margaret Bicknell	E
12 May 1713	The Wife of Bath	John Gay	Gay	Mountfort	P
24 Nov 1713	The Apparition	"a gentleman of Christ Church College in Oxford"	n/a	Santlow	E

6. Female Solidarity

Autumn 1663	Love's Kingdom	Richard Flecknoe	n/a	"Venus"	P
c.1666	St Cecily, or The Converted Twins	E.M.	n/a	"Augusta, Palinodio, Phantasio, Meretricio"	E
18 Dec 1668	Catiline's Conspiracy	Ben Jonson	n/a	Gwyn in "Amazonian Habit"	P

(continued)

Date	Play Title	Author of Play	Author of Prologue or Epilogue	Actress	Prologue or Epilogue
18 Dec 1668	Catiline's Conspiracy	Ben Jonson	n/a	Nell Gwyn	E
June 1669	Tyrannick Love	Dryden	Dryden	Gwyn	E
Spring 1670	The Womens Conquest	Edward Howard	Howard	"Queen of Amazons"	E
20 Sept 1670	The Forc'd Marriage	Behn	Behn	a woman (at least after line 41)	P
24 Feb 1671	The Amorous Prince	Behn	Behn	"Cloris and Guilliam"	E
6 Mar 1671	The Six Days Adventure	Howard	Howard	a woman	P
6 Feb 1672	The Gentleman Dancing-Master	William Wycherley	Wycherley	"Flirt"	E
June or July 1672	Secret-Love	Dryden	Dryden	Boutell	P
June 1672	Philaster (all-female prod.)	Beaumont & Fletcher	n/a	R. Marshall	E
3 July 1673	Empress of Morocco	Settle	Earl of Rochester	Lady Elizabeth Howard	P2
Nov 1674	Love and Revenge	Settle	Settle	"Nigrello in a Man's Habit"	E
12 Jan 1675	The Country Wife	Wycherley	Wycherley	Knep	E
c.1675–1700	The Lovers Stratagem	n/a	n/a	"Macquerella"	P
c.1675–1700	The Lovers Stratagem	n/a	n/a	"Dianora"	E
c.1675–1676	Beauties Triumph	Duffett	Duffett	a young lady	P
c.1676–1677	Cytherea	John Smith	Smith	"Venus"	P
c.1676–1677	Cytherea	Smith	Smith	"Venus in a bower"	E
Sept 1677	The Siege of Babylon	Samuel Pordage	Pordage	M. Betterton	E
28 May 1678	The Counterfeits	John Leanerd?	Leanerd?	Barry	E
June 1678	Squire Oldsapp	D'Urfey	D'Urfey	Currer	E
20 June 1678	Huntington Divertisement	n/a	n/a	"Huntingtonia"	E
8 Apr 1679	misc. pro. found in Bodleian ms.	n/a	n/a	a woman	P

Date	Title	Author		Speaker/Note	
Sept or Oct 1679	The Merry Milkmaid of Islington	n/a	n/a	a woman	E
c.Mar 1681	Tamerlane the Great	Charles Saunders	Dryden	maybe a woman?	E
c.Oct 1681	The False Count	Behn	Behn	Barry	E
mid-Oct 1681	Mithridates, King of Pontus	Lee	Lee	Mrs Cox and Carlell Goodman	E
Oct or Nov 1681	Sir Barnaby Whigg	D'Urfey	D'Urfey	a new actress	E
11 Mar 1682	The Heir of Morocco	Settle	Settle	"Spoken by Mrs. Coysh's girl, as Cupid"	E
Apr 1682	*The City-Heiress*	*Behn*	*n/a*	*Butler*	*E*
18 July 1682	Epilogue spoken by Mrs Moyle at Oxford	n/a	n/a	Moyle	E
10 Aug 1682	Romulus and Hersilia; or, The Sabine War	Behn	Behn	Lady Slingsby	E
28 Nov 1682	The Duke of Guise	Dryden and Lee	Dryden	Cooke	E
28 Nov 1682	The Duke of Guise (2nd epilogue)	Dryden and Lee	Dryden	an actress	E
Dec 1682	*The Princess of Cleve*	*Lee*	*Dryden*	*a woman*	*P*
Dec 1682	The Princess of Cleve	Lee	Dryden	a woman	E
31 May 1683	Dame Dobson; or, The Cunning Woman	Ravenscroft	Ravenscroft	Currer	P
c.1683–1684	The Indian Empress	16 year old writer	same	"some young Ladyes at Green-wich"	P1
Feb 1684	*Valentinian*	*Rochester*	*Behn*	*Cooke*	*P1*
Jan 1686	The Banditti; or, A Ladies Distress	D'Urfey	D'Urfey	a woman	P
c.July 1686	An Epilogue. Spoken to University of Oxon	n/a	n/a	Cooke	E
July 1687	Epilogue spoken at Oxford	n/a	prob. Wm. Mountfort	Mountfort	E

(continued)

Date	Play Title	Author of Play	Author of Prologue or Epilogue	Actress	Prologue or Epilogue
Early May 1688	Squire of Alsatia	Shadwell	Shadwell	Mountfort	E
4 Dec 1689	Don Sebastian, King of Portugal	Dryden	Dryden	Mountfort	P2
Dec 1689	The Late Revolution	n/a	n/a	Madame Celiers	E
Jan 1690	The Successful Straingers	Mountfort	Mountfort	Bracegirdle	P
Jan 1690	The Treacherous Brothers	Powell	Mountfort	Butler	E
Mar 1690	*The Amorous Bigotte*	*Shadwell*	*Shadwell*	*Bracegirdle*	*E*
June 1690	Belphegor; or, The Marriage of the Devil	John Wilson	Wilson	"Imperia"	E
21 Oct 1690	Amphitryon	Dryden	Dryden	Bracegirdle	P
Dec 1690	Alphonso King of Naples	Powell	D'Urfey	Knight	E
Dec 1690	The Scowrers	Shadwell	Shadwell	prob. Barry or Bracegirdle	E
mid-Dec 1690	The Mistakes, or, The False Report	Harris (& maybe Mountfort)	Tate	Butler	E
Mar 1691	Bussy D'Ambois	D'Urfey	D'Urfey	n/a	E
May or June 1691	King Arthur; or, The British Worthy	Dryden	Dryden	Bracegirdle	E
Dec 1691	The Wives Excuse	Southerne	Southerne	Barry	E
June 1692	Regulus	Crowne	Crowne	Bracegirdle	E
Nov 1692	The Volunteers; or, The Stock-Jobbers	Shadwell	D'Urfey	Bracegirdle	P
Feb 1693	The Maid's Last Prayer	Southerne	Southerne	Barry	P
Feb 1693	The Maid's Last Prayer	Southerne	Southerne	Bracegirdle	E
mid-Apr 1693	The Richmond Heiress	D'Urfey	D'Urfey	a woman	E
mid-Jan 1694	Love Triumphant; or, Nature will Prevail	Dryden	Dryden	Mountfort	E

Date	Title				
Feb 1694	The Fatal Marriage	Southerne	Southerne	Verbruggen	E
30 Apr 1695	*Love for Love*	*Congreve*	*Congreve*	*Bracegirdle*	*P*
30 Apr 1695	Love for Love	Congreve	Congreve	Bracegirdle	E2
Nov 1695	Oroonoko	Southerne	Southerne	Verbruggen	E
Dec 1695	Philaster	Settle (adaptation)	Settle	a girl	E
Dec 1695	The Lover's Luck	Dilke	Dilke	Howard	E
Jan 1696	*Love's Last Shift*	*Cibber*	*Cibber*	*Cross*	*E*
Mar 1696	The City Bride; or, the Merry Cuckold	Harris	Harris	Bowman	E
Mar 1696	The Lost Lover, or, The Jealous Husband	Manley	Manley	Cross	E
Apr 1696	Pausanias	Norton	Henley	Verbruggen	E
c.late spring 1696	Ibrahim, The 13th Emperour of the Turks	Pix	Pix	Cross	P
c.late spring 1696	*Ibrahim*	*Pix*	*n/a*	*Cross*	*P2*
Oct 1696	Brutus of Alba, or, Augusta's Triumph	n/a	n/a	Diana Temple	E
Oct 1696	Rule a Wife and Have a Wife	Fletcher	n/a	prob. a woman	P
late 1690s	An Epilogue, for Mrs. Verbruggan	n/a	n/a	Verbruggen	E1 & E2
Nov 1696	*The Relapse; or, Virtue in Danger*	*Vanbrugh*	*Vanbrugh*	*Cross*	*P1*
Nov 1696	The Relapse; or, Virtue in Danger	Vanbrugh	Vanbrugh	Verbruggen	P2
Dec 1696	Aesop	Vanbrugh	Vanbrugh	"Aesop, Oronces, Euphronia"	E20
Feb 1697	The Mourning Bride	Congreve	Congreve	Bracegirdle	E
Feb or Mar 1697	The Triumphs of Virtue	n/a	n/a	Rogers	E

(continued)

Date	Play Title	Author of Play	Author of Prologue or Epilogue	Actress	Prologue or Epilogue
May 1697	The Intrigues at Versailles	D'Urfey	D'Urfey	Barry	E
June 1697	The Novelty	Motteux and others	Motteux	Prince	E
Late Apr 1698	Beauty in Distress	Motteux	Motteux	Bracegirdle	E
May or June 1698	Fatal Friendship	Trotter	Trotter	Barry	E
Feb 1699	The Island Princess	Motteux	Motteux	Mr Will Pinkethman and Rogers	E1
Feb 1700	The Generous Choice	Manning	n/a	Porter	E
Jan 1701	The Ladies Visiting-Day	William Burnaby	Burnaby	Prince	E
4 Feb 1701	The Unhappy Penitent	Trotter	Trotter	Oldfield	P
Dec 1702	The Twin Rivals	Farquhar	Farquhar	Hook	E
Apr 1703	The Fickle Shepherdess	n/a	n/a	Porter	P
Apr 1703	The Fickle Shepherdess	n/a	Burnaby	Barry	E
c.Nov 1703	The Different Widows	Pix	Pix	Porter	E
Jan 1704	Abra Mule; or, Love in Empire	anon (Joseph Trapp)	Trapp	Bracegirdle	E
Nov 1704	The Biter	Rowe	Rowe	Bracegirdle	E
16 Feb 1705	Gibraltar; or, The Spanish Adventures	Dennis	"a Friend"	"Leonora, a young Spanish Lady"	E
30 Oct 1705	The Confederacy	Vanbrugh	Vanbrugh	Barry	E
23 Nov 1705	Ulysses	Rowe	Rowe	Bracegirdle	E
3 Dec 1705	Perolla and Izadora	Cibber	Maynwaring	Oldfield	E
27 Dec 1705	The Mistake	Vanbrugh	Motteux	Porter	E
Nov 1706	Platonick Lady	Centlivre	Thomas Baker	Bracegirdle	E
21 Apr 1707	Phaedra and Hippolytus	Smith	Smith	Oldfield	E
5 June 1708	The Maid the Mistress	William Taverner	Taverner	a woman (Danchin: prob. Knight)	E

Date	Title	Author	Attribution	Performer	Code
27 Mar 1710	A Bickerstaffe's Burial	Centlivre	n/a	a woman?	E[21]
c.Feb 1712	The Mohocks	John Gay	Gay	"the person who should have play'd Joan Cloudy"	E
17 Mar 1712	The Distrest Mother	Ambrose Philips	Addison/Budgell	Oldfield	E
Early 1713	The Fall of Tarquin	William Hunt	a "gentlewoman of York"	Pearson	E2
12 May 1713	The Wife of Bath	Gay	Gay	Bicknell	E
2 Feb 1714	Tragedy of Jane Shore	Rowe	Rowe	Oldfield	E1
2 Feb 1714	Tragedy of Jane Shore	Rowe	Pope	Oldfield	E2
1714	The Wonder: A Woman Keeps a Secret	Centlivre	A. Philips	Santlow	E
25 Jun 1714	The Puritan	"Written by Shakespeare"	Henry Carey	Miss Younger, who played "Miss Molly"	E

7. Social Critique Type 1: Mocking Masculinity

Date	Title	Author	Attribution	Performer	Code
Mar 1664	The Comical Revenge; or, Love in a Tub	George Etherege	Etherege	"the Widow" (prob. Mrs Long)	E
20 Feb 1668	The Duke of Lerma	Sir Robert Howard	Howard	Nell Gwyn & Mrs Knepp	P
spring 1670	The Womens Conquest	Edward Howard	Howard	Queen of Amazons	E
June 1671	Juliana; or, The Princess of Poland	Crowne	Crowne	"Paulina and Landlord"	E
June 1671	The Generous Enemies	Corye	Corye	actress in breeches	E
June 1672	New Poems (only printed)	Duffet	n/a	a woman	E
c.June 1672	The Parson's Wedding (all female)	Killigrew	Killigrew	Marshall	P
June/July 1672	Secret-Love	Dryden	Dryden	Recves	E

(continued)

Date	Play Title	Author of Play	Author of Prologue or Epilogue	Actress	Prologue or Epilogue
c.1673–1674	Concealed Royalty	n/a	n/a	Right Honorable Lady Christian Bruce	P
9 Nov 1674	Love and Revenge	Settle	Settle	"Nigrello in a Man's Habit"	E
12 Jan 1675	*The Country Wife*	*Wycherley*	*Wycherley*	*Knep*	*E*
c.1675–1700	The Lovers Stratagem	n/a	n/a	"Macquerella"	P
28 May 1675	The Conquest of China by the Tartars	Settle	Settle	Lee	E
Nov 1676	Titus and Berenice	Otway	Otway	Lee "when she was out of Humour"	E
Feb 1677	The Debauchee	Behn?	n/a	a woman	P
Summer 1677	The Counterfeit Bridegroom	maybe Betterton or Behn	n/a	Currer	P
17 Jan 1678	Sir Patient Fancy	Behn	Behn	Quin	E
Late Feb 1678	The Rambling Justice	Leanerd	Leanerd	"Flora"	P
5 Apr 1678	Friendship in Fashion	Otway	Otway	Barry	E
20 June 1678	Huntington Divertisement	n/a	n/a	"Huntingtonia"	E
8 Apr 1679	misc. pro. found in Bodleian ms.	unknown	unknown	a woman	P1
8 Dec 1680	Lucius Junius Brutus	Lee	Lee	Barry	E
mid-Oct 1681	Mithridates, King of Pontus	Lee	Lee	Elizabeth Cox and Mr Goodman	E
c.Oct 1681	The False Count	Behn	Behn	Barry	E
Apr 1682	*The City-Heiress*	*Behn*	*Behn*	*Butler*	*E*
Dec 1682	The Princess of Cleve	Lee	Dryden	a woman	E
Nov 1683	The London Cuckolds	Ravenscroft	"W.C."	a woman	P2
20 Nov 1689	The Widdow Ranter	Behn	Dryden	a woman	E

		Dryden	Dryden	Mountfort	P2
4 Dec 1689	Don Sebastian, King of Portugal				
Sept 1690	Sir Anthony Love	Southerne	Southerne	Butler	E
Dec 1690	Alphonso King of Naples	Powell	D'Urfey	Knight	E
Feb 1692	*The Rape; or, The Innocent Imposters*	*Brady*	*Shadwell*	*Bracegirdle*	*E*
late Apr 1693	A Very Good Wife	Powell	Powell	Knight	E
Oct 1693	The Double Dealer	Congreve	Congreve	Bracegirdle	P
Oct 1693	The Double Dealer	Congreve	Congreve	Mountfort	E
30 Apr 1695	*Love for Love*	Congreve	Congreve	Bracegirdle	P
Sept 1695	The Mock-Marriage	Scott	Scott	Knight	E
Nov 1695	Don Quixote III	D'Urfey	D'Urfey	"Mary the Buxome" (Verbruggen)	E
Jan 1696	*Love's Last Shift*	*Cibber*	*Cibber*	*Cross*	*E*
Mar 1696	The City Bride; or, the Merry Cuckold	Harris	Harris	Bowman	E
Feb or Mar 1697	The Triumphs of Virtue	n/a	n/a	Allison	P
Feb or Mar 1697	The Triumphs of Virtue	n/a	n/a	Rogers	E
Apr 1697	The Provok'd Wife	Vanbrugh	Vanbrugh	Bracegirdle	P
Apr 1697	The Provok'd Wife	Vanbrugh	Vanbrugh	Barry and Bracegirdle	E
May 1697	The Intrigues at Versailles	D'Urfey	D'Urfey	Barry	E
June 1697	The Novelty	Motteux and others	Motteux	Prince ("Theodosia")	E
May 1699	The Rise and Fall of Massaniello 1	D'Urfey	D'Urfey	Rogers	E
5 Mar 1700	The Way of the World	Congreve	Congreve	Bracegirdle	E
Jan 1701	The Ladies Visiting-Day	Burnaby	Burnaby	Prince	E
c.Mar 1701	The Czar of Muscovy	anon (Pix)	Lee/Burnaby	a woman	E

(continued)

Date	Play Title	Author of Play	Author of Prologue or Epilogue	Actress	Prologue or Epilogue
Apr 1701	Love's Victim; or, The Queen of Wales	anon (Gildon)	Burnaby	Porter	E
Dec 1701	Altemira	Charles Boyle	Boyle	Porter	E
Apr 1703	The Fickle Shepherdess	anon	Burnaby	Barry	E
Nov 1706	Platonick Lady	Centlivre	Thomas Baker	(written for Bracegirdle)	E
1709	Love and Liberty	Johnson	Lee/Burnaby	a woman	E
19 Feb 1713	Cinna's Conspiracy	n/a (adaptation of Corneille's *Cinna*)	n/a	Porter	E

8. Social Critique Type 2: Critiques of Love and Marriage

Date	Play Title	Author of Play	Author of Prologue or Epilogue	Actress	Prologue or Epilogue
c.June 1672	Henry the Third of France	Shipman	n/a	a woman	E
c.June 1672	Epilogue by a woman	Duffett	Duffett	a woman	E
9 Nov 1674	Love and Revenge	Settle	Settle	"Nigrello"	E
11 Dec 1680	The Sicilian Usurper (History of Richard II)	Tate	Tate	Mrs. Cook	E
Apr 1682	*The City-Heiress*	*Behn*	*Behn*	*Mrs Butler*	*E*
Jan 1686	The Banditti; or, A Ladies Distress	D'Urfey	D'Urfey	a woman	P
4 Mar 1686	The Devil of a Wife	Thomas Jevon	Jevon	Jevon and Susannah Percival	E
Jan 1691	Love For Money, or, The Boarding School	D'Urfey	D'Urfey	Mountfort and Mrs Butler	E
Dec 1691	The Wives Excuse	Southerne	Southerne	Barry	E
8 Nov 1692	Henry II, King of England	Bancroft or Mountfort	Dryden	Bracegirdle	E1

Feb 1693	The Maid's Last Prayer	Southerne	Southerne	Bracegirdle	E
mid-Apr 1693	The Richmond Heiress	D'Urfey	D'Urfey	a woman	E
mid-Jan 1694	Love Triumphant; or, Nature will Prevail	Dryden	Dryden	Mountfort	E
21 Mar 1694	The Ambitious Slave	Settle	Settle	Knight	P
Nov 1695	Oroonoko	Southerne	Congreve	Verbruggen	E
Late Aug 1696	Spanish Wives	Pix	Pix	Verbruggen	E
May or June 1698	Fatal Friendship	Trotter	Trotter	Barry	E
May 1699	The Rise and Fall of Massaniello 1	D'Urfey	D'Urfey	Rogers	E
23 Nov 1700	Love at a Loss	Trotter	Trotter	"Lesbia"	E
Apr 1701	Love's Victim; or, The Queen of Wales	anon (Gildon)	Burnaby	Porter	E
Nov 1701	Antiochus the Great	Jane Wiseman	"a Friend"	Barry	E
Feb 1703	Love Betray'd	Burnaby	Burnaby	Barry	E
Mar 1703	The Fair Penitent	Rowe	Rowe	Bracegirdle	E
16 Feb 1704	The Amorous Widow	Betterton	Maynwaring	Oldfield	E
14 Jun 1705	Sir Solomon Single	John Caryll	Caryll	Susanna Mountfort II	E
30 Oct 1705	The Confederacy	Vanbrugh	Vanbrugh	Barry	E
3 Dec 1705	Perolla and Izadora	Cibber	Maynwaring	Oldfield	E
27 Dec 1705	The Mistake	Vanbrugh	Motteux	Mrs Porter	E
11 Feb 1706	The Revolution of Sweden	Trotter	Trotter	a woman	E
Nov 1707	The Royal Convert	Rowe	Rowe	Oldfield	E
5 June 1708	The Maid the Mistress	Taverner	Taverner	a woman (Danchin: prob. Mrs Knight)	E
3 May 1709	The Modern Prophets	D'Urfey	D'Urfey	Bicknel & Porter	E
12 Dec 1709	The Man's Bewitch'd	Centlivre	Cibber	Oldfield	E
27 Mar 1710	A Bickerstaffe's Burial	Centlivre	n/a	a woman?	E
30 Dec 1710	Marplot	Centlivre	Centlivre	a woman	E

(continued)

Date	Play Title	Author of Play	Author of Prologue or Epilogue	Actress	Prologue or Epilogue
12 Nov 1711	The Wives Relief	C. Johnson	Maynwaring	Oldfield	E
c.Feb 1712	The Mohocks	Gay	Gay	"the person who should have play'd Joan Cloudy"	E
28 Nov 1712	The Heroick Daughter	Cibber	Cibber	"Ximena" (Oldfield)	E
6 Jan 1713	The Female Advocates	Taverner	Taverner	a woman	E
12 May 1713	The Wife of Bath	Gay	Gay	Bicknell	E
25 Jun 1714	The Puritan	"Written by Shakespeare"	Carey	Younger, who played "Miss Molly"	E
9. Social Critique Type 3: Complaints of Male Infidelity/Mistreatment of Women					
c.1670	unknown play	Jonson?	Shadwell?	a woman (and a man)	P
20 Sept 1670	The Forc'd Marriage	Behn	Behn	A woman (at least after line 41)	P
June 1672	Philaster (all-female prod.)	Beaumont & Fletcher	n/a	Marshall	E
July 1673	Empress of Morocco	Settle	Lord Lumnley	Lady Elizabeth Howard	P1
3 July 1673	Empress of Morocco	Settle	Settle	Howard	P2
late Aug 1676	Tom Essence; or, The Modish Wife	Thomas Rawlins?	Rawlins	a woman	E
18 Jan 1677	The Destruction of Jerusalem by Titus, part II	John Crowne	Crowne	R. Marshall	E
July 1677	The Constant Nymph	n/a	n/a	Lee	P
June 1678	Squire Oldsapp; or, The Night	Thomas D'Urfey	D'Urfey	Currer	E
Sept 1679	The Politick Whore; or, The Conceited Cuckold	n/a	n/a	"Portia, the Politick Whore"	E
Apr 1682	The City-Heiress	Behn	Behn	Butler	E

July 1682	epilogue spoken by Mrs Moyle at Oxford	n/a	n/a	Moyle	E
28 Nov 1682	The Duke of Guise (2nd epilogue)	Dryden and Lee	Dryden	a woman	E
late 1680s	epilogue by a Woman leaving the Stage	n/a	n/a	a woman	E
late Mar 1690	The Amorous Bigotte	Shadwell	Shadwell	Bracegirdle	E
21 Oct 1690	Amphytrion	Dryden	Dryden	Mountfort ("Phaedra")	E
June 1692	Regulus	Crowne	Crowne	Bracegirdle	E
Apr 1693	The Richmond Heiress	D'Urfey	D'Urfey	a woman	E
2 Feb 1714	Tragedy of Jane Shore	Rowe	Finch	Oldfield	E[3]
1714	The Wonder: A Woman Keeps a Secret	Centlivre	Philips	Santlow	E

10. Bawdy (but nonrevived) epilogues to tragedies

1663–1664	Heraclitus Emperour of the East	Monsieur de Corneille	n/a	"Leontina"	E
20 Feb 1668	The Great Favorite; or, The Duke of Lerma	Howard	Howard	Gwyn	E
18 Dec 1668	Catiline's Conspiracy	Jonson	n/a	Gwyn	E
1670–1671	The Religious Rebell; or, The Pilgrim-Prince	n/a	n/a	"witty Matilda"	E
8 Dec 1680	Lucius Junius Brutus	Lee	Lee	Barry	E[22]
late Oct 1690	Distres'd Innocence	Settle	Montfort	Knight	E
Feb 1697	The Mourning Bride	Congreve	Congreve	Bracegirdle	E
Late Apr 1698	Beauty in Distress	Motteux	Motteux	Bracegirdle	E
Mar 1703	The Fair Penitent	Rowe	Rowe	Bracegirdle	E[23]
17 Mar 1712	*The Distrest Mother*	*Philips*	*Addison/Budgell*	*Oldfield*	*E*

(continued)

Date	Play Title	Author of Play	Author of Prologue or Epilogue	Actress	Prologue or Epilogue
Early 1713	The Fall of Tarquin	William Hunt	a "gentlewoman of York"	Pearson	E2
17 Apr 1713	Cato	Addison	Dr Garth	Porter	E
2 Feb 1714	Tragedy of Jane Shore	Rowe	Rowe	Oldfield	E1
2 Feb 1714	Tragedy of Jane Shore	Rowe	Pope	Oldfield	E2
11. Other Exposed					
c.1662–1663	A Witty Combat	T.P.	n/a	"Madam Moders"	E
mid-Oct 1663	The Step-Mother	Stapylton	Stapylton	"the Step-Mother"	E
c.1663–1664	The Ungrateful Favourite	Person of honour	n/a	"Tragedie" and others	P
25 Jan 1674	The Indian Queen	Howard & Dryden	n/a	Indian boy and girl	P
25 Jan 1664	The Indian Queen	Howard & Dryden	n/a	Montezuma	E
c.1666	St Cecily, or The Converted Twins	E.M.	n/a	"Augusta, Palinodio, Phantasio, Mereretricio"	E
Feb 1663	The Slighted Maid	Stapylton	Stapylton	Gibbs	E
Late Feb 1667	Secret-Love	Dryden	Dryden	Gwyn	E
c.1668–1669	Life of Mother Shipton	Thomas Thompson	n/a	"Mother Shipton"	E
1670	Querer por Solo Querer	Don Antonio de Mendoza	n/a	Isabella Velasco & Isabella Guzman	P
c.Spring 1672	Sodom	n/a (Settle, Rochester, Fishbourne?)	n/a	"Cunticula"	E

Date	Title	Author		Role/Character	
c.Spring 1672	Sodom	n/a (Settle, Rochester, Fishbourne?)	n/a	"Fuckadilla"	E
c.Spring 1672	Sodom	n/a (Settle, Rochester, Fishbourne?)	n/a	"Madam Swivia"	E
30 Mar 1674	Ariane, ou le Mariage de Bacchus	Pierre Perrin	Perrin	"Thamis," 3 nymphs as rivers	P
c.Late spring 1674	The Mock Tempest	Duffett	Duffett	"Miranda"	E
26 Nov 1674	The Triumphant Widow	William Cavendish	Cavendish	a woman	E
15 Feb 1675	Calisto	Crowne	Crowne	3 nymphs + 4 parts of the world	P
c.Spring 1675	The Martial Queen	R. Carleton	Carleton	Lady Christian Bruce	P
11 Dec 1676	The Plain Dealer	Wycherley	Wycherley	"Widow Blackacre"	E
c.1676–1677	Cytherea	Smith	Smith	"Venus, wearing a flaming girdle"	P
c.1676–1677	Cytherea	John Smith	Smith	"Venus in a bower"	E
29 May 1677	Rare en Tout	Madame de la Roche-Guilhen	n/a	"L'Europe, La Thamise," others	P
June 1678	Brutus of Alba	Tate	Tate	"Ragusa"	E
Sept 1679	The Virtuous Wife	D'Urfey	D'Urfey	Barry, Tony Leigh, James Nokes	P
Dec 1679	The Loyal General	Tate	Tate	Currer, the "Queen"	E
Dec 1681	Ingratitude of a Commonwealth	Tate	Tate	"Valeria"	E
c.Dec 1681	The Roundheads	Behn	Behn	"Lady Desbro"	E
c.1681–1682	Venus and Adonis, a masque	Blow	Blow	"Cupid, Shepherds, Shepherdesses"	P

(continued)

Date	Play Title	Author of Play	Author of Prologue or Epilogue	Actress	Prologue or Epilogue
1681–1682	Romes Follies	n/a	n/a	Florimel	E
c.1688–1689	The Benefice	Robert Wild	Wild	"Ceres, the Goddess of Harvest"	P[24]
c.1688–1689	The Benefice	Wild	Wild	"Ceres" & someone else	E
Apr 1689	Bury-Fair	Shadwell	Shadwell	Mountfort	E
Dec 1689	Dido and Aeneas	Tate & Purcell	n/a	"Phoebus and Nereids"	P
Dec 1689	The Late Revolution	n/a	n/a	Madame Celiers	E
1690–1691	Win Her and Take Her	John Smyth and Underhill?	D'Urfey	Butler	E
Jan 1692	Marriage-Hater Match'd	D'Urfey	D'Urfey	Mr W. Mountfort & Bracegirdle	P
Jan 1692	Marriage-Hater Match'd	D'Urfey	D'Urfey	"La Pupsey" (Butler) & "her Lap-Dog in Masquerade"	E
mid-June 1693	"Dublin epilogue"	n/a	n/a	Butler	E
Late May 1694	Don Quixote II	D'Urfey	D'Urfey	"Sancho and Mary the Buxome" (Underhill & Mrs Verbruggen)	E
14 Nov 1696	The Anatomist	Ravenscroft	n/a	"Thalia and Erato"	P2
Dec 1696	Aesop	Vanbrugh	Vanbrugh	"Aesop, Oronces, Euphronia"	E
Dec 1696	Cinthia and Endimion; or, The Loves of the Deities	D'Urfey	D'Urfey	Several female and male characters	P
Apr 1697	The Provok'd Wife	Vanbrough	"by another hand"	"Lady Brute and Bellinda"	E
c.1697–1698	The Puritanical Justice (unacted)	n/a	n/a	"Mrs Sneak"	P
Feb 1699	The Island Princess	Motteux	Motteux	Pinkethman and Mrs Rogers	E1

Date	Title		Author	Character/Role	
Feb 1699	The Island Princess	Motteux	Motteux & Clarke	Mary Lindsey	E2[25]
Mar 1700	The Reform'd Wife	Burnaby	a friend	"the Sickly Lady"	E
31 May 1701	The Bath	D'Urfey	D'Urfey	"Crab and Gillian" (Cibber & S. Verbruggen)	E
Mar 1703	The Old Mode and the New	D'Urfey	D'Urfey	Moor	E
24 June 1704	The Wit of a Woman	Thomas Walker	n/a	a woman	P1
13 Nov 1704	Zelmane; or, The Corinthian Queen	Pix?	n/a	Bowman "dressed like Victory"	E
3 Jan 1706	The Faithful General	"a young lady"	"a young lady"	Bradshaw	E
5 Apr 1706	The Wonders in the Sun	D'Urfey	D'Urfey	"the Satyr", the "Genius of Poetry," "Apollo, Calliope, Orpheus, Eurydice"	P
25 Feb 1710	The Fair Quaker of Deal	Charles Shadwell	Shadwell	"the Fair Quaker" (Santlow)	E
15 Apr 1710	The Royal Merchant	Beaumont & Fletcher, adapted	n/a	Bradshaw	P
17 Aug 1711	The City Ramble; or A Playhouse Wedding	Settle	Settle	Many incl. councilman's wife, daughter, and an actress	P
c.Jan 1712	The General Cashiered	n/a	n/a	"Fame and Envy"	P
Early 1713	The Fall of Tarquin	William Hunt	Dr Towne	"Clelia"	E1
c.Jul 1713	The Players Epilogue	n/a	n/a	Willis	E

Notes

1. Danchin does not attribute a sex. I suspect it is a female epilogue because of the reference to pregnancy in the first line.

2. Political, but also self-referential.

3. Bracegirdle's character does die at the end of this play, but the epilogue entirely features Bracegirdle's perspective, not that of her character.

4. Discusses comic epilogues to tragedies.

5. The exception to the rule: this is the one "revived prologue."

6. Danchin thinks the speaker is either Poppea or Nero. The line "'Twould please You to see Pretty Miss reviv'd" makes me think the speaker is female. See Jane Wiseman, *Antiochus the great; or, the fatal relapse*, 1st ed. (London: William Turner and Richard Bassett, 1702), A3r: 1–2.

7. Barry was supposed to deliver this epilogue but got sick during the play; Boutell delivered it instead. This must have caused confusion given that Barry's character Barzana was the only woman to die in the play.

8. Epilogue takes place in the process of Aspasia dying.

9. This is likely a breeches prologue, since in the performance Long played the cross-dressed part of Hypolito.

10. This is not a breeches prologue per se; Gwyn dresses in a broad-brimmed hat and belt to parody James Nokes. I have included it in this section because Gwyn likely wore breeches as part of her costume.

11. Wentworth played Jupiter, a breeches part, at court. In this epilogue she has returned to her female form but comments on the breeches role.

12. Content-wise this reads as a cloaked epilogue, but Barry's character Camilla was wearing breeches at the end of act 5.

13. This prologue was later used as the prologue to Charles Johnson's *Love and Liberty* (1709).

14. This is Susannah Mountfort, daughter of William and Susannah Mountfort.

15. This epilogue features an older woman advertising young girls' developing sexuality.

16. The boy and girl do not otherwise appear in the play, but they refer here to the convention of the revived epilogue.

17. This may or may not be an epilogue, but given its resemblance to the genre I have chosen to include it. Danchin excludes it. For further discussion, see Pierre Danchin, *The Prologues and Epilogues of the Restoration, 1660–1700*, 4 vols. (Nancy: Presses Universitaires de Nancy, 1981–1988), 2:680.

18. *The Merry Milkmaid of Islington, Love Lost in the Dark*, and *The Politick Whore* are published together in *The Muse of Newmarket* (London, 1680).

19. Danchin: this is largely the same epilogue as that spoken by Elizabeth Barry to *Lucius Junius Brutus* on 8 December 1680, later used in a slightly different form in *The Czar of Muscovy* in 1701. For a discussion of variants, see Vander Motten, "An Unnoticed Restoration Epilogue," *English Studies* 67, no. 4 (1986): 308–10.

20. Danchin considers this a scene rather than an epilogue.

21. It is my conjecture that the speaker is a woman.

22. Barry's character committed suicide, but the epilogue entirely features Barry's perspective, not that of her character.

23. Bracegirdle's character does die at the end of this play, but the epilogue entirely features Bracegirdle's perspective, not that of her character.

24. Follows lengthy induction.

25. A song.

Bibliography

Adam, Michel. "L'utilisation des actrices dans les prologues et epilogues sur la scene anglaise de 1668 a 1689." In *De William Shakespeare a William Golding: Melanges dedies a la memoire de Jean-Pierre Vernier*, edited by Sylvere Monod, 65–76. Rouen: Rouen University Press, 1984.

Anon. *Animadversions on Mr. Congreve's Late Answer to Mr. Collier*. London: John Nutt, 1698.

———. "The Friendly vindication of Mr Dryden from the censure of the Rota." Cambridge, 1673.

———. *The Player's Tragedy. Or, Fatal Love*. London, 1693.

———. *Poems on Affairs of State*. Vol. 4. London, 1707.

Apte, Mahadev. *Humor and Laughter: An Anthropological Approach*. Ithaca, NY: Cornell University Press, 1985.

Aston, Anthony. *A Brief Supplement to Colley Cibber, Esq. His Lives of the Late Famous Actors and Actresses*. London, 1747.

Auslander, Philip. "Comedy about the Failure of Comedy: Stand-Up Comedy and Postmodernism." In *Critical Theory and Performance*, edited by Janelle G. Reinelt and Joseph R. Roach, 196–204. Ann Arbor: University of Michigan Press, 1992.

Austin, J. L. *How to Do Things with Words*. Edited by J. O. Urmson and Marina Sbisa. Cambridge, MA: Harvard University Press, 1975.

Avery, Emmett. *The London Stage, 1660–1800*. Vol. 2, *1700–1729*. Carbondale: Southern Illinois University Press, 1960.

———. "Rhetorical Patterns in Restoration Prologues and Epilogues." In *Essays in American and English Literature Presented to Bruce Robert McElderry, Jr.*, edited by Max Schulz, with William D. Templeman and Charles R. Metzger, 221–37. Athens: Ohio University Press, 1967.

Avery, Emmett L., and Arthur H. Scouten. "Introduction." in *The London Stage*, edited by William Van Lennep. Carbondale: Southern Illinois University Press, 1965.

Ballaster, Rosalind. *Seductive Forms: Women's Amatory Fiction from 1684–1740*. Oxford: Oxford University Press, 1992.

Bancroft, John. *Henry the Second, King of England, with the Death of Rosamond*. London: Jacob Tonson, 1693.

———. *King Edward the Third, with the Fall of Mortimer*. London: Hindmarsh, 1691.

Banks, John. *Cyrus the Great: or, the Tragedy of Love*. 1st ed. London: Richard Bentley, 1696.

———.*The Unhappy Favourite, or, the Earl of Essex*. London: Lintot, 1699.

Barreca, Regina. *Last Laughs: Perspectives on Women and Comedy*. New York: Gordon and Breach, 1988.

Bashar, Nazife. "Rape in England between 1550 and 1700." In *The Sexual Dynamics of History*, edited by London Feminist History Group, 28–42. London: Pluto, 1983.

Bate, W. J., John M. Bullitt, and L. F. Powell, eds. *The Yale Edition of the Works of Samuel Johnson*. Vol. 2. New Haven, CT: Yale University Press, 1963.

Beach, Adam R. "Carnival Politics, Generous Satire, and Nationalist Spectacle in Behn's *The Rover*." *Eighteenth-Century Life* 28, no. 3 (2004): 1–19.

Behn, Aphra. "The Rover." In *The Works of Aphra Behn*. Electronic edition, edited by Janet Todd. Charlottesville, VA: InteLex Corporation, 2004.

Bennett, Susan. "Decomposing History (Why Are There So Few Women in Theater History?)." In *Theorizing Practice: Redefining Theatre History*, edited by W. B. Worthen and Peter Holland, 71–87. Hampshire: Palgrave Macmillan, 2003.

———. *Theatre Audiences: A Theory of Production and Reception*. 2nd ed. London: Routledge, 2001.

———. "Theatre History, Historiography and Women's Dramatic Writing." In *Women, Theatre and Performance*, edited by Maggie B. Gale and Viv Gardner, 46–59. Manchester: Manchester University Press, 2000.

Bevis, Richard. *English Drama: Restoration and Eighteenth Century, 1660–1789*. New York: Longman, 1988.

Blount, Charles. "Mr Dreyden vindicated in a reply to the friendly vindication of Mr Dreyden: with reflections on the Rota." London: T. D., 1673.

Bodens, Charles. *The Modish Couple*. London: J. Watts, 1732.

Bond, Donald Frederic. *The Spectator*. 5 vols. Oxford: Clarendon, 1965.

Boswell, James. *Life of Johnson*. Edited by R. W. Chapman. Oxford: Oxford University Press, 1990.

Bourke, Mary. "Comedy Cabaret: Downstairs at the King's Head." Crouch End, London, 2002.

Bower, George Spencer. *A Study of the Prologue and Epilogue in English Literature from Shakespeare to Dryden*. London: Kegan, Paul, Trench, 1884.

Bowers, Toni. *The Politics of Motherhood: British Writing and Culture, 1680–1760*. Cambridge: Cambridge University Press, 1996.

Brady, Nicholas. *The Rape: or, the Innocent Impostors.* 1st ed. London: R. Bentley, 1692.

Brown, John Russell, ed. *The Oxford Illustrated History of Theatre.* Oxford: Oxford University Press, 2001.

Brown, Laura. "The Defenseless Woman and the Development of English Tragedy." *Studies in English Literature* 22 (1982): 429–43.

Brown, Tom. *Amusements Serious and Comical, Calculated for the Meridian of London.* 2nd ed. London: John Nutt, 1702.

———. "Bully Dawson to Bully Watson." In *A Continuation or Second Part of the Letters from the Dead to the Living.* London, 1703.

———. "Elegy on Mounfort." Huntington Library, 1693.

———. "From the Worthy Mrs Behn the Poetess to the Famous Virgin Actress." In *A Continuation or Second Part of the Letters from the Dead to the Living.* London 1703.

Bruster, Douglas, and Robert Weimann. *Prologues to Shakespeare's Theatre: Performance and Liminality in Early Modern Drama.* London: Routledge, 2004.

Bush-Bailey, Gilli. "Breeches Role." In *Oxford Encyclopedia of Theatre and Performance,* edited by Dennis Kennedy. Oxford: Oxford University Press, 2003. Reprint, 2005.

———. *Treading the Bawds: Actresses and Playwrights on the Late-Stuart Stage.* Manchester: Manchester University Press, 2006.

Cameron, Kenneth M. "Jo Haynes, Infamis." *Theatre Notebook* 24, no. 2 (1969): 56–67.

Cameron, William J., ed. *Poems on Affairs of State.* Vol. 5. New Haven: Yale University Press, 1971.

Canfield, J. Douglas, ed. *The Broadview Anthology of Restoration and Eighteenth-Century Drama, Concise Edition.* Peterborough: Broadview, 2001. Reprint, 2004.

Carver, Larry. "Rochester's *Valentinian.*" *Restoration and Eighteenth Century Theatre Research* 4, no. 1 (1989): 25–38.

Castle, Terry. *Masquerade and Civilization.* Stanford, CA: Stanford University Press, 1986.

Cibber, Colley. *An Apology for the Life of Colley Cibber.* Edited by B. R. S. Fone. New York: Dover, 1968. Reprint, 2000.

———. *Love's Last Shift, or, the Fool in Fashion.* 1st ed. London: H. Rhodes, R. Parker, S. Briscoe, 1696.

Collier, Jeremy. *A Short View of the Immorality, and Profaneness of the English Stage.* 1st ed. London: S. Keble, 1698. Reprint, 1996.

Collington, Tara L., and Philip D. Collington. "Adulteration or Adaptation? Nathaniel Lee's "'Princess of Cleve'" and Its Sources." *Modern Philology* 100, no. 2 (2002): 196–226.

Congreve, William. *Love for Love: A Comedy.* 1st ed. London: Tonson, 1695.

———. *Love for Love.* Edited by M. M. Kelsall. 2nd ed. London: Ernest Benn, 1999.

———. *The Way of the World.* 1st ed. London: Tonson, 1700.

Congreve, William. *The Works of William Congreve.* Edited by D. F. McKenzie. 3 vols. New York: Oxford University Press, 2011.

The Constant Nymph, or, the Rambling Shepherd, a Pastoral. London: Langley Curtis, 1678.

Cordner, Michael. *Four Restoration Marriage Plays.* Oxford: Oxford World's Classics, 1995.

Cunningham, Peter. *The Story of Nell Gwyn and the Sayings of Charles II.* New York: F. P. Harper, 1896.

Curll, Edmund. *Memoirs of the Life of Mrs. Oldfield.* London, 1731.

D'Urfey, Thomas. *The Intrigues at Versailles.* London: Saunders, Buck, and Parker, 1697.

———. *The Marriage-Hater Match'd.* London: Richard Bentley, 1692.

Danchin, Pierre. "Le Développement du Spectaculaire sur le Theatre Anglais (1660–1800): le Role des Prologues et Épilogues." *Medieval English Theater* 16 (1994).

———. *The Prologues and Epilogues of the Eighteenth Century.* 4 vols. Nancy: Presses Universitaires de Nancy, 1990; 1994.

———. *The Prologues and Epilogues of the Eighteenth Century: The Third Part, 1737–1760.* 2 vols. Paris: Editions Messene, 1997.

———. *The Prologues and Epilogues of the Restoration 1660–1700.* 6 vols and index. Nancy: Presses Universitaires de Nancy, 1981–1988.

Davies, Christie. "Exploring the Thesis of the Self-Deprecating Jewish Sense of Humor." *Humor* 4, no. 2 (1991): 189–209.

Dawson, Mark S. *Gentility and the Comic Theatre of Late Stuart London.* Cambridge: Cambridge University Press, 2005.

Dearing, Vinton A., ed. *The Works of John Dryden.* Vol. 16. Berkeley: University of California Press, 1996.

Derrida, Jacques. *Limited, Inc.* Evanston, IL: Northwestern University Press, 1988.

Dilke, Thomas. *The Lover's Luck.* London: Playford and Tooke, 1696.

Dryden, John. *King Arthur: or, the British Worthy.* 1st ed. London: Jacob Tonson, 1691.

———. *Tyrannick Love.* London: T. W. for Jacob Tonson and Thomas Bennet, 1702.

Erickson, Robert A. "Lady Fullbank and the Poet's Dream in Behn's Lucky Chance." In *Broken Boundaries: Women and Feminism in Restoration Drama,* edited by Katherine M. Quinsey, 89–110. Lexington: University Press of Kentucky, 1996.

Erskine-Hill, Howard. *William Congreve.* London: Routledge, 1995.

Faller, Lincoln B. *The Popularity of Addison's Cato and Lillo's The London Merchant.* New York: Garland, 1988.

Fisher, Judith W. "Audience Participation in the Eighteenth-Century London Theatre." In *Audience Participation: Essays on Inclusion in Performance,* edited by Susan Kattwinkel, 55–69. Westport, CT: Praeger, 2003.

Fitzgerald, Percy. *A New History of the English Stage.* London: Tinsley Bros., 1882.

Fodstad, Lars August. "Refurbishing the Doll's House?" *Ibsen Studies* 6.2 (2006): 149–87.

Freud, Sigmund. *Jokes and Their Relation to the Unconscious.* New York: Norton, 1960.

Frye, Northrop. *Anatomy of Criticism; Four Essays.* New York: Atheneum, 1966.

Gallagher, Catherine. *Nobody's Story: The Vanishing Acts of Women Writers in the Marketplace, 1670–1820*. Berkeley: University of California Press, 1994.

Gardner, William Bradford. *The Prologues and Epilogues of John Dryden*. New York: Columbia University Press, 1951.

Gay, Penny. "'So Persuasive an Eloquence'? Roles for Women on the Eighteenth-Century Stage." In *The Public's Open to Us All: Essays on Women and Performance in Eighteenth-Century England*, edited by Laura Engel, 12–29. Newcastle, UK: Cambridge Scholars, 2009.

Gelber, Michael Werth. *The Just and the Lively: The Literary Criticism of John Dryden*. Manchester: Manchester University Press, 1999.

Genest, John. *Some Account of the English Stage, from the Restoration in 1660 to 1830*. 10 vols. London: H. E. Carrington, 1832.

Genette, Gerard. *Narrative Discourse: An Essay in Method*. Translated by Jane E. Lewin. Ithaca, NY: Cornell University Press, 1980.

———. *Paratexts: Thresholds of Interpretation*. Translated by Jane E. Lewin. Cambridge: Cambridge University Press, 1997.

Gilbert, Joanne. *Performing Marginality: Humor, Gender, and Cultural Critique*. Detroit: Wayne State University Press, 2004.

Gildon, Charles. *A Comparison between the Two Stages*. London, 1702.

———. *The Lives and Characters of the English Dramatick Poets*. London: Nick Cox and William Turner, 1699.

Gill, Pat. *Interpreting Ladies: Women, Wit, and Morality in the Restoration Comedy of Manners*. Athens: University of Georgia Press, 1994.

Girard, Rene, and Yvonne Freccero. *Deceit, Desire, and the Novel; Self and Other in Literary Structure*. Baltimore: Johns Hopkins Press, 1965.

Goff, Moira. "The Incomparable Hester Santlow." In *Performance in the Long Eighteenth Century: Theatre, Music, Dance*. Edited by Jane Milling and Kathryn Lowerre. Burlington, VT: Ashgate, 2007.

Goffman, Erving. *Frame Analysis: An Essay on the Organization of Experience*. Cambridge, MA: Harvard University Press, 1974.

Gollapudi, Aparna. "Seeing Is Believing: Performing Reform in Colley Cibber's *Love's Last Shift*." *Restoration and Eighteenth-Century Theatre Research* 19, no. 1 (2004): 1–21.

Gould, Robert. "The Play-House. A Satyr." In *Poems, chiefly consisting of satyrs and satyrical epistles*, 161–85. London, 1689.

Gousseff, James William. *The Staging of Prologues in Tudor and Stuart Plays*. PhD diss. Northwestern, 1962.

Hackett, Helen. *Virgin Mother, Maiden Queen: Elizabeth I and the Cult of the Virgin Mary*. New York: St. Martins, 1995.

Haward, Sir William. "Ms. Don. B. 8." Bodleian Library.

Highfill, Philip H., Kalman A. Burnim, and Edward A. Langhans. *A Biographical Dictionary of Actors, Actresses, Musicians, Dancers, Managers and Other Stage Personnel in London, 1660–1800*. 16 vols. Carbondale: Southern Illinois University Press, 1973.

Holland, Peter. *The Ornament of Action: Text and Performance in Restoration Comedy.* Cambridge: Cambridge University Press, 1979.

The Honey-Suckle; Consisting of Original Poems, Epigrams, Songs, Tales, Odes, and Translations. Edited by "A Society of Gentlemen." London: Charles Corbett, 1734.

Hook, Lucyle. "Anne Bracegirdle's First Appearance." *Theatre Notebook* 13 (1959): 135.

———. "Mrs. Elizabeth Barry and Mrs. Anne Bracegirdle, Actresses. Their Careers from 1672 to 1695: A Study in Influences." PhD diss., New York University, 1949.

Hopkins, Charles. *Boadicea Queen of Britain.* London: Tonson, 1697.

Howe, Elizabeth. *The First English Actresses: Women and Drama, 1660–1700.* Cambridge: Cambridge University Press, 1992.

Hughes, Derek. *English Drama 1660–1700.* Oxford: Clarendon, 1996.

———. "Rape on the Restoration Stage." *Eighteenth Century* 46, no. 3 (2005): 225–36.

———. *The Theatre of Aphra Behn.* Houndmills, Basingstoke, Hampshire: Palgrave, 2001.

Hume, Robert D. *The Development of English Drama in the Late Seventeenth Century.* Oxford: Clarendon, 1976.

———. "The Satiric Design of Nat. Lee's *The Princess of Cleve.*" *Journal of English and Germanic Philology* 75 (1976): 117–38.

Hume, Robert D., and Harold Love, eds. *Plays, Poems, and Miscellaneous Writings Associated with George Villiers, Second Duke of Buckingham.* Vol. 1. Oxford: Oxford University Press, 2007.

Johnson, Samuel. "Ambrose Philips." In *The Lives of the Most Eminent English Poets.* London: C. Bathhurst et al., 1781.

———. "Life of Philips." In *Lives of the English Poets,* edited by George Birkbeck Hill. Oxford: Clarendon, 1905.

Kaufman, Anthony. "The Smiler with the Knife: Covert Aggression in Some Restoration Epilogues." *Studies in the Literary Imagination* 17, no. 1 (1984): 63–74.

Kenny, Shirley Strum. "The Playhouse and the Printing Shop: Editing Restoration and Eighteenth-Century Plays." *Modern Philology* 85, no. 4 (1988).

Kewes, Paulina. *Authorship and Appropriation: Writing for the Stage in England, 1660–1710,* Oxford English Monographs. Oxford: Clarendon Press, 1998.

Kinservik, Matthew. *Discipling Satire.* Lewisburg, PA: Bucknell University Press, 2002.

Knapp, Mary Etta. *Prologues and Epilogues of the Eighteenth Century.* New Haven, CT: Yale University Press, 1961.

Knight, Charles A. *Joseph Addison and Richard Steele: A Reference Guide, 1730–1991.* New York: Simon and Schuster, 1994.

Kotthoff, Helga. "Gender and Humor: The State of the Art." *Journal of Pragmatics* 38 (2006): 4–25.

Lafler, Joanne. *The Celebrated Mrs. Oldfield.* Carbondale: Southern Illinois University Press, 1989.

Langdell, Cheri Davis. "Aphra Behn and Sexual Politics: A Dramatist's Discourse with Her Audience." In *Drama, Sex, and Politics*, edited by James Redmond, 109–28. Cambridge: Cambridge University Press, 1985.

Langhans, Edward A. "Tough Actresses to Follow." In *Curtain Calls: British and American Women and the Theater, 1660–1820*, edited by Mary Anne Schofield and Cecilia Macheski. Athens: Ohio University Press, 1991.

Laqueur, Thomas. *Solitary Sex: A Cultural History of Masturbation*. New York: Zone Books, 2003.

Latham, Robert, and William Matthews. *The Diary of Samuel Pepys*. 11 vols. Vol. 7. London: G. Bell and Sons, 1976.

Lee, Nathaniel. *The Rival Queens, or the Death of Alexander the Great*. Chadwyck-Healey ed. London: James Magres and Richard Bertley, 1677.

Lewis, Peter. "Fielding's *The Covent-Garden Tragedy* and Philips's *The Distrest Mother*." *Durham University Journal* 37 (1976): 33–46.

Lewis, W. S., Warren Hunting Smith, and George L. Lam, eds. *Horace Walpole's Correspondence with Sir Horace Mann and Sir Horace Mann the Younger*. 48 vols. Vol. 25. New Haven, CT: Yale University Press, 1971.

Loftis, John, and David Stuart Rodes, eds. *The Works of John Dryden*. Edited by Vinton A. Dearing. 20 vols. Vol. 11. Berkeley: University of California Press, 1978.

Loughlin, Marie H. *Hymeneutics: Interpreting Virginity on the Early Modern Stage*. Lewisburg, PA: Bucknell University Press, 1997.

Love, Harold. "Was Lucina Betrayed at Whitehall?" In *That Second Bottle: Essays on John Wilmot, Earl of Rochester*, edited by Nicholas Fisher, 179–90. Manchester: Manchester University Press, 2000.

———. "Who Were the Restoration Audience?" *Yearbook of English Studies* 10 (1980): 21–44.

Lowenthal, Cynthia. *Performing Identities on the Restoration Stage*. Carbondale: Southern Illinois University Press, 2003.

———. "Sticks and Rags, Bodies and Brocade: Essentializing Discourses and the Late Restoration Playhouse." In *Broken Boundaries: Women and Feminism in Restoration Drama*, edited by Katherine M. Quinsey, 219–33. Lexington: University of Kentucky Press, 1996.

Markley, Robert. "Aphra Behn's *The City Heiress*: Feminism and the Dynamics of Popular Success on the Late Seventeenth-Century Stage." *Comparative Drama* 41, no. 2 (2007): 141–66.

———. "'Be Impudent, Be Saucy, Forward, Bold, Touzing, and Leud': The Politics of Masculine Sexuality and Feminine Desire in Behn's Tory Comedies." In *Cultural Readings of Restoration and Eighteenth-Century English Theater*, edited by J. Douglas Canfield and Deborah C. Payne, 114–40. Athens: University of Georgia Press, 1995.

Marsden, Jean I. *Fatal Desire: Women, Sexuality, and the English Stage, 1660–1720*. Ithaca, NY: Cornell University Press, 2006.

———. "Rape, Voyeurism, and the Restoration Stage." In *Broken Boundaries: Women and Feminism in Restoration Drama*, edited by Katherine M. Quinsey, 185–202. Lexington: University Press of Kentucky, 1996.

Maus, Katharine Eisaman. "'Playhouse Flesh and Blood': Sexual Ideology and the Restoration Actress." *English Literary History* 46 (1979): 595–617.

McCallum, Paul. "Cozening the Pit: Prologues, Epilogues, and Poetic Authority in Restoration England." In *Prologues, Epilogues, Curtain-Raisers, and Afterpieces: The Rest of the Eighteenth-Century London Stage*, edited by Daniel J. Ennis and Judith Bailey Slagle, 33–69. Newark: University of Delaware Press, 2007.

McKenzie, D. F. *The London Book Trade in the Later Seventeenth Century*. Sandars Lectures. Cambridge: Typescript. British Library, 1976.

Memoirs of the Life of Count de Grammont: Containing the Amorous Intrigues of the Court of England in the Reign of King Charles II. Translated by Anthony Hamilton. London: Thomas Payne, 1760.

Meyerhold, Vsevolod Emilevich. *Meyerhold on Theatre*. Translated by Edward Braun. New York: Hill and Wang, 1969.

Mikalachki, Jodi. *The Legacy of Boadicea: Gender and Nation in Early Modern England*. London: Routledge, 1998.

Milhous, Judith. *Thomas Betterton and the Management of Lincoln's Inn Fields, 1695–1708*. Carbondale: Southern Illinois University Press, 1979.

Milhous, Judith, and Robert D. Hume. "Theatrical Politics at Drury Lane: New Light on Letitia Cross, Jane Rogers, and Anne Oldfield." *Bulletin of Research in the Humanities* 85, no. 4 (1982): 412–29.

Miner, Earl, and Vinton Dearing. *The Works of John Dryden*. Vol. 3. Berkeley: University of California Press, 1969.

Mintz, Lawrence E. "Standup Comedy as Social and Cultural Mediation." In *American Humor*, edited by Arthur P. Dudden. New York: Oxford University Press, 1987.

A Modest survey of That Celebrated Tragedy the Distrest Mother, so often and so highly applauded by the ingenious Spectator. London: Redmayne and Morphew, 1712.

Morton, Richard. "Textual Problems in Restoration Broadsheet Prologues and Epilogues." *Library* 12, no. 3 (1957): 197–203.

Motten, Vander. "An Unnoticed Restoration Epilogue." *English Studies* 67, no. 4 (1986): 308–10.

Mountfort, William. *The Injur'd Lovers*. 1st ed. London: Sam Manship, 1678.

Mulvey, Laura. "Visual Pleasure and Narrative Cinema." *Screen* 16, no. 3 (1975): 6–18.

Nicoll, Allardyce. *A History of Early Eighteenth Century Drama, 1700–1750*. 2nd ed. Cambridge: Cambridge University Press, 1929.

Nielsen, Wendy C. "Boadicea Onstage before 1800, a Theatrical and Colonial History." *Studies in English Literature* 49, no. 3 (2009): 595–614.

Novak, Maximillian E., and George R. Guffey. *The Works of John Dryden*. Vol. 10. Berkeley: University of California Press, 1970.

Nussbaum, Felicity. *Rival Queens: Actresses, Performance, and the Eighteenth-Century British Theater*. Philadelphia: University of Pennsylvania Press, 2010.

Oldys, William, and Edmund Curll. *The History of the English Stage, from the Restauration to the Present Time*. London: E. Curll, 1741.

Ollard, Richard. *Pepys: A Biography*. London: Hodder and Stoughton, 1974.

Orr, Bridget. *Empire on the English Stage 1660–1714*. Cambridge: Cambridge University Press, 2001.

Otway, Thomas. *The Works of Thomas Otway*. Edited by J. C. Ghosh. 2 vols. Vol. 2. Oxford: Clarendon, 1968.

Owen, Robert. *Hypermnestra*. 1st ed. London: Lintott, 1703. Reprint, 1722.

Owen, Susan. "Behn's Dramatic Response to Restoration Politics." In *The Cambridge Companion to Aphra Behn*, edited by Derek Hughes and Janet Todd, 68–82. Cambridge: Cambridge University Press, 2004.

———. *Restoration Theatre and Crisis*. Oxford: Clarendon, 1996.

Pacheco, Anita. "Rape and the Female Subject in Aphra Behn's *The Rover*." *English Literary History* 65, no. 2 (1998): 323–45.

Parker, Andrew, and Eve Kosofsky Sedgwick. *Performativity and Performance*. Essays from the English Institute. New York: Routledge, 1995.

Parker, Derek. *Nell Gwyn*. Phoenix Mill, Britain: Sutton, 2000.

Parnell, Paul E. "*The Distrest Mother*, Ambrose Philips" Morality Play." *Comparative Literature* 11, no. 2 (1959): 111–23.

Payne, Deborah. "Reified Object or Emergent Professional? Retheorizing the Restoration Actress." In *Cultural Readings of Restoration and Eighteenth Century English Theater*, edited by J. Douglas Canfield and Deborah C. Payne. Athens: Georgia University Press, 1995.

Pearson, Jacqueline. *The Prostituted Muse: Images of Women and Women Dramatists, 1642–1737*. New York: St Martin's Press, 1988.

Peck, James. "Albion's '"Chaste Lucrese"': Chastity, Resistance, and the Glorious Revolution in the Career of Anne Bracegirdle." *Theatre Survey* 25, no. 1 (2004).

Pfister, Manfred. *The Theory and Analysis of Drama*. Cambridge: Cambridge University Press, 1994.

Philips, Ambrose. *The Distrest Mother*. 1st ed. London: Sam. Buckley, 1712.

Powell, George. *Alphonso King of Naples*. 1st ed. London: Abel Roper and Thomas Bever, 1691.

Pullen, Kirsten. *Actresses and Whores: On Stage and in Society*. Cambridge: Cambridge University Press, 2005.

Purcell, Henry. *Orpheus Britannicus*. London: J. Heptinstall for Henry Playford, 1698.

Quinsey, Katherine M. "Introduction." In *Broken Boundaries: Women and Feminism in Restoration Drama*, edited by Katherine M. Quinsey, 1–10. Lexington: University Press of Kentucky, 1996.

Randall, Dale B. J. *Winter Fruit: English Drama 1642–1660*. Lexington: University Press of Kentucky, 1995.

Rapin, Rene. *Reflections on Aristotle's Treatise of Poesie. Containing the necessary, rational, and universal rules for Epick, dramatick, and the other sorts of poetry.* London: T. N. for H. Herringman, 1674.

Richardson, Samuel. *Pamela, or, Virtue Rewarded.* 6th ed. Vol. 4. London, 1772.

Ritchie, Fiona. "'Jilting Jades'? Perceptions of Female Playgoers in the Restoration, 1660–1700." In *Theatre and Culture in Early Modern England, 1650–1737,* edited by Catie Gill, 131–44. Surrey, UK: Ashgate, 2010.

The Riverside Shakespeare. Edited by Herschel Baker et al. Boston: Houghton Mifflin, 1997.

Roach, Joseph R. *It.* Ann Arbor: University of Michigan Press, 2007.

———. "The Performance." In *The Cambridge Companion to English Restoration Theatre,* edited by Deborah Payne Fisk, 19–39. Cambridge: Cambridge University Press, 2000.

Roberts, David. *The Ladies: Female Patronage of Restoration Drama, 1660–1700.* Oxford: Clarendon, 1989.

Robinson, J. W. "Elegy on the Death of Joseph Haines." *Theatre Notebook* 35, no. 3 (1981): 99–100.

Rogers, Pat. "The Breeches Part." In *Sexuality in the Eighteenth Century,* edited by Paul-Gabriel Boucé, 244–58. Manchester: Manchester University Press, 1982.

Rosenfeld, Sybil. *Strolling Players and Drama in the Provinces, 1660–1765.* Cambridge: Cambridge University Press, 1939.

Rosenthal, Laura. "'Counterfeit Scrubbado': Women Actors in the Restoration." *Eighteenth Century* 34, no. 1 (1993): 3–22.

Rothstein, Eric. *Restoration Tragedy: Form and the Process of Change.* Westport, Conn.: Greenwood Press, 1978.

Rowe, Nicholas. *The Ambitious Step-Mother.* London, 1701.

———. "The Ambitious Step-Mother." In *The Works of Nicholas Rowe,* 1–91. London, 1728.

Rubin, Gayle. "The Traffic in Women: Notes on the "'Political Economy' of Sex." In *The Second Wave: A Reader in Feminist Theory,* edited by Linda Nicholson, 27–62. New York: Routledge, 1997.

"Satyr on the Whigs and Tories." In *MS Harleian,* 237–47: British Library, 1683.

Schechner, Richard. *Essays on Performance Theory, 1970–1976.* New York: Drama Book Specialists, 1977.

Scott, Thomas. *The Unhappy Kindness: or a Fruitless Revenge.* London: H. Rhodes, S. Briscoe, and R. Parker, 1697.

Scott-Douglass, Amy. "Aphra Behn's *Covent Garden Drollery*: The First History of Women in the Restoration Theatre." In *The Public's Open to Us All: Essays on Women and Performance in Eighteenth-Century England,* edited by Laura Engel, 98–127. Newcastle: Cambridge Scholars, 2009.

Sedgwick, Eve Kosofsky. *Between Men: English Literature and Male Homosocial Desire.* Gender and Culture. New York: Columbia University Press, 1992.

Senelick, Laurence. *The Changing Room: Sex, Drag, and Theatre.* London: Routledge, 2000.

Settle, Elkanah. *The Distres'd Innocence: or, the Princess of Persia.* 1st ed. London: E. J. for Abel Roper, 1691.

———. *The Heir of Morocco, with the Death of Gayland.* London: Cademan, 1682.

———. *The World in the Moon.* London: Roper, 1697.

Shade, Ruth. "Take My Mother-in-Law: 'Old Bags,' Comedy and the Sociocultural Construction of the Older Woman." *Comedy Studies* 1, no. 1 (2010): 71–83.

Shadwell, Thomas. *The Amorous Bigotte.* 1st ed. London: James Knapton, 1690.

Shirley, James. *The Coronation.* London, 1640.

Snyder, Henry L. "The Prologues and Epilogues of Arthur Maynwaring." *Philological Quarterly* 50 (1971): 610–29.

Southerne, Thomas. *Sir Anthony Love.* London: Joseph Fox and Abel Roper, 1691.

———. *The Works of Thomas Southerne.* Edited by Robert Jordan, and Harold Love. 2 vols. Vol. 1. Oxford: Clarendon, 1988.

The Spouter's Companion. London: J. Cook, ca.1770.

Staves, Susan. *Players' Scepters: Fictions of Authority in the Restoration.* Lincoln: University of Nebraska Press, 1979.

Stern, Tiffany. *Documents of Performance in Early Modern England.* Cambridge: Cambridge University Press, 2009.

———. *Rehearsal from Shakespeare to Sheridan.* Oxford: Clarendon, 2000.

———. "'A Small-Beer Health to His Second Day': Playwrights, Prologues, and First Performances in the Early Modern Theater." *Studies in Philology* 101, no. 2 (2004): 172–99.

Straub, Kristina. *Sexual Suspects; Eighteenth-Century Players and Sexual Ideology.* Princeton, NJ: Princeton University Press, 1992.

Straznicky, Marta. "Restoration Women Playwrights and the Limits of Professionalism." *English Literary History* 64, no. 3 (1997): 703–26.

Strong, Roy. *The Cult of Elizabeth: Elizabethan Portraiture and Pageantry.* Berkeley: University of California Press, 1977.

Styan, J. L. *Restoration Comedy in Performance.* Cambridge: Cambridge University Press, 1986.

Sutherland, James. "Prologues, Epilogues, and Audience in the Restoration Theatre." In *Of Books and Humankind: Essays and Poems Presented to Bonamy Dobree,* edited by John Butt, J. M. Cameron, D. W. Jefferson, and Robin Skelton. London: Routledge and Kegan Paul, 1964.

Thorn-Drury, G. "Some Notes on Dryden." *Review of English Studies* 1, no. 3 (1925): 324–30.

Thorson, James. "The Dialogue between the Stage and the Audience: Prologues and Epilogues in the Era of the Popish Plot." In *Compendious Conversations: The Method of Dialogue in the Early Enlightenment,* edited by Kevin L. Cope, 331–45. Frankfurt: Peter Lang, 1992.

Todd, Janet. *The Works of Aphra Behn*. Vol. 1. Columbus: Ohio State University Press, 1992.

Trotter, Catharine. *Agnes de Castro*. London: Rhodes, Parker, Briscoe, 1696.

Van Lennep, William, ed. *The London Stage, 1660–1800*. 5 vols. Vol. 1. Carbondale: Southern Illinois University Press, 1965.

Vieth, David M. "The Art of the Prologue and Epilogue: A New Approach Based on Dryden's Practice." *Genre* 5, no. 3 (1972): 271–92.

Villiers, George, Duke of Buckingham. *The Works of His Grace, George Villiers, Late Duke of Buckingham*. Vol. 2. London: Sam Briscoe, 1715.

Walker, Garthine. *Crime, Gender and Social Order in Early Modern England*. Cambridge: Cambridge University Press, 2003.

Walker, Nancy. "Agelaste or Eiron: American Women Writers and the Sense of Humor." *Studies in American Humor* 4, no. 1/2 (1985): 105–25.

Wandor, Michelene. "Cross-Dressing, Sexual Representation and the Sexual Division of Labour in Theatre." In *The Routledge Reader in Gender and Performance*, edited by Lisbeth Goodman and Jane de Gay, 170–75. New York: Routledge, 1998.

Wanko, Cheryl. *Roles of Authority: Thespian Biography and Celebrity in Eighteenth-Century Britain*. Lubbock: Texas Tech University Press, 2003.

Warner, William B. *Licensing Entertainment: The Elevation of Novel Reading in Britain, 1684–1750*. Berkeley: University of California Press, 1998.

Wheatley, Christopher J. "Tragedy." In *The Cambridge Companion to English Restoration Theatre*, edited by Deborah Payne Fisk, 70–85. Cambridge: Cambridge University Press, 2000.

Wheatley, Katherine Ernestine. *Racine and English Classicism*. Austin: University of Texas Press, 1956.

Wiley, Autrey Nell. "Female Prologues and Epilogues in English Plays." *Publications of the Modern Language Association (PMLA)* 48 (1933): 1060–79.

———. *Rare Prologues and Epilogues 1642–1700*. London: George Allen and Unwin, 1940. Reprint, Port Washington, NY: Kennikat, 1970.

Wilmot, John, 2nd Earl of Rochester. *Valentinian*. 1st ed. London: Timothy Goodwin, 1685.

Wilson, John Harold. *All the King's Ladies; Actresses of the Restoration*. [Chicago]: University of Chicago Press, 1958.

———. *Court Satires of the Restoration*. Columbus: Ohio State University Press, 1976.

Winn, James Anderson. *John Dryden and His World*. New Haven, CT: Yale University Press, 1987.

Wiseman, Jane. *Antiochus the Great; or, the Fatal Relapse*. 1st ed. London: William Turner and Richard Bassett, 1702.

Womersley, David. *Restoration Drama: An Anthology*. Oxford: Blackwell, 2000.

Wycherley, William. *The Country Wife*. Edited by James Ogden. London: A. and C. Black, 1991.

General Index

Page numbers for illustrations are in italics.

actors, plight of, 4–5, 93, 161
actresses: actress-audience relationship, 2, 9, 11–12; actress-playwright relationship, 9; and female public participation, 6, 11–13, 15, 27, 45, 53, 55, 107; and prostitution, 81, 90, 93, 136–39, 162, 163n14; reputations of, 28–29, 32n27, 55, 59, 78, 81, 90, 124, 135–62, 167n91, 172–73; rise of the actress, 6, 11, 15, 40, 43, 143. *See also* celebrity; *specific names*
Addison, Joseph, 24, 27, 29, 169–87, 188n15; *Cato*, 187, 220
Allison, Betty, 152, 201, 203, 215
"Animadversions on Mr. Congreve's Late Answer to Mr. Collier," 140
Another Prologue at a Boarding School, 201
The Apparition, 207
Apte, Mahadev, 15, 65
"Ariadne": *She Ventures and He Wins*, 201, 206

ass epilogue. *See under* Haines, Joseph (Jo)
Aston, Anthony (Tony), 141–42, 152, 155; *The Coy Shepherdess*, 43
Auslander, Philip, 14, 106
Austin, J. L., 40, 66n3
Avery, Emmett, 10, 33n49, 47, 66n4

Babb, Mrs., 70n59, 204
Baker, Robert: *The Mad-House*, 64
Baker, Thomas, 122, 212, 216; *The Fine Lady's Airs*, 198
Bancroft, John: *Henry II, King of England*, 154, 156–57, 199, 206, 216
Banks, John, 47, 205; *Cyrus the Great: Or Tragedy of Love*, 76, 202; *The Destruction of Troy*, 205
Barreca, Regina, 15
Barry, Elizabeth, 70n53, 157, 158, 161, 163n15, 168n93, 196–221 *passim*, 224n7; and breeches roles, 53–54, 126; and cloaked paratexts, 45, 53–57, 129n23; and Earl of Rochester, 56,

111, 129n19; partnership with Anne
Bracegirdle, 137–39; and political
critique, 45, 53–57, 116–17, 122;
and rape, 142, 144, 146; and revived
epilogues, 76; sexual reputation of,
55, 139, 163n14, 164n34; and social
critique, 116–17, 122
bawdy epilogues. See under paratexts
Beaumont, Francis: The Faithful
Shepherdess, 201; Philaster, or, Love
Lies a Bleeding, 202, 204, 208, 211,
218; The Royal Merchant, 64, 223
Behn, Aphra, 27, 48, 70n53, 70n57,
155, 182, 196–221 passim; Abdelazer;
or, The Moor's Revenge, 67n20,
201; The Amorous Prince, 208;
arrest of, 12, 23, 39, 65n1; The
City-Heiress, 7–8, 55–56, 57, 105,
117–21, 131n56, 196–218 passim;
and cloaked paratexts, 48, 53–55;
Covent Garden Drollery, 23; The
Debauchee, 214; The Emperour of
the Moon, 70n57, 196; The False
Count, 121, 209, 214; The Feign'd
Curtizans; or, A Night's Intrigue,
205; and female self-expression, 28,
33n40, 55; and female spectatorship,
105–6, 110–14; The Forc'd Marriage;
or, Jealous Bridegroom, 33n40, 204,
208, 218; Like Father, Like Son, 205;
and political commentary, 12, 23,
39–40, 53–56, 65n1; and revived
epilogues, 39, 76, 101n32; Romulus
and Hersilia; or, the Sabine War, 12,
23, 39–40, 101n32, 196, 198, 200,
209; The Roundheads, 221; The Rover,
54, 55, 118–19, 141, 143, 149, 196;
The Second Part of the Rover, 54,
196; Sir Patient Fancy, 24, 48, 121,
214; social critique paratexts, 116,
118–19, 121, 127, 136; and virgin
paratexts, 88, 139, 155; The Widdow
Ranter, 67n20, 205, 214; The Young
King, 53–55, 196

Bellamy, George Anne, 173
Bennett, Susan, 10, 11, 17, 23, 34n55
Betterton, Mary Saunderson, 54, 83,
137, 142–43, 164n34, 172, 208
Betterton, Thomas, 22, 68n34, 109–10,
137, 158–59, 202, 214, 217; actor-
audience relationship, 47–48, 50;
The Amorous Widow, 172, 217;
and cloaked paratexts, 47–50;
collaboration with Aphra Behn,
121; The Counterfeit Bridegroom, 121,
214; and exposed paratexts, 68n37;
and the United Company, 138, 161,
163n15
Bickerstaff, Miss, 201, 203
Bicknell, Margaret, 207, 213, 218
Blount, Charles: Mr Dreyden Vindicated,
16
Blow, Dr John: Venus and Adonis, a
Masque, 221
Bodens, Charles: The Modish Couple,
171
Bononcini, Giovanni, 198
Booth, Barton, 86
Boothby, Frances: Marcelia, 60
Boutell, Elizabeth (Betty), 139, 142,
147, 164n34, 196, 199, 204, 208,
232n7
Bowen, William, 60, 61, 109
Bowman, Elizabeth, 96–98, 201–23
passim
Bowman, John, 97–98
Boyle, Charles, 216
Boyle, Roger, Earl of Orrery, 108;
Altemira, 216
Bracegirdle, Anne, 22, 32n34, 68n34,
109, 197–222 passim, 224n3,
225n23; and breeches paratexts, 85,
87; celebrity of, 28–29, 172; revived
epilogues, 76, 101n32; social critique
paratexts, 116, 122, 125; tendentious
paratexts, 94–95; virginal reputation
of, 29, 87–88, 135–68 passim, 175;
and William Congreve, 137

Marlborough, Duke of, 86
marriage, critique of, 117–21, 216–18
Marsden, Jean, 82, 95, 104n82, 107,
142, 145, 147, 164n33, 166n62
Marshall, Rebecca, 138–39, 142,
164n34, 199, 204, 208, 213, 218
Marten, John, 176
masculinity, 96, 116; critique of, 121–
25, 213–16; and impotence, 51–52,
121–25. *See also* cuckoldry; male
mistreatment of women
masturbation, 176
Maus, Katherine Eisaman, 15, 30n3, 96,
136–37
Maynwaring, Arthur, 173, 175, 177,
178, 188n18, 190n39, 212, 217, 218
McKenzie, D. F., 22, 168n98
media event, 190nn53–54
*Memoirs of the Life of Count de
Grammont*, 111, 129n20
The Merry Milkmaid of Islington, 205,
209, 224n18
Middleton, Thomas, 16; *A Mad World
My Masters*, 118
Milhous, Judith, 18, 189n31
*Miscellaneous Works of . . . George, Late
Duke of Buckingham*, 63
*A Modest Survey Of that Celebrated
Tragedy The Distrest Mother, So
often and so highly Applauded by the
Ingenious Spectator*, 179, 189n26
Monmouth, Duke of, 12, 29n2, 39,
65n1, 131n56
Moor, Henrietta, 207, 223
Mordaunt, Lady Mary, 201
Motteux, Peter, 143, 167n74, 197–223
passim; *Beauty in Distress*, 212, 219;
The Island Princess, 212, 222, 223;
The Novelty, 212, 215; *The Rape of
Europa*, 143; *The Temple of Love*, 198
Mountfort, Susannah. *See* Verbruggen,
Susannah

Mountfort, Susannah II (daughter of
Susannah Verbruggen), 201, 217,
224n14
Mountfort, William, 49, 139–40, 142,
144–47, 155–56, 199–222 *passim*,
224n14; *Greenwich Park*, 200;
The Injur'd Lovers, 142, 144; *The
Successful Straingers*, 206, 210
Moyle, Mrs., 125, 209, 219
Mr. Turbulent, 196
Mulvey, Laura, 145
Murphy, Arthur: *The Citizen*, 43
mutuality, 110

Neale, Thomas: *The Wheel of Fortune*,
203
Nine Years' War, 148, 166n65
Nokes, James, 19, 50, 59, 60, 68n39,
221, 224n10
Norton, Richard: *Pausanias*, 197, 211
Nussbaum, Felicity, 19, 136–37, 173

Oates, Titus, 55–57, 69n51. *See also*
Popish Plot
obscenity, 88, 128n6, 186
Oldfield, Anne, 188n14, 188n20, 198–
220 *passim*; and bawdy epilogues, 29,
169, 171–86 *passim*, 189n29; and
celebrity, 21, 172–73; reputation of,
137, 175, 177–78; and tendentious
epilogues, 95
Oldmixon, John: *The Governor of
Cyprus*, 197
*Onania; or, Heinous Sin of Self Pollution,
and all its Frightful Consequences, in
both SEXES Considered*, 176
onanism. *See* masturbation
Otway, Thomas, 55–56, 70n53, 137,
142, 196–214 *passim*; *Alcibiades*, 28,
82–83, 198; *Don Carlos*, 88, 201,
202; *Friendship in Fashion*, 205, 214;
The History and Fall of Caius Marius,

Index of Plays

Index of Actresses

~

About the Author

Diana Solomon is assistant professor of English at Simon Fraser University.